Judaism and Its Social Metaphors

Judaism and Its Social Metaphors

Israel in the History of Jewish Thought

JACOB NEUSNER

Brown University

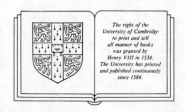

The right of the
University of Cambridge
to print and sell
all manner of books
was granted by
Henry VIII in 1534.
The University has printed
and published continuously
since 1584.

CAMBRIDGE UNIVERSITY PRESS

Cambridge

New York   New Rochelle   Melbourne   Sydney

Published by the Press Syndicate of the University of Cambridge
The Pitt Building, Trumpington Street, Cambridge CB2 1RP
32 East 57th Street, New York, NY 10022, USA
10 Stamford Road, Oakleigh, Melbourne 3166, Australia

© Cambridge University Press 1989

First published 1989

Printed in the United States of America

Library of Congress Cataloging-in-Publication Data
Neusner, Jacob, 1932–
Judaism and its social metaphors / Jacob Neusner.
   p.   cm.
Includes index.
1. Judaism – History – Talmudic period, 10–425.
2. Rabbinical literature – History and criticism.   3. Sociology, Jewish.
4. Jews – Identity.   I. Title.
BM177.N474   1989
296.3–dc19   88–17057

British Library Cataloguing-in-Publication Data
Neusner, Jacob, 1932–
Judaism and its social metaphors.
1. Jewish doctrine.   Israel
I. Title
296.3´87

ISBN 0 521 35471 4

For

ANDREW GREELEY

whose profound grasp of the nature of religion
and deep understanding of the activity of religion in society
have enlightened an entire generation.

A tribute to his remarkable union of scholarship,
intellect, imagination, and perception

in the the quest for
what it means for us to be
"in our image, after our likeness"
all together and all at once.

Contents

Proposition 3: *The systemic importance of the category
"Israel" depends on the generative problematic – the
urgent question – of the system builders, and not on
their social circumstance. The place of "Israel" within
the self-evidently true response offered by the system will
prove congruent to the logic of the system and that
alone.*

Hypothesis: *The system builders' social (including political) circumstance defines the generative problematic that
imparts self-evidence to the systemically definitive logic,
encompassing its social component.*

Preface

In this book I ask a small question about a large subject: How does a religious system bring to concrete and vivid expression a definition of those who live within that system – how does it characterize its members as a distinctive sort of social entity? In the authoritiative writings of every Judaism known in history, the term "Israel" is critical. What a Judaism means by the term entails the sort of social group it associates with "Israel" and the way it imagines and portrays "Israel." An investigation of both aspects can provide insight into the solution of a much broader issue – the relationship, in the formation of a religious system, between circumstance and context, social facts and the social imagination.

By religious system I mean a cogent composition of three things: a worldview, a way of life, and an address to a defined entity. A religious system addresses a group of people with an account of a worldview, a way of life, and a theory about the social entity constituted by the group of people at hand. The ethos, ethics, and social theory all together raise a fundamental and urgent question and then answer that question with a cogent and (to the system's framers) self-evidently valid statement. This study considers how a Judaic system (or "a Judaism") explained the social entity to which that system addressed itself, how in context it gave an account of what an "Israel" is. For in any Judaism, the social entity will be called "Israel," and hence any Judaism will encompass in its cogent statement a clear account of what an "Israel" is.

The relevance of this study hardly requires spelling out. Every morning's headlines bring new testimony to the definitive position of the issue at hand. The question of who, and what, is (an) "Israel" today troubles the peace of Israel, the Jewish state, and the definition of who is a Jew continues to preoccupy the Judaic authorities of the diaspora as well. But the matter of "Israel" – what sort of social entity "Israel" is, who an "Israel" is, to what genus we refer when we speak of the species, "Israel" – enjoys more than merely current relevance. In point of fact the category, "Israel," and its definition define a shibboleth of the history of Judaism. The identification of "Israel" has preoccupied thinkers of all Judaisms from the beginning to the present. The making of Judaic systems commenced with the formation of the Pentateuch in the aftermath of the destruction of the first Temple of Jerusalem in 586 B.C.E. From that time to the present day the definition of "Israel" – who belongs, who does not, and to what sort of social entity do "Israelites" adhere in forming (an) "Israel" – has formed a remarkably pervasive theme in all Judaisms. When we take up the systemic treatment by a Judaism of the category "Israel," we address one critical and indicative issue of the Judaic system under study. The centrality of thought on "Israel" for all Judaisms from then to now may be assessed not only in the encounter with the record of the past.

For all Judaisms – systems comprising a way of life and a worldview addressed to a particular social entity – have always faced the problem of defining that social entity, which all have called "Israel." Each Judaism, of course, provided its own definition of what an Israel is, as well as of who an Israel[ite, that is, in modern language, a Jew] is. The urgency of confronting the question invariably derived from the requirement, facing all Judaisms, to specify a theory of "Israel" that explained who belonged, and who did not belong. But that explanation formed a critical component of the systemic definition to begin with. So to say that the issue of "Israel" settles who is in and who is out is to make a redundant statement out of the fact that the systemic definition states the generative principle of a system in the limited terms of its social component. That is why, when we know who and what a system construes an Israel to be, we find our way deep into the thought processes of the system at its deepest generative levels. Given the diversity of Judaisms past and present, we cannot find it astonishing that the name for the social entity constituted by Jews, the name "Israel," has carried a variety of meanings, and, as we shall soon understand, each of these served not as concrete description of real people living in the here and now, a merely factual statement of how things are, but as a metaphor. The metaphor might take genealogical or political or supernatural or taxonomical or hierarchical or ontological or epistemological character, as systems varied. An "Israel" in a given system might enjoy no counterpart among social entities here on earth; sui generis, "Israel" then framed its own (of necessity, unintelligible) metaphor.

This social entity, this Israel, therefore may constitute a family of a particular order – that is, all Jews descend from Abraham, Isaac, and Jacob, Sarah, Rebecca, Leah, and Rachel. Then we invoke the metaphor of family. Or, it may be held, Israel constitutes a people or a nation, in which case to be "Israel" is to be part of a political unit of one kind or another, comparable with other such social groups based on, or in, a shared political being, and that will dictate thought on the nature of Israel, whether or not the Jews at a given time and place constituted a political entity at all. We find, furthermore, the claim that the social entity at hand simply is not like any other, a genus unto itself. "Israel" as "unique" has no counterpart among the nations: on one side of the social equation of humanity are all the nations all together; on the other side, Israel, all alone. These and other metaphors serve as the vehicles for the social thought of the Judaic systems, or Judaisms, of the ages. These abstract observations have now to be made concrete for a Judaism.

Everyday conversation with my beloved colleague, Professor Calvin Goldscheider, Program in Judaic Studies and Department of Sociology, Brown University, was essential for this project. He asked tough questions and also provided thoughtful definitions and points of clarification of theory. His influence on Chapter 1 is evident in every line. Talks from day to day with Professor William Scott Green, University of Rochester, proved equally productive, particularly in the design of the whole. I found benefit in the warnings of my colleague, Professor Wendell S. Dietrich, not to stray into theological pastures sown with weeds. The sustaining friendship of Professor Ernest S. Frerichs illumines this, as it does every other, work of mine. My graduate student, now Professor Paul Virgil Flesher, Northwestern University, provided not only a good hearing for ideas but also thoughtful responses and valued criticism. Those colleagues who read Chapter 11 and commented on it are mentioned in the appropriate passages.

Providence, Rhode Island   JACOB NEUSNER

Abbreviations

A.Z.	Abodah Zarah	M.S.	Maaser Sheni
Ar.	Arakhin	Mak.	Makkot
B.B.	Baba Batra	Mal.	Malachi
B.M.	Baba Mesia	Men.	Menahot
B.Q.	Baba Qamma	Mic.	Micah
Ber.	Berakhot	Ned.	Nedarim
Bes.	Besah	Neg.	Negaim
Bik.	Bikkurim	Nid.	Niddah
Chron.	Chronicles	Num.	Numbers
Col.	Colossians	Ob.	Obadiah
Dem.	Demai	Pes.	Pesahim
Deut.	Deuteronomy	Prov.	Proverbs
Ed.	Eduyyot	Ps.	Psalms
Er.	Erubin	Qid.	Qiddushin
Est.	Esther	R.	Rabbi; or Rabbah (as in
Ex.	Exodus		Gen. R.)
Ez.	Ezekiel	R.H.	Rosh Hashanah
Gal.	Galatians	Rom.	Romans
Gen.	Genesis	Sam.	Samuel
Gen. R.	Genesis Rabbah	Shab.	Shabbat
Git.	Gittin	Sheb.	Shebi'it
Hab.	Habakkuk	Sheq.	Sheqalim
Hal.	Hallah	Song	Song of Songs; Song of
Hor.	Horayyot		Solomon
Hos.	Hosea	Sot.	Sotah
Is.	Isaiah	Suk.	Sukkah
Jer.	Jeremiah	T.	Tosefta tractate
Josh.	Joshua	Ta.	Taanit
Ket.	Ketubot	Ter.	Terumot
Kgs.	Kings	Uqs.	Uqsin
Lam.	Lamentations	Y.	Yerushalmi
Lev.	Leviticus	Yad.	Yadayim
Lev. R.	Leviticus Rabbah	Yeb.	Yebamot
M.	Mishnah tractate	Zeb.	Zebahim
M.Q.	Moed Qatan	Zech.	Zechariah

Introduction

When, to explain who they are, several people or families who live in a village call themselves "villagers," or "people who live in such-and-such a village," they speak of the simple, palpable facts of their everyday life. But when they call themselves "Israel," and mean by that the same group of which the Hebrew Scriptures or "Old Testament" speaks, they claim for themselves a standing and a status that the simple facts of daily life do not, and cannot, validate. They compare themselves to some other social group and allege that they are like that other group or continue it or embody it in the here and now. In so doing, they evoke in explaining who they are what we may call a metaphor. For the statement, "we are Israel," means to allege, "we are like that Israel of old" of which the Scriptures speak. The same is so when Christian residents of a given locale call themselves "the Church," or "the body of Christ." Then they speak of what is not seen, though very real. In both of these cases, the claim that "we" are "Israel," or "we" are "the body of Christ," forms instances of metaphors invoked to explain the character and standing of a social entity. Social metaphors, therefore, refer to the things with which a group of people compare themselves in accounting for their society together. These two instances, "Israel" and "Church," therefore supply familiar examples of how people invoke a metaphor in identifying the social entity that they constitute. Why insist on regarding as metaphors these ways in which people imagine themselves together? The reason is that what we examine are ways of comparing the abstract to the concrete, the unknown and inconceivable to the known and the palpable and the understood.

When people explain to themselves the character and calling of the social entity that they compose and the life they lead together, they may produce for themselves an encompassing picture, which I call a

1

system if three necessary components are present: an account of a worldview, a prescription of a corresponding way of life, and a definition of the social entity that finds definition in the one and description in the other. Those components sustain one another in explaining the whole of a social order, hence constituting the theoretical account of a system. Systems defined in this way work out a cogent picture, for those who make them up. That picture comprises how things are correctly to be sorted out and fitted together, explains why things are done in one way rather than in some other, and defines who they are that act and understand matters in this particular way. When, as is common, people invoke God as the foundation for their worldview, maintaining that their way of life corresponds to what God wants of them and projecting their social entity in a particular relationship to God, then we have a *religious system.*

What about the notion of a *Judaism,* which constitutes the third important building block of this study? When a religious system appeals as an important part of its authoritative literature or canon to the Hebrew Scriptures of ancient Israel, or "Old Testament," we have a Judaism. That usage, *a* Judaism, is unfamiliar but critical. When people use the word "Judaism," they use it only in the singular, and they assume that the word refers to a single religion, or religious tradition, extending (if not from creation) from Sinai to the present. Along these same lines, people assume that we all know what we mean when we refer to "Israel." Instead, in this book I refer not only to *a* Judaism but, more commonly, to a Judaic *system*. And the premise of this inquiry is that when people say "Israel," they may mean, "an Israel," a species of a genus, Israel. That is to say, I define in categories not broadly understood the genus of which I speak, a religion, as well as the species of that genus, a Judaism. So too, I treat "Israel" as an unknown entity, to be defined inductively by a search for the meanings imputed to that entity or word in a literature of a quite specific and concrete character. A Judaism always applies to the social entity that forms the third necessary component of its system, the title "Israel," and this is a book, in particular, about how a particular Judaism conceived of its "Israel."

We may now put together the conception of a Judaism, or a Judaic system, and the idea of a metaphor for a social entity and in that way grasp what is at issue in this book – (a) Judaism and its social metaphors. For any Judaism the fundamental act of metaphorization is the comparison of the Jews of the here and now with the "Israel" of which the received Scriptures common to all Judaisms speak. Treating the social entity – two or more persons – as other than they are in the present or as more than a (mere) given means that the group perceives itself, its life together, as something else than what it appears to be. And that supererogatory act of imagination constitutes the metaphorical reading of the social entity. Prior to all the specific metaphors we shall survey comes that act of metaphorization. For no facticity or givenness explains why people should treat the fact that, as a social entity, they form a group that bears specific definition beyond everyday traits (e.g., of location or individual composition) as extraordinary. Why, after all, should it be natural or self-evident that the social group forms more than an "us" – more than "our village," "our household," or perhaps people like "us" in other villages or other households? These, the hardest social facts, stand on their own. Any meaning imputed to the group beyond these statements of the "us" of the here and now by definition constitutes an act of metaphorization of two or more persons, treating them as a group and explaining what and who, as a group, they are. So much for (a) Judaism and its social metaphors. But which Judaism?

Here we deal with only one Judaism, the Judaism of the dual Torah, written and oral, that took shape in late antiquity.[1] We know about that system from the holy books of Judaism produced between the second and the seventh centuries C.E. The Judaism of the dual Torah was hardly the only Judaic system, or Judaism, that over time Jews have worked out for themselves. The Essene community of Qumran presented a quite different Judaic system that was equally cogent and well crafted, and the authorship of the Pentateuch in ca. 450 B.C.E. produced a still more encompassing Judaic system. These two systems in antiquity have counterparts in modern times, each claiming to be "just" Judaism: Reform, or Orthodoxy, or Zionism, or Reconstructionism each has a definition of a way of life, its distinctive worldview, and its own account of who, and what, is (an) "Israel." Like all Judaisms, the Judaism of the dual Torahs called its social entity "Israel," and invested "Israel" with a full and encompassing statement of definition of the social entity – group, class, caste, family, nation, and the like – that that Judaism proposed to address.

I call that Judaism "the Judaism of the dual Torah" because its principal symbolic statement invoked the myth that at Sinai God revealed the Torah, or revelation, in written and oral forms. The one in writing is today contained in the Hebrew Scriptures. The one formulated and transmitted orally, commonly called Oral Torah, was originally memorized but is now written down, according to this Judaism, in the Mishnah, a philosophical law code brought to closure at ca. 200 C.E., to which the (Babylonian) Talmud forms the authoritative commentary; in fact, the memorized Torah in late antiquity encompassed a variety of writings. These writings form the sole evidence on the basis of which we may describe the Judaism of the dual Torah. They fall into two parts: those centered upon the Mishnah, and those that amplify Scripture. (In a moment we shall divide them chronologically.) Those dealing with the Mishnah included the Tosefta, a corpus of supplements to statements in the Mishnah, organized around the framework of the Mishnah, and expressed in the language and cadences of the Mishnah; the Talmud of the Land of Israel, called the Yerushalmi, a systematic commentary to thirty-nine tractates of the sixty-two tractates of the Mishnah, brought to closure at ca. 400 C.E., and, finally, the Bavli, or Talmud of Babylonia, of ca. 600 C.E., which comments on thirty-seven tractates of the Mishnah (and not the same ones addressed in the Yerushalmi). Among the commentaries to the written Torah that came to closure in this same period were three that cite the Mishnah and imitate its language and cadences and may have reached their conclusion by ca. 300 C.E. – Sifra to Leviticus, Sifré to Numbers, and Sifré to Deuteronomy – and three that took shape in the period of the formation of the Yerushalmi – Genesis Rabbah, ca. 400, Leviticus Rabbah, ca. 450 C.E., and Pesiqta deRab Kahana, organized around synagogue lections for various special holy days, ca. 500 C.E. While these documents do not encompass the entirety of the writings included within the framework of the sector of the Torah called "oral," they do form the heart of the matter. Using this corpus of writings, I shall conduct an inquiry into how the word "Israel" functioned, the type of entities deemed to constitute an "Israel," and the circumstances in which a given mode of thinking about "Israel" served or did not serve.

The writings of the dual Torah fall into two groups, each with its own plan and program. The first begins with the Mishnah, a philosophical law book brought to closure at ca. 200 C.E., later on called the first statement of the oral Torah. In its wake, the Mishnah drew tractate Abot, ca. 250 C.E., a statement concluded a generation after the Mishnah on the standing of the authorities of the Mishnah; Tosefta, ca. 300 C.E., a compilation of supplements of various kinds to the statements in the Mishnah; and three systematic exegeses of books of Scripture or the written Torah – Sifra to Leviticus, Sifré to Numbers, and Sifré to Deuteronomy – of indeterminate date but possibly concluded by 300 C.E. These books overall form one stage in the unfolding of the Judaism of the dual Torah, which emphasized issues of sanctification of the life of Israel, the people, in the aftermath of the destruction of the Temple of Jerusalem in 70 C.E., in which, it was commonly held, Israel's sanctification came to full realization in the bloody rites of sacrifice to God on high. I call this system a Judaism without Christianity, because the issues found urgent in the documents of this phase address questions not pertinent to the Christian *défi* of Israel.

The second set of writings begins with the Talmud of the Land of Israel, or Yerushalmi, generally supposed to have come to a conclusion at ca. 400 C.E.; Genesis Rabbah, assigned to about the next half century; Leviticus Rabbah, ca. 450 C.E.; Pesiqta deRab Kahana, ca. 450–500 C.E; and, finally, the Talmud of Babylonia or Bavli, assigned to the late sixth or early seventh century, ca. 600 C.E. The two Talmuds systematically interpret passages of the Mishnah, and the other documents, as is clear, do the same for books of the written Torah. Some other treatments of biblical books important in synagogue liturgy, particularly the Five Scrolls – Lamentations Rabbati, Esther Rabbah, and the like – are supposed to have reached closure at this time as well. This second set of writings introduces, alongside the paramount issue of Israel's sanctification, the matter of Israel's salvation, with doctrines of history, on the one side, and the Messiah, on the other, given prominence in the larger systemic statement. I call this stage a Judaism despite Christianity, because it lays points of stress and emphasis that, in retrospect, appear to respond to, and to counter, the challenge of Christianity. From the beginning of the legalization of Christianity in the early fourth century, to the establishment of Christianity at the end of that same century, Jews in the Land of Israel found themselves facing a challenge that, prior to Constantine, they had found no compelling reason to consider. The specific crisis came when the Christians pointed to the success of the Church in the politics of the Roman state as evidence that Jesus Christ was king of the world, and that his claim to be Messiah and King of Israel had now found vindication. When the Emperor Julian in 361–3 C.E. apostasized and renewed state patronage of paganism, he permitted the Jews to begin to rebuild the Temple, part of his large plan of humiliating Christianity. His prompt death on an Iranian battlefield supplied further evidence for heaven's choice of the Church and the truth of the Church's allegations concerning the standing and authority of Jesus as the Christ. The Judaic documents that reached closure in the century after these events attended to questions of salvation, such as the doctrine of history and of the Messiah, and the authority of the sages' reading of Scripture as against the Christians' interpretation, that had earlier not enjoyed extensive consideration. In all, this second Judaism met the challenge of the events of the fourth century. The Judaic system of the dual Torah, expressed in its main outlines in the Yerushalmi and associated compilations of biblical exegeses concerning Genesis, Leviticus, and some other scriptural books, culminated in the Bavli, which emerged as the authoritative document of the Judaism of the dual Torah from then to now.

Before we proceed, let us take up and dismiss a minor problem. In today's world the word "Israel" commonly is made to refer to the State of Israel, and the word "Israeli" to a citizen of that nation. "Israel" also may refer to a particular place, namely, the State of Israel or the Land of Israel. But that narrow and particularly political, "enlandized" meaning is new, beginning, as it does, in 1948. Long prior to that time, and even today, there has been a second and distinct meaning, "Israel" as "all Jews everywhere," the people of Israel. This "Israel" defined as "the Jewish people," sometimes capitalized as "the Jewish People," identifies "Israel" with a trans-national "community." It is a very important meaning of the word, for Scripture's many references to "Israel," as in "the Guardian of Israel does not slumber or sleep," then are taken to refer to that people or People. Throughout the liturgy of the synagogue, "Israel" always refers to the people, wherever they live, and not to the State of Israel today. The fact that these two meanings, the one particular to a state, the other general to a scattered group, contradict one another alerts us to a problem. It is that a single word may stand for two things. As we shall see in the pages of this book, it may stand for many more. Indeed, thinking about "Israel" leads us deep into the generative processes of the system at hand. In their reflection on that to which "Israel" is to be compared and contrasted, in their selection of a particular set of comparisons from a repertoire of metaphors available from Scripture, in their mode of thought on the matter, whether philosophical and abstract, whether political and concrete, the framers of the Judaic systems before us portray in this detail the character and conscience of their entire systems.

I want to find out how people bring to concrete and vivid expression their thought about the social entity that in their minds they imagine that they constitute, along with their families and others of like opinion and life pattern. When they speak of "Israel," to what sort of social group do they refer, and how do they think about that group? The answer can help solve a much larger issue, the way in which systems take shape, the relationship, in the formation of systems, between circumstance and context, contents and convictions. What we address, therefore, in this study is a striking example of how people explain to themselves who they are as a social entity. For religion is a powerful force in human society and culture, and is realized not only or mainly in theology; religion works through the social entity that embodies that religion. Religions form churches or peoples or nations or communities or other entities that, in the concrete, constitute the "us," as against "the nations" or merely "them." And religions carefully explain, in deeds and in words, who that "us" is – and they do it every day. If we wish to know how that "we" or "us" attains concrete definition within the larger religious worldview and way of life of a particular religious system, we do well therefore to invoke the case of Judaic systems or Judaisms, because in nearly all known Judaisms the "us" of "Israel" forms an indicative and critical element.

NOTES

1 At no point in this book do I address issues that pertain to the world beyond late antiquity, defined as the age from the first to the seventh centuries C.E. I have dealt with the Judaic systems of modern times in my *Death and Birth of Judaism* (New York: Basic Books, 1987), and with the foundations of the paradigm of Judaic systems in my *Self-Fulfilling Prophecy: Exile and Return in the History of Judaism* (Boston: Beacon Press, 1987). These are quite separate problems, which do not impinge upon this book in any way.

CHAPTER 1

Imagining Society, Re-visioning "Israel"

i. Imagining Society

We do not experience but only imagine "society," because "society" viewed whole is something too abstract and remote from everyday life to afford a concrete encounter. We know individual people. But we generalize and so in our minds conceive, or imagine, that the concrete persons we encounter represent or form part of that abstraction, society. Thus we make sense of the world beyond the here and the now of everyday life. We move from what we know, the concrete and immediate, to what we do not know. Whatever lies beyond our experience, encompassing all modes of abstraction and all conceptions of not merely event but process, demands to be set into relationship with what we already know. Connections that we make, abstractions that we perceive only in their concrete manifestations, processes that we can imagine but not identify – not the blow but power, not the caress but love – these form the raw material of mind. Accordingly, when we name and treat as real and concrete what are in fact abstractions and intangible processes, we impose upon ourselves the need to compare the abstract to the concrete. We therefore think in a process of analogy, contrast, comparison, and metaphor about something that, to begin with, we ourselves have identified and so made up in our minds.

Take a group, for example. When two or more persons perceive themselves to bear traits in common and to constitute a group on account of those indicative traits, they face a range of choices in thinking about the classification and character of that social entity that they imagine they compose. It can be immediate, but it does not have to be. A family, a village, a neighborhood, a town – these form part of felt experience; we can walk in the streets, recognize relationship with persons we know and our relationship to whom we can name, and trace the outer limits of the settled area. But when people identify with others they have not met and may never meet, the process of the search for appropriate metaphors to take the place of absent experience in the everyday world begins. In thinking about such abstractions as social entities, people appeal to comparisons between the concrete things they know and the abstract things they seek to explain and express for themselves.[1]

When we speak of such large abstractions as society, or people, or nation – for instance, use the word "family" to mean a social entity or aggregate of persons beyond the one in which we grew up and to which we bear blood relationships, or call a friend or a political ally a "brother" – we move onward from the concrete to the abstract. That metaphorical mode of thought permits us to speak about things though we cannot point in diurnal encounter to the concrete experience of those things. A principal abstraction therefore constitutes a social entity that transcends the concrete experience and pragmatic knowledge of two or more people together. How we think about those abstractions that in the most general and indeterminate terms we may call "social entities" – the result of generalization from the here and now to the out-there, the outcome of a process of imagination, fantasy, and reflection, or the results of that intellectual process – lends substance to our perception, through now-real and concrete expectation, of the hitherto unknown and unfelt but merely imagined. In these processes of thought we resort to metaphor so as to treat as a thing what originates out of process or abstraction. That is how reflection and imagination about the commonalities of specific things form an exercise in metaphorical thought.

How does a religious system serve as a mode of the nurture of metaphors for interpreting our social experience of the concrete? We recall the difference between caress, the concrete, and love, the abstraction. How we move from the immediate to the general forms the problem of reflection and, through reflection, generalization. People are used to thinking of philosophy and also of science as modes of rigorous generalization. But religion, no less than philosophy and science, also forms a principal mode of profound thought about process and abstraction, mediating between immediate encounter and the abstract and generalizing theology. For religion gives concrete definition to what lies beyond immediate experience, as much as to what is formed of concrete encounter. For example, religion has the power of transforming cells of like-minded persons into believers, and believers into a Church or the saved or holy people or a supernatural family or (as is most common) even a social entity that is altogether sui generis. Religion as a mode of thought competes with philosophy and science because all three exercise that same power of turning ineffable abstraction, intangible relationship, or a process beyond palpable perception into a thing we can define and identify. Religion exercises this power, whether it addresses God in heaven or speaks of humanity in the home, street, and town; identifies a building as holy; defines a properly performed gesture as sanctifying; or declares two or three individuals to form a society, a holy entity, for instance, that is the embodiment here and now of God's people or God's own person or body.

Among the many supernatural works of enchantment accomplished by religion, the one studied here is the capacity of religion to transform individuals and families into a corporate body, imputing relationships other than those natural to location or family genealogy. Religion can name and treat as real the otherwise-random confluence, in belief and behavior, of isolated groups of people, to persuade those families that they form part of something larger than their limited congeries, even though no one in those families has ever seen, or can ever encompass in a single vision, the entirety of that something more, that entire nation or mystical body. In simple terms, religions speak of social entities made up of their devotees. These they turn from concrete entity in the here and now into abstractions merely represented, in the here and now, by the present exemplar. The social entity turns into a symbol for something more. So the social group (defined presently) is transformed from what the world sees to what the eye of faith perceives, becoming, in the case of a Judaism, an "Israel."

Thinking about the social entity in particular demands metaphorical thinking because a social group that does not rest, for its being, upon constant and palpable interaction exists mainly in the abstract. It is as an abstraction that is (merely) exemplified by the group near at hand, the one that does consist of individuals who do interact. When people think about that abstraction – about the Church or the Israel or "the nation of Islam" of which they form a part – they invoke a variety of concrete metaphors. Whatever metaphors they use, they are engaged in a transaction of a symbolic character, in which they propose to express their sense not by reference to what they can see and touch, but to what, in the things they can see and touch, corresponds to that social entity.

ii. The Social Entity of a Religious System

By "social entity," using the most general language I can find, I mean "social group," defined as two or more persons who exhibit the traits of a group – that is, traits that emerge when the participants form a common identity and express a feeling of unity concerning common goals and shared norms. The social group involves direct interaction and communication, actions designed to carry out a system of values, and may be a family, a village, or any other entity in which there is a concrete encounter among two or more persons who perceive themselves to form such a group. At this point, the process of abstraction begins.

Specifically, a social group may take shape among persons who do not necessarily interact and communicate with one another, but who do share a common system of values. It may derive from an intangible process, with the result that participants in the group invoke metaphors from the known social world (e.g., family) to explain that unknown fact of social life that, in their minds, they now have constituted. That sort of social group differs from the one formed by a family, in which there is interaction, or a village or a neighborhood of like-minded persons, in which there are shared values among persons who see one another and form their sense of constituting a group on the basis of everyday activity. In the context of a religious system, this more abstract social group constitutes an entity defined by common goals and shared norms, but – and this explains the metaphorical character of thought about that entity – one in which all its individual members do not interact.

Such social groups may prove formal or informal, but a social group constituted by a religion at its essence is formal, for it is very carefully defined with imposed norms of faith and action. A social group may appeal to extended kinship. By definition religious systems are not made up of genealogical units, though they may identify the social group formed by the religion as a family or an extended family. When they do posit shared ancestry, they engage in a symbolic transaction, once more requiring us to investigate how the *is* becomes the *ought,* how the everyday shades into the abstract. Along these same lines, a social group may appeal to the society formed of the encounter among individuals who never, in fact, meet. Here too the encounter is one in theory and in the abstract, joining in a single social group persons who imagine that they know and understand one another but who in reality do not intersect.

A further instance of the power of metaphor shows us how a

group may in its own mind define its relationship with the outside world. People who share traits with others may determine that they are separate from those others and constitute a minority, as against the majority formed by those "others." In its own mind, therefore, a social group may be classified as a minority group, finding definition in contrast with another, larger group, defined within the same larger classification. By definition a religious system will create such a minority group, in that the world beyond will be made up of many such groups, of which the one at hand is not likely to form the largest, that is, to constitute a numerical majority. The symbolic transaction commences when the group defines itself by contrast to other groups, when it conceives of itself to constitute a minority-group type of group. In all of these ways, it is through metaphors evoked in description of the social group that we see the working of the imagination.

These symbolic transactions are realized through shared imagination or perception held in common – hence, in the metaphors by which abstractions such as "society" or "nation" reach concrete form in intellect and expectation alike. When broadly construed, these metaphors form gossamer threads, yet bond persons who do not commonly meet at all. The same act of imagination imposes upon persons the consciousness, and concrete character, of community. Symbolic transactions pertinent to the group life posited by a religious system constitute the social theory of that system[2] – the social entity to which and of which the system speaks. Because the symbolic transactions come to concrete expression in metaphors – hence, "social metaphors" – we find ourselves sorting out those metaphors that serve, and those that do not, in a given religious system.

In all, we deal with people who come together from time to time but who see themselves as forming a lasting society. Although they do not constitute a population or occupy a given territory, they see themselves as a society. They do not have large-scale, enduring political organizations or social institutions to draw them together, though, in their conception of the group, they will imagine both and call themselves a nation or a people. They are more than a crowd and far more than a mere category of society, such as people of a given age or occupation. But they also are much less in the concrete social facts of their existence than they conceive themselves to be. Hence comes the abstraction with which we deal under the title, "social entity of a religious system," or, in the case of a Judaism, an "Israel." And our interest is in that conception of the social entity, the social group, that forms the centerpiece of the religious system at hand.

iii. Re-visioning (an) "Israel" in Particular

In the literature under review, definition of an "Israel" and who belongs to it takes the form of spelling out the rules of relationship, which draws us squarely into our consideration of the relevance of metaphorical thinking. For to define one social entity, an "Israel," the authorships we encounter not only explain how that entity relates to some other. They also – and especially – compare and contrast that entity to some other. Accordingly, when our authorships wish to think about "Israel" or "an Israel," their ordinary mode of thought is to ask with what is "Israel" or "an Israel" to be compared; hence, in what ways it is like, and in what ways it is unlike, that with which it is compared. These then form the contrastive and analogical processes of reflection that I characterize as metaphorical thinking. Social metaphors refer to both the things to which authorships resort when thinking about the social entity, "Israel," and also the way in which they carry on their processes of thought. On the basis of that fixed mode of thought, I conceive the appropriate mode of inquiry to be an examination of metaphors of social entities, or social metaphors.

A second consideration also justifies appeal to metaphor, specifically, metaphors pertinent to society, as the means of making sense of sages' thinking about, and therefore doctrine of, Israel. As we shall see, when sages composed their consensus, it was as an act of stating in common the outcome of shared processes of imagination. To understand this matter, the reader must recall that the writings before us are not by individual authors, but derive from a consensus of a group concerning what should be said and how it should be stated. This collective literature, therefore, stands for not an author but an authorship, and it represents a social group – sages, at various times and places – thinking together and stating the consensus it has reached. This same literature deriving from a social group then undertakes to state what a still larger social group is and does; consequently, this literature represents – as a matter of utter facticity – a social group (sages) thinking about a social group ("Israel"). The systematic thought of a religious system about the social entity tells us about the social group to which that system's framers imagined that they addressed themselves. The social teachings of diverse religious systems form a considerable and commonplace subject of study.[3] In choosing a small chapter of that large subject, I do not innovate. But the ways in which a religious system defines its own society, in particular the modes of thought and processes of imagination that yield one picture of the social entity and not some other – that is not a routine inquiry.

iv.   "*An* Israel" and "*a* Judaism": A Social Metaphor in a Religious System

A social metaphor tells a group how to identify itself in two ways. First, the metaphor identifies the type of social group at hand, the genus; and, second, it will consequently define the species of the genus or type at hand. The process involves a number of pertinent questions: Is the social entity a family? Then how does it compare with other families? Is it a nation? Then in what way does it differ from other nations, and in what context does the category, nation, take on its definitive sense and meaning? Or a social group may declare itself sui generis, not like any other social group at all, but a genus unto itself, a third possibility between two available choices.

A set and sequence of social groups living in different times and places and not continuous with one another, Jews commonly told themselves tales of how in recorded time they had come into existence as a single social entity, "Israel," in a unitary and harmonious history. In these stories Jews appealed to various social metaphors, of two basic classifications. First, some held that the Jews – Israel – were sui generis, of a type of social entity lacking all counterpart, and thus not of a type into which all other social groups could be classified. Second, others maintained that Israel formed a distinct species of a common genus, whether family or nation or people. But under what conditions or circumstances will one metaphor take priority, and when will a different metaphor appear self-evidently compelling? Also, if a given metaphor serves, does it carry in its wake a variety of other metaphorical consequences in the way in which the group that invokes the metaphor thinks about itself and explains its collective existence? To state matters simply, if I know the operative metaphor, what else do I know about the group's thinking about itself beyond the metaphor? How can I form rules of predicting what traits a theory of a social group will carry in the wake of the generative metaphor of the group?

v.   The Ecology of Judaisms and the Centrality of the Social Metaphor

We can understand the religious system composed by the Judaism of the dual Torah only if we form a clear picture of the doctrine of "Israel." Why the importance of the social metaphor in the Judaism of the dual Torah?[4] The reason is that the doctrine of what is "Israel" and who is Israel, as worked out over seven hundred years, forms the critical component that held the whole system together. The ecological reason for the paramount concern with explaining the nature of the group, Israel, derives from two factors. The first was this Judaism's matrix, within the larger world of the Jews of the Land of Israel and their Scripture. The second was the point of origin of this particular Judaism, beyond the destruction of the temple in 70 C.E..

The story begins after 586 B.C.E. From that time forward all Judaisms that came into being framed a theory of "Israel," meaning, the group that a given Judaism identified as its social base. From the reconstitution of the Jews in the Land of Israel some three generations after the destruction of the first temple in 586 B.C.E., reflection on the character and composition of that social entity began with the self-conscious question: Who is Israel and what are the conditions for being Israel? Every Judaism required answers to that question, which formed a definitive trait of the social ecology in which all Judaisms took shape. The urgency of the issue, "Israel," may be explained by reference to the reconstruction of the story of the group accomplished, out of materials referring to the period before 586 B.C.E., by authorships after that turning point. Specifically, that point of entry into reflection on the issues of group life – the identification of an appropriate definition, a social metaphor for the group – was dictated by the interpretation placed upon the events of the sixth century by the emergent scripture, the Pentateuch or Five Books of Moses. That document, composed in part from revised materials deriving from the period before the destruction in 586 B.C.E., treated as critical the issues of the ongoing life of the community, seen as not a given but a gift, and its relationship to the land that it possessed, interpreted as subject to diverse stipulations. The upshot was the doctrine of the experience of exile and return, and that doctrine imparted to the social entity formed by the Jews of the Land a heightened reality, treating as problematic and uncertain what, in the view of others, was simply another fact of the social life of humanity in that region. Accordingly, any Judaism required for a complete statement of its system a doctrine of who and what is Israel, the social group.

Every Judaism from the beginning, between 586 B.C.E. with the destruction of the first temple and 450 B.C.E. with the return to Zion, the rebuilding of the temple, and the promulgation of the Torah of Moses as the governing document, addressed the issue of who is Israel. Each appealed to its social metaphor in stating an answer to that question. The reason that the definition of what, and who, (an) Israel is played so critical role a in all Judaism is not difficult to imagine. It was, specifically, the unsettling and disorienting experience selected and composed into an account of Israelite society by the authorship of Scripture in its final version. That authorship selected as normative two experiences – the one, the exile from Jerusalem and destruction of the temple, the other, the return to Zion and rebuilding of the temple. The paradigm of exile and return made it difficult to think of the life of the group as a given, a fixed star in the firmament of reality. Rather, that unsettling account of the life of the group portrayed the group's collective existence as a gift and not a given, as something subjected to stipulations and conditions, for example, a covenant with God. The terms of the covenant – involving life on the land endowed with moral traits, uncertainty of the ongoing existence of the group unless certain conditions were met, and the notion that the group came from somewhere and was en route to some farther destination – highlighted the issue of who is Israel, and what an Israel is.

That framing of events into the pattern at hand represents an act of powerful imagination and interpretation, what I have called a symbolic transaction. It is an experience that is invented, because no one person or group both went into "exile" and also "returned home." Diverse experiences have been sorted out, various persons have been chosen, and the whole has been worked into a system by those who selected history out of happenings, and models out of masses of persons. I say "selected," because no Jews after 586 B.C.E. actually had experienced what in the aggregate Scripture says happened. Scripture does not record a particular person's experience. More to the point, if it is not autobiographical, writing for society at large the personal insight of a singular figure, it also is not an account of a whole nation's story. Because the original exile encompassed mainly the political classes of Jerusalem and some useful populations alongside, many Jews in the Judea of 586 B.C.E. never left. And, as is well known, a great many of those who ended up in Babylonia stayed there, with only a minority returning to Jerusalem. Consequently, the story of exile and return to Zion encompasses what happened to only a few families, who identified themselves as the family of Abraham, Isaac, and Jacob, and their genealogy as the history of Israel. Those families that stayed and those that never came back, had they written the Torah, would have told as normative and paradigmatic a different tale altogether.

That experience of the few that formed the paradigm for Israel beyond the restoration taught as normative lessons of alienation. Let me emphasize the lessons people claimed to learn out of the events they had chosen for their history: The life of the group is uncertain, subject to conditions and stipulations. Nothing is set and given, but all things are a gift, land and life itself. But what actually did happen in that uncertain world – exile but then restoration – marked the group as special, different, select. There were other ways of seeing things, and the pentateuchal picture was no more compelling than any other. Those Jews who did not go into exile and those who did not "come home" had no reason to take the view of matters that characterized the authorship of Scripture. The life of the group need not have appeared more uncertain, more subject to contingency and stipulation, than the life of any other group. The land did not require the vision that imparted to it the enchantment, the personality, that, in Scripture, it received: "The land will vomit you out as it did those who were here before you." And the adventitious circumstance of Iranian imperial policy – a political happenstance – did not have to be recast into return. So nothing in the system of Scripture – exile for reason, return as redemption – followed necessarily and logically. Everything was invented or interpreted, much as with the force and power of metaphor.

That experience of the uncertainty of the life of the group in the century or so from the destruction of the first temple of Jerusalem by the Babylonians in 586 B.C.E. to the building of the second temple of Jerusalem by the Jews, with Persian permission and sponsorship returned from exile, formed the paradigm. With the promulgation of the "Torah of Moses" under the sponsorship of Ezra, the Persians' viceroy, at ca. 450 B.C.E., all future Israels would then refer to that formative experience as it had been set down and preserved as the norm for Israel in the mythic terms of that "original" Israel, the Israel not of Genesis and Sinai and the end at the moment of entry into the promised land, but the "Israel" of the families that recorded as the rule and the norm the story of both the exile and the return. In that minority genealogy, that story of exile and return, alienation and remission, imposed on the received stories of preexilic Israel and adumbrated time and again in the Five Books of Moses and addressed by the framers of that document in their work over all, we find that paradigmatic statement in which every Judaism, from then to now, found its structure and deep syntax of social existence, the grammar of its intelligible message.

To be (an) "Israel" – the social component of a Judaism – from then to now has meant to ask what it means to be Israel. The original pattern meant that an Israel would be a social group the existence of which had been called into question and affirmed – and therefore always would be called into question and remained perpetually to be affirmed. Every Judaism then would find as its task the recapitulation of the original Judaism. That is to say, each made its own distinctive statement of the generative and critical resentment contained within that questioning of the given, that deep understanding of the uncertain character of the existence of the group in its normal location and under circumstances of permanence that (so far as the Judaic group understood things) characterized the life of every other group but Israel. What for everyone else (so it seemed to the Judaisms addressed to the Israels through time) was a given for Israel was a gift. What all the nations knew as how things *must* be Israel understood as how things *might not be:* exile and loss, alienation and resentment, but, instead of annihilation, renewal, restoration, reconciliation, and (in theological language) redemption. So that paradigmatic experience, the one beginning in 586 and ending in ca. 450 B.C.E., written down in that written Torah of Moses, made its mark. That pattern, permanently inscribed in the Torah of God to Moses at Sinai, would define for all Israels over all time that matter of resentment demanding recapitulation: leaving home, coming home. An "Israel" – any "Israel" – would then constitute a social entity engaged by exile and return. But that covered a wide range of possibilities.[5]

NOTES

1 I hope in these brief remarks to exempt myself from the interesting discussions on metaphor carried on in literary criticism, as distinct from the discussion in the area of social thought. Among the papers assembled by Sheldon Sacks, ed., *On Metaphor* (Chicago: University of Chicago Press, 1978), the one I find most helpful is that by David Tracy, who points toward the study of literary genres not merely "as classificatory or taxonomic devices but as genuinely productive of meaning" (p. 95). That, of course, is the upshot of my analysis of metaphors in Jews' thinking about the social entity formed by them.

2 In Part II I introduce the notion of a comprehensive theory of society, whole and in all of its parts and details as distinct from a system's social theory. The importance of that notion will be explained in due course.

3 The teachings concerning the society constituted by a particular religious group define a familiar and perfectly routine subject of description, analysis, and interpretation. I have in mind not only the teachings concerning society, but the very definition of society, and this for its part is not a common subject in the history of religion.

4 This brief summary alludes to the findings of *Judaism: The Evidence of the Mishnah* (Chicago: University of Chicago Press, 1981) and *Self-Fulfilling Prophecy: Exile and Return in the History of Judaism* (Boston: Beacon Press, 1987).

5 In the concluding chapter I offer a criterion for assessing the importance of the social metaphor in a religious system. It is by no means a subjective judgment, and, therefore, reflection on the social entity, in different religious systems. This is shown in concrete cases of Judaisms.

PART I

"Israel" in the First Statement of Judaism, 70–300 C.E.

CHAPTER 2

"Israel" in Relationship to Heaven

i. The Judaism of Sanctification

The doctrine of "Israel" implicit through the Mishnah, ca. 200 C.E., and explicit in many of its details may be stated very simply: The community now stands in the place of the temple of Jerusalem, destroyed in 70 C.E. What that meant is that the word for the social entity, "Israel," would now serve, within the systemic structure at hand, as had the temple. The temple walls had marked the boundaries between holy and ordinary. So now did "Israel." As in the vision of Ezekiel in chapters 40–47, the temple had marked the boundaries among the hierarchy of society, with the high priest going to the innermost sanctum, then the priests going closest to the holiest place, with others approaching in hierarchical distance: Levites, Israelite males, women, and onward outward. So now did "Israel" serve this second, inner-facing task of social hierarchization, as well as the outer-facing task of political differentiation of "Israel" from everyone else, "the nations." Let me spell out the origins, sources, and structure of that metaphor of "Israel" as a social entity wholly apart and holy.

The Judaic system of the dual Torah began the first of the two stages of its formative history, the one marked by the Mishnah and related writings with an event comparable with the generative crisis of the pentateuchal system of ca. 586–450 B.C.E. It was yet another destruction of a Jerusalem temple, this one in 70 C.E. Specifically, the crisis precipitated by the destruction of the temple of Jerusalem in 70 C.E. centered attention on what can have endured beyond disaster. The Jews had organized their theory of themselves and their society around that temple for the preceding six hundred years, a span of time that separates America from pre-Columbian times and Europe

21

from the Hundred Years War.[1] People endured. Processes of abstract thought took that concrete fact – Jews were still around – and transformed the survivors into continuators, "Israel" of old, now, and to the end of time. Why focus attention on that category or social group, "people"? We recall the established conviction, critical to the pentateuchal system, that "Israel" was special, singular, selected, so that what happened to "Israel" signified God's will. What emerged in the Mishnah, which formed the climax and conclusion of one process of thought beginning with the destruction, was the sustained exegesis, in exhaustive detail, of the meaning of "Israel" as the holy people of God – that is, "Israel" in relationship to Heaven. To state matters simply, a theological anthropology, expressed in the powerful metaphor, "in our image, after our likeness," found its counterpart in a theological sociology of "Israel" as the social group that lived a way of life in the image and after the likeness of heaven: a holy way of life.[2] To understand this fundamental trait of "Israel" as a social metaphor within the Judaism of the dual Torah in its first phase, we begin with the generative paradigm within which events found meaning.

That transformation of the existing social group into metaphor, turning "Israel" into the holy people living the holy life, marked a recapitulation of the typical and fundamental characteristic of the original, and generative, paradigm. (Some) Jews, calling themselves "Israel," because of their (in their mind) amazing experience from 586 to 450 B.C.E. of loss and restoration, death and resurrection, had attained remarkable self-consciousness. This sense of the (selected) persons as a social group came to expression in the Pentateuch. As we just noted, the pentateuchal writings, received as the Torah revealed by God to Moses at Sinai, underlined that point. In the life of a nation that had ceased to be a nation on its own land and then once more had regained that condition, the present calamity rehearsed once more the paradigm of the death and resurrection. Consequently, the truly fresh and definitive component of the new system, after 70 C.E., in fact restated in contemporary terms the fixed and established doctrine, confronting the framers of all Judaic systems, with which the first Judaism, the Judaism of the Torah of "Moses" after 450 B.C.E., had commenced.

The Mishnah's system did not begin on its own. Just as its authorship drew upon the paradigms of Scripture, so they received from prior systems[3] important modes of thought (in particular, generative metaphors) from their immediate predecessors. Profound reflection on who and what is "Israel" derived from one of the contributory partners in the new Judaism, nascent after 70 C.E. That antecedent was Pharisaism, a sect within the Jews of the Land of

"Israel" during the last century and a half prior to the destruction of the temple. For the Judaism of the dual Torah, culminating in the publication of the Mishnah as its first literary component in ca. 200 C.E., did not begin at 70 C.E., any more than the pentateuchal story of exile and return had commenced the telling in 450 B.C.E. Just as the ultimate statement of 450 B.C.E. drew upon received materials, even upon some from the period before 586 B.C.E., all of which to be sure were recast in the final version of matters, so the Mishnah's system inherited important components from the Pharisaism of the period before the destruction of the Jerusalem temple and end of its sacrificial rite in the year 70 C.E. Pharisaism framed one important component of the social theory of the Judaic system of the dual Torah represented, in its initial statement, by the Mishnah. When we grasp the issue critical to the Mishnah's larger system, we see the component of the system contributed by Pharisaism – the implicit theory of "Israel."

The theory of "Israel" implicit in Pharisaic practice, particularly the well-documented way of life involving observance of the purity laws that govern the temple cult in the streets and homes of the country far beyond the temple walls, marks "Israel" as holy, as much as the Temple and Land were holy. For Pharisaic practice points toward the theory that Jews beyond the temple – that is, "Israel" outside of the priesthood – were to keep the purity laws. The implicit conviction is that everyone should eat in accord with the rules of the temple altar: food fit for holy rite, consumed by persons made ready for holy deeds. To translate the matter into more general terms, Pharisaism before 70 C.E. had laid its stress upon the sanctification of all "Israel." Its doctrine of "Israel" encompassed as candidates for sanctification every Jew in the Holy Land. All were conceived to be subject to those rules of sanctification through cultic purity that, in the levitical statement of Scripture, originally pertained only to the priesthood, and then only when the priests engaged in the work of the temple and its sacrificial cult or in consuming their share of the sacrifices.

When the authorship of the Mishnah took as a critical issue the question of whether, in the aftermath of the destruction of the temple, "Israel" remained holy, and, if so, how that holiness inhered, that authorship carried forward an established theme. What now changed is that the issue became urgent, no longer a theme or an opportunity, but an inexorable and everyday concern. The centrality of "Israel" in the analogy of a people holy as the temple was holy, marked the Mishnaic system. "Israel" was a species of the genus, people or nation. But, in the system of the Mishnah's authorship, "Israel," the genus, possessed only the sole species, Israel. Other matters demanding attention included the meanings imputed to the category "Israel," the definition of that social entity, and how that entity was to be described in relationship to other such entities or entirely on its own. It is hardly surprising that thought on these issues formed the centerpiece of the Mishnah's system in the aftermath of the crisis that began with the destruction of Jerusalem and reached its climax in the defeat of Bar Kokhba in 135 C.E., three generations later, with its forceful and final result, the clear recognition that restoration would not come soon.

Identification as critical to the system of the Mishnah of the issue of "Israel" as a holy nation does not depend merely upon our reading, in theory, of the requirements of the political circumstances of the moment. In point of fact, the document itself, the Mishnah, makes its concerns abundantly known. Specifically, from the issues on which they concentrated their attention, we know that the issue of who and what is "Israel" profoundly troubled the Mishnah's authorship. For the question that provoked sustained thought finds definition in the points of emphasis of the document as a whole. An authorship that, with great force and in stupefying detail, maintained that the holiness of the life of "Israel," the people, a holiness that had formerly centered on the temple, now endured and transcended the physical destruction of the building and the cessation of sacrifices, clearly found urgent the question of sanctification after the destruction. The premise of the Mishnah's system and its recurrent message stated in countless details that "Israel" the people was holy, the medium and the instrument of God's sanctification. What required sanctification, in particular, were the modalities of life lived in community (and none conceived of a holy life in any other mode, such as monachism, lying outside the imagination of this authorship): procreation, nourishment, family, land, time, village, temple. The system then instructed "Israel" to act as if "Israel," the Jewish people, like the temple of old, formed a utensil of the sacred. That is why I maintain the view that, for the Mishnah's authorship, one critical, generative and urgent issue centered upon the definition and status of "Israel." That approach to thinking about "Israel," stressing the everyday life as the locus of sanctification, derived, to begin with, from Pharisaism.

Pharisaism, with its notion that ordinary people could and should obey the rules of sanctification and so pretend to be of the priestly caste, therefore formed one of the two principal antecedents of the group that, after 70 C.E., began the processes of reflection and legislation which culminated, in 200 C.E., with the publication of the Mishnah and its legislation as the law for the Jews of the Land of Israel and of Babylonia as well. Pharisaism shared with pre–70 C.E. scribism responsibility for the foundations of the first stage in the Judaism of the dual Torah, the one contributing method, the other, content. By "scribism" I mean the professional ideal of the pre–70 C.E. scribes, a profession of clerks and lawyers who interpreted and applied pertinent passages of Scripture to the practical life of the community of the day. Joined to the Pharisaic mode of looking at life, now centered in the doctrine of the holiness of "Israel" the holy people, was the substance of the scribal ideal, the stress on learning of Torah and carrying out its teachings. The emerging system would in due course claim, like the scribes of old, that it was possible to serve God not only through sacrifice, but also through study of Torah. So the precipitating question was the question of the priests and Pharisees: How to serve God? And the ultimate answer was the answer of scribes: through Torah learning. The impact upon the definition of "Israel" need hardly be spelled out: "Israel" would then be the people that received and studied the Torah. But we look in vain in the pages of the Mishnah for sayings that drew that consequence or even rested on that premise.

Whatever the gifts of the Pharisees and scribes, the doctrine of society, "Israel," as the locus of the sacred that we do find central to the Mishnaic statement nonetheless is essentially fresh. Turning "Israel" into a metaphor of a particular order, and treating the metaphor "Israel" as paramount in the symbolic system of the Mishnah defines one distinctive trait of the Mishnah's authorship's ultimate statement. To understand the originality of that fundamental definition through metaphor of the social group as transcending the perceived family, household, and village, we recall a decisive fact. Neither of the two principal contributors to the system had under-stood themselves as encompassing social entities – for example, as entire or "all Israel," in the way in which, as we shall see,[4] the Essenes of Qumran did. There is not a shred of evidence that the Pharisaic group regarded outsiders as "non-Israel," only as cultically unclean. People with whom one will not eat lunch are not therefore gentiles, merely different in that they are not suitable companions for lunch. So Pharisaism was not understood, so far as we can see, by its devotees to form or define an "Israel." Quite to the contrary, Pharisaism had laid its stress upon *universal* keeping of the law, obli-gating every Jew to do what only the elite caste, the priests, were normally expected to accomplish. Pharisaism therefore represented an alternative theory of the social hierarchization of "Israel," not a fresh conception of "Israel." Scribes for their part had posited as critical the study of the Torah and the centrality of the learned person in the religious system. But scribes formed a profession, not imagining that their ideal was to be realized – so far as we can see – by everyone in society. And by definition scribes did not, could not, conceive of themselves as coextensive with "Israel."

The received conception found itself transformed in the Mishnaic system, which held out the ideal of sanctification as pertinent not solely to the home and village, the limits of the imagination of the Pharisaic system, let alone to the procedures of certain limited social transactions, such as had occupied the attention of the scribes. The excruciating detail of humble life subjected to the exegesis of the Mishnaic hermeneutic of the sanctification of "all 'Israel'" defined "all Israel," that is, "everybody," as holy in the here and now, in a way in which the temple priests, the Pharisees, and (in their context) the scribes prior to 70 C.E. did not.

True, the Mishnaic system carried to the logical conclusion the mode of social thought of both Pharisaism and scribism, bringing to its fulfillment the fundamental direction of the thinking of both groups. But the something more in the Mishnah's doctrine of "Israel" that differentiated the nascent system from its progenitors was the sustained interest the larger polity of "Israel" beyond the home and family, beyond the village and its petty transactions, such as Pharisaism and scribism took into account. The modalities of the sacred under circumstances after 70 C.E. – that is, conditions by definition unaffected by Pharisaic doctrine, now prevailing in the everyday life of all "Israel," meaning every Jew in the Land of "Israel" – now entered the realm of sanctification subject to the discourse of the new system. The authorship of the Mishnah concurred that "Israel" in its entirety must frame a kingdom of priests and a holy people, but to that authorship, sanctification now flowed outward, over and beyond the ruined walls of the Jerusalem temple.

The concrete meaning of the hermeneutic that defined "Israel" as holy in the Mishnaic system is readily seen in the expansion of the received topical program of sanctification. It formed a vast re-definition accomplished by the Mishnah's framers for their system. Pharisaism for its part had earlier concerned itself with food and family – that is, sustaining life, creating life.[5] After 70 C.E., issues of the everyday life of commerce and agriculture, civil exchanges and politics, became subject to that same concern of effecting sanctification. The range of legislation in the second-century layers of thought expanded in ways unprecedented in the first century.[6] It seems well established that Pharisaism had earlier concerned itself with procreation and nourishment; marriages and meals conformed to the regulations understood as sanctifying. But nothing now in hand suggests that Pharisaism proposed doctrines affecting other areas of the common life. The Mishnah in its ultimate, encompassing, and socially comprehensive statement offered a political vision of its "Israel." Scribism before 70 C.E. (if once again we may dignify a professional doctrine and ideal as an *-ism*) for its part had dealt with Scripture, with documents, with details – but not with the main issues of national life, whether political or salvific, so far as we can now discern (here matters are still less certain). And the social vision of a profession did not carry outward to the notion that everyone in society must become qualified to join that profession. It was one thing to deem the Torah authoritative for everyone – so neutral and banal a statement cannot have provoked disagreement in Jewry at large. It was quite another to call upon everyone to master what the profession knew. That hardly represents an interest of scribism.

So, to state matters simply, if the worldview stressing Torah learning came from the scribes, and the way of life stressing universal observance of the law from the Pharisees, the encompassing and detailed doctrine of who is "Israel," expressed in the entire universe to which the Mishnah's authorship addressed itself, proves fresh and unpredictable. The arena for sanctification, *surviving* "Israel," holy to the Lord, encompassing the whole of the Jewish people beyond the caesura marked by the destruction of the temple, corresponded to the broadest frontiers of the Jews' social entity. What made the Judaic system aborning after 70 C.E. more than the sum of its primary components, Pharisaism and scribism, was that very doctrine, which neither Pharisaism nor scribism can have contributed: The exegesis of the entirety of the collective life of that social entity, in all of its humble and commonplace affairs, as the opportunity for sanctification. That is why I maintain, in the Judaism of the dual Torah in the first of its two phases, the centrality of the metaphor of "Israel." It is simply what makes the system work.[7]

The Mishnaic theory of "Israel" defined the system's urgent question that received a self-evidently valid answer. The reason is that the standing and even definition of "Israel" formed the critical and generative concern, with the temple in ruins and the prior political system ("state") no longer pertinent. The urgent issue of the second century, the standing and status of the defeated nation, now deprived of its connection to Heaven through the ancient cult, required a judgment on the sanctity of "Israel" now without that cult that, in the pentateuchal picture, signified the holiness of the people, "Israel." Scripture had said that God maintained the Presence in "Israel" within the tent of meeting, which was the temple of Jerusalem, where "Israel" provided nourishment through the upward-rising smoke of the altar fires, and whence the lines of natural and social order extended outward across the face of the villages of the holy land. The issue at hand was met head-on in the exegetical outreach of the Mishnah's authorship. The ruin of the cult, so the implicit judgment of the system maintained, did not mark the end of the collective, holy life of "Israel." What survived was the sanctity of the holy people, and hence originated the doctrine of "Israel" as it would come to richly detailed realization as the centerpiece of the system of the Judaism of the dual Torah.

The genius of the Mishnah's authorship's Judaic system of sanctification was to recognize that the holy people for the interim might reconstitute the temple in the sanctity of its own community life. Therefore the people had to be made holy, as the temple had been holy. The people's social life had to be sanctified, now also as the surrogate for what had been lost. That is why – much later on, long after the closure of the Mishnah – the rabbinic reading of the Judaism of the dual Torah would further maintain that all "Israel" must master the Torah, with the consequence that the rabbi served as the new priest, the study of Torah substituted for the temple sacrifice, and deeds of loving kindness were the social surrogate for the sin offering; thus personal sacrifice replaced animal sacrifice. All things fit together to construct out of two of the old Judaisms the worldview and way of life of the new and enduring system, the one that ultimately became the Judaism of the dual Torah. But that was not just yet. Before proceeding to the second stage in the formation of Judaism, we have to describe the first stage in its full, literary statement. And that brings us to the Mishnah, its contents, character, and system of sanctification of "Israel," viewed not as abstraction but as metaphor – that is, as a people, the genus, that was holy, the species.

ii.   The Mishnah's System of Sanctification

To understand the substance of the metaphor of "Israel" as holy, we have to revert to the issues of sanctification in the earliest phases of the unfolding system of the Mishnah. Two points of ordinary life formed the focus for concrete, social differentiation in the foundations of the Mishnah's system of sanctification: food and sex, the latter governing valid marriage. What people ate, how they conducted their sexual lives, and whom they married or to whom they gave their children in marriage would define the social parameters of their group. These facts indicate who was kept within the bounds, and who was excluded and systematically maintained at a distance. That is why and how sanctification functions to define the social thinking and therefore to lend shape to metaphors of the social entity of a system.

In the context of the Pharisees, who formed one initial component of the system of the Mishnah, these are the only things subject to the independent control of the small group. The people behind the laws at the earliest strata of the Mishnah's linear, sedimentary, and incremental unfolding,[8] after all, could not tell people other than their associates in their own group what to eat or whom to marry. But they could make their own decisions on these important, but mundane, matters. By making those decisions in one way and not in some other, they moreover could keep outsiders at a distance and those who originally adhered to the group within bounds. Without political control, they could not govern the transfer of property or other matters of public interest. But without political power, they could and did govern the transfer of their women. It was in that intimate aspect of life that they firmly established the outer boundary of their collective existence. The very existence of the group and the concrete expression of its life, therefore, comes under discussion in the transfer of women. Here we confront a theory of the place of women that is joined to a theory of the transfer of property and the definition of ownership. When the system takes a keen interest in women, it is primarily at that point in their life cycle where they move from one man to another – that is, at the interstices of their social existence. There is no tractate on the woman in marriage or the woman as daughter or the woman as widow, and scarcely a chapter on the woman as mother. But there are tractates on the betrothal of a woman, on the marriage agreement associated with the transfer of a woman from father to husband, on the dissolution of a marriage and transfer of property from the husband's to the woman's domain, on the standing of a woman vis-à-vis the deceased childless husband's brothers (levirate connection), on the woman as accused adulterer. Five of the seven tractates in the division called "women," meaning, of course, family, concerned that single issue of the transfer of women and the concomitant transfer of property.

The political status enjoyed by the continuators, after the destruction of the temple and again after the Bar Kokhba war was lost, broadened the horizons of the system builders. For, later on, in the mid-second century, the sages' group, serving as clerks in the government of the Jews' ethnarch in Palestine, whom the Jews knew as *nasi* or patriarch in the Land of "Israel," expanded in power and interest. Then, too, the range of systemic interests vastly broadened. Rules were generated in particular by doctrines defining the institutions of government, both civil and cultic, expressed in king and high priest and temple rite and upkeep, and the administration of all civil affairs, torts, damages, criminal law, and rules of conduct in the village and in the cult at appointed seasons and on holy time. The limited inherited concerns were therefore broadened in scope to take in the entirety of social life as sages imagined it. But the basic theory, established in the earlier phases of a continuous and linear process of expansion of the law, governed. Consequently the model of the original sect defined as holy dictated the shape of the law of the community as a whole, as the Mishnah's authorship stated that law. And that law then formed the detailed expression of a single overriding metaphor for "Israel."

The working out of the metaphor of "holy people" expressed in symbolic behavior principles of belief. Viewed systemically, the social entity shaped the worldview and way of life. Why was that the case? Because the issue taken to form the centerpiece of existence by the Mishnah's framers (but not necessarily by everyone else in their setting) concerned the standing and status of a social entity deprived of its former definitive institutions and indicative traits. Once the social issue came to predominate, then other components of the system as a whole would contribute to the sorting out of the details.[9] These constituents of the system then expressed in detail that generative logic framed within the metaphor for the social entity, which then served as the metaphor for the system as a whole.[10] These matters of stress on sanctification, early and late in the process of the formation of the Mishnah's system, point to a profound conviction about the Land, people, produce, condition, and context of nourishment. The setting was holy. The actors were holy. What they did that had to be protected in holiness was, at the outset, procreation and eating, and later, matters of civic and political concern. What was at stake at the very foundations may be grasped in the matter of eating, to which I have already alluded. When, we recall, the Jews ate their food at home, they were supposed to eat it the way priests did (so the book of Leviticus maintained) in the temple. And the way priests ate their food in the temple – that is, following the cultic rules and conditions observed in that setting – compared with the way God ate his food in the temple. Thus – again with our focus only on nourishment – God's food and locus of nourishment were to be protected from the same sources of danger and contamination, preserved in the same exalted condition of sanctification.

We may generalize on this matter, working our way outward from the temple toward the social boundaries of "Israel," as a holy nation in the analogy of the temple. By acting (initially, eating) like God, "Israel" may become like God in those ways in which humanity may attain godliness, not in essence but in process, not in consubstantiality but in way of life: the imitation of God. That is what I mean by a theological anthropology. That would yield a pure and perfect incarnation, on earth in the Land that was holy, of the model of Heaven. "Israel" then would form a social group that lived in accord with the disciplines of Heaven, "like God," "in our image, after our likeness," with that "our" supplying for the group a theological sociology to match the theological anthropology that compares the human being to God.

What is at stake in both anthropological and sociological theologies of the Judaism of the dual Torah is worked out in the ongoing cult of sacrifice of the produce of the holy land to God in heaven above. To begin with the cult is the point of struggle between the forces of life and nourishment and the forces of death and extinction: meat, grain, oil, and wine, against corpse matter, dead creeping things, blood in the wrong setting, semen in the wrong context, and the like. Then, on the occasions when meat was eaten, mainly at the time of festivals or other moments at which sin offerings and peace offerings were made, people who wished to live ate their meat, and at all times ate the staples of wine, oil, and bread, in a state of life and so generated life. They kept their food and themselves away from the state of death as much as possible. And this heightened reality pertained at home, as much as in the temple, where most rarely went on ordinary days. The temple was the font of life, the bulwark against death. At the outset eating food was the critical act and occasion, just as the priestly authors of Leviticus and Numbers had maintained when they made laws governing, for example, slaughtering beasts and burning up their flesh, baking pancakes and cookies with and without olive oil and burning them on the altar, pressing grapes and making wine and pouring it out onto the altar. The nourishment of the Land – meat, grain, oil, and wine – was set before God and burned ("offered up") in conditions of perfect cultic antisepsis.

So much for the original conception, which, in its foundations, concerned not the social group, that is, "Israel," or a caste within "Israel," but a statement of anthropology: Who is humanity, what can a human being become? But the theological anthropology did yield what I have called a theological sociology: a theory of "Israel." As time passed, that same analogy, the notion of the imitation of God by obeying the rules of sanctification, overspread many other aspects of the life of the social group, so far as the authorship of the Mishnah could conceive that life. The consequence, by the mid-second century, was a fully worked-out metaphor for not the human being alone but "Israel" as a whole, the society or nation – the genus now does not matter – in the model of Heaven, that is, a theory for the sanctification of "Israel" and therefore a governing analogy: To constitute "Israel" is to form, on earth, a social group analogous to the court and community of Heaven.

Thus, the Mishnah presents a worldview that speaks of transcendent things, a way of life in response to the supernatural meaning of what is done, a heightened and deepened perception of the sanctification of "Israel" in deed and in deliberation. Sanctification in context meant two things, first, distinguishing "Israel" in all its dimensions from the world in all its ways; second, establishing the stability, order, regularity, predictability, and reliability of "Israel" in the world of nature and supernature in particular at moments and in contexts of danger. Danger meant instability, disorder, irregularity, uncertainty, and betrayal – experiences drawn from the just-passed encounter with Rome on the battlefield. Each topic of the system as a whole takes up a critical and indispensable moment or context of social being. Through what is said in regard to each of the Mishnah's principal topics, what the system of norms as a whole wishes to declare is fully expressed. Yet if the parts severally and jointly give the message of the whole, the whole cannot exist without all of the parts, so well joined and carefully crafted are they all.

iii. A Teleology without Eschatology for an "Israel" beyond History

The effect of the Mishnaic system was to limit the impact, upon the politics of the Jews in the Land of Israel, of the disruptive events of the late first and second century. The crisis precipitated by the destruction of the second temple and the failure of the second revolt, led by Bar Kokhba three generations later, to regain Jerusalem and rebuild the temple, therefore affected both the nation and the individual. For, in the nature of things, what happened in the metropolis of the country inevitably touched affairs of home and family. What connected the individual fate to the national destiny was the long-established conviction that the fate of the individual and the destiny of the Jewish nation depended upon the moral character both of the one and of the other. Disaster came about because of the people's sin, so went the message of biblical history and prophecy. The sins of individuals and of nation alike ran against the revealed will of God, the Torah. So reflection upon the meaning of the recent catastrophe inexorably followed paths laid out long ago, trod from one generation to the next. But we look in vain in the Mishnaic statement for attention to these matters as a principal concern. Not salvation consequent upon the remission of sin but the sanctification of "Israel" through the sustaining, holy way of life represented the choice of the Mishnah's authorship. The silence of that authorship proves suggestive when we contemplate the emphases of other authorships of the same age.

While, as we recall, in the same period, from before 70 C.E. onward, as the Mishnah took shape, the Gospels were being written, we look in vain in the Mishnah's corpus of issues at the end of the first century for response to the presence of the followers of Jesus within "Israel," the Jewish nation, in its Land. Christian writers addressed issues generated by the logic of their several distinct systems. When they considered their systemic "Israels," in the encounter with their setting, they defined for themselves an "Israel" of their own perceptions.[11] Paul's "Israel" of course proved the most subtle;[12] the later *adversus judaeos* writers made up an "Israel" for the purposes of argument, from the repertoire of Justin's dialogue with Trypho onward covering an established and conventional program of debate with an "Israel" that existed for polemical purposes. And the same is so, as we have seen, for the authorship of the Mishnah. It follows, for example, that what mattered about the Pharisees to the Christian writers derived from what mattered in general to those writers. This had to do with the (systemically important) contrast between purity laws and a different sort of purity altogether. We look in the Mishnah in vain for evidence that issues presented by the Christian group within the Jewish social entity of the Land of "Israel" received attention within those circles that, over time, nurtured the conceptions ultimately written down in the Mishnah. Later on, as we shall see in part two of this book, the agenda of Christian theologians and Judaic sages did converge; political conditions necessitated response by both parties to the same theological issues. But no political facts in the first and second centuries required the Mishnah's authorities to address matters urgent to Christian authors. The reason was that, before the legalization of Christianity by Constantine at the beginning of the third century, the development of the Christian communities contained nothing of compelling interest to the Mishnah's sages. I cannot point to a single issue critical to Christian writers on which Mishnah's sages laid down a central and definitive doctrine. We shall understand the impact of Christianity's political triumph in the fourth century upon the second phase of the Judaic system of the dual Torah only when we see how utterly remote from the Christian *défi* was the urgent question and the compelling response of the first phase of that same Judaic system.

The Mishnah's system therefore presents a cultic Judaism of sancti-

fication, temporarily without a temple that emerged in a world in
which there (to the framers) was no Christianity. Here we see the
Judaism that flowed from the critical question framed by the destruction of the temple. What that Judaism did not find necessary – for
example, a doctrine of the authority of Scripture and a systematic
exegetical effort at the linking of the principal document, the Mishnah, to Scripture, or a doctrine of history and eschatology such as
who the Messiah is and when the Messiah will come – is as interesting
as what it did define as its principal focus. The system of the Mishnah,
a Judaism for a world in which nascent Christianity played no considerable role, laid no considerable stress on the symbol of the Torah,
though, of course, the Torah as a scroll, as a matter of status, and as
revelation of God's will at Sinai, enjoyed prominence. It produced a
document, the Mishnah, so independent of Scripture that, when the
authors wished to say what Scripture said, they chose to do so in their
own words and in their own way. Whatever their intent, the
authorships of the documents of the first phase in the Judaism of the
dual Torah clearly did not need to explain to a competing "Israel,"
heirs of the same Scriptures of Sinai, just what authority validated the
document, and how the document related to Scripture. That same
system took slight interest in the Messiah and presented a teleology
lacking all eschatological, therefore messianic, focus.

Later on, when Christianity in the hour of its political triumph
would represent an acute challenge to the "Israel" framed by sages,
that theory would respond, in its way, to the larger concerns of the
hour. In the theoretical system at hand, the abstractions of an "Israel"
that was holy and of a process of sanctification were realized in
concrete instances of the exegesis of the everyday in the hermeneutics of the sacred. This "Israel" took on a rather abstract form,
matched by the utter abstraction of the intellectual process that
effected sanctification. At the opposite dimension of the system, far
on the other side of reality, came exceedingly concrete details of pots
and pans, excretions and baths, gored oxen and disputed real estate.

The Mishnaic system, we shall now see, defined all matters in
relationship to all other matters in a structure given force and energy
by the task of classification and taxonomy. Lost in the middle range
was a theory of the social entity covering that material and concrete
"Israel" in the here and now. That middle-range metaphor of "Israel"
would come to expression in the analogy of the social entity to the
extended family of Jacob, or in the equally concrete "Israel" as an
entity to be compared and contrasted with the material and political
"Rome." These two metaphorical constructions represent concrete
ways of thinking about the entity – that (abstract) group transcending

(perceived and palpable) household and village – that lay between the household, down here, and the processes of classification and hierarchy under the aspect of Heaven, up there, expressed in the meanings and uses of "Israel" we shall survey in the Mishnah. "Israel" as family, encompassing even "Rome" as sibling, and "Israel" as nation or society absolutely sui generis, take up a prominence in the second stage in the formation of Judaism denied to them in the first. The system expressed in the successor writings of the Yerushalmi, an exegesis of the Mishnah, and associated exegeses of Scripture, for its part, would define "Israel" not in relationship but on its own, a category bearing absolute meaning even when not set into relationship with other categories of its genus – and, in consequence, would read "Israel" also as sui generis.

We shall return to these matters in due course. Let us now return to the Mishnah and our survey of its framing of "Israel," the metaphors of a social character it introduces in that inquiry. Our interest now is not theory and abstraction, but concrete use of language: which words, how used. When we listen to the silences of the Mishnah, as much as to its points of stress, we hear a single message, a message of a Judaism that answered a single encompassing question: What, in the aftermath of the destruction of the holy place and holy cult, remained of the sanctity of the holy caste, the priesthood, the holy land, and, above all, the holy people and its holy way of life? The answer – sanctity persists, indelibly, in "Israel," the people, in its way of life, in its land, in its priesthood, in its food, in its mode of sustaining life, in its manner of procreating and so sustaining the nation – would endure.

NOTES

1 I count backward from 70 C.E. to ca. 500 B.C.E. That is the period in which the pentateuchal system imposed its structure of order in politics, culture, and cult alike. We do not have contemporary accounts of the cultural systems that predominated prior to 586 B.C.E., so we cannot say much about the role of the temple prior to that time, except as that role was portrayed afterward. But if we entertain the notion that, from the time of its building by Solomon, the temple and its cult proved a paramount definitive component in Israelite life, then the destruction in 70 C.E. marked a conclusion of a continuous politics of approximately one thousand years. We should have to point to a counterpart, in Western civilization, that served as both a paramount and a palpable institution from ca. 1000 C.E., and, apart from the papacy, I can think of none. The counterpart parallels for Asian and African history lie beyond my knowledge. But even this rough sketch suggests what was at stake in 70. C.E.

2 And that theological sociology finds its exact counterpart in the theological anthropology that defines "Israel" as the model for humanity in the image, after the likeness. I shall spell this out in the third part of this study. But for the moment I wish only to introduce the notion that sociology and anthropology, in the theology of the Judaism of the dual Torah, form inseparable companions. To say whether the theory of society is prior to the theory of what is the human being seems to me beyond the limits even of logic. My own insistence is simply that in the theological system of the Judaism of the dual Torah anthropology forms the particularity of which sociology states the general. All this will come to clarification in due course.

3 In concrete terms, among the earliest authorities of the group after 70 C.E. that ultimately produced the Mishnah were Pharisees, named as such in contemporary writings, such as Gamaliel II. But not all the figures known in the founding generation beyond 70 C.E. are identified as Pharisees. More than that, as a matter of fact, we cannot say.

4 In Chapter 11.

5 But its political program, clearly a premise in the Gospels' and Josephus' picture of the group, scarcely left a mark on those passages of the Mishnah that derive from the period before 70 C.E. And the Mishnah's political program in no way accords with the politics of the Pharisees as Mark, Matthew, and Luke, and Josephus, portray their politics.

6 This is the upshot of my *History of the Mishnaic Law* (Leiden: Brill, 1974–85) in forty-three volumes divided into five parts, covering *Appointed Times, Women, Damages, Holy Things, and Purities.* I summarize the matter of the stages in the unfolding of the law in my *Judaism: The Evidence of the Mishnah* (Chicago: University of Chicago Press, 1981).

7 That is the argument of Chapter 11.

8 For that is how I have been able to trace the history of the Mishnaic law.

9 In Chapter 11 we shall examine systems of thought in which the social issue did not take priority by contrast to those in which it did. Paul's and the Mishnah's form the one kind, Philo's a different kind. To Philo's system of thought, the definition of "Israel" and the place of "Israel" in the whole hardly contributed definitive data. He had other concerns entirely. And, among the system builders, he was hardly alone. To give another example, the pentateuchal Judaism deemed the relationship of people to land, the holiness of the land itself, to form the centerpiece of existence and to indicate the status and standing of much else. The generative problematic of that system concerned not the standing of its "Israel" on its own but the relationship between its "Israel" and its "land of Israel." It was in a very concrete sense a profoundly Zionist Judaic system, in a way in which the Mishnah's system was not. For the Mishnah's system saw the land as inert and acted upon, the Israel(ite) as the active force and power. For the

pentateuchal Judaism, by contrast, the land could even "vomit up" its inhabitants and throw them out. The treatment of the land as enchanted and active in the priestly component of the pentateuchal Judaism has no counterpart in the Mishnah's system.

10 In Chapter 11 we shall see how this same process comes to exemplification in other Judaisms.

11 We do not have to entertain the chimera of a single "Christianity," any more than we can locate a single "Judaism." But the description, analysis, and interpretation of the diverse Christian systems have not yet gotten underway.

12 We shall deal with that "Israel" in the conclusion.

CHAPTER 3

"Israel" in Relationship to "Non-Israel"

i. "Israel" for the Mishnah's Authorship

This general account of "Israel" as principal sector of the Mishnah's authorship's thought on sanctification brings to the surface the implicit premises of the system as a whole. But when we come to the place and role of "Israel" as these are explicitly defined, the picture changes considerably. True, "Israel" forms the ubiquitous premise of discourse, being the individual person, the "enlandized" nation, the universal and transnational, nonlocative people, society, social group, caste or class that the context requires. In that way "Israel" ordinarily defines the locus of discourse. But the categorically determinative traits of an, or any, "Israel" rarely dictate details let alone the sheltering context.

At the foundations of the entire Mishnaic system and structure stands the conception of Israel as God's unique and holy people. Yet, so far as the notion of Israel as a holy and supernatural social entity circulated, it played a remarkably slight *explicit* role in the Mishnah. When "Israel" is explicitly treated as supernatural and holy, the entity constitutes a mere category and serves as the premise for the numerous and commonplace exercises in the distinction of Israel and gentile – part of the vast exercise of ordering and hierarchization that the Mishnah's authorship proposed to accomplish. So as we shall see, "Israel" defines a category among categories, but plays no generative or explicit role. The work of hierarchization forms the staple of the Mishnah's authorship's thought on Israel: in the same genus as other nations or peoples, but different from them as to species – that is to say, "Israel" is an entity that is acted upon, not actor; the fact, not the factor. Like the abstraction "woman," as the term is used in the Mishnah,[1] the abstraction "Israel" forms a passive constituent, not an active component, of thought. Like a woman's traits – for example, those of a taxonomic sort – an "Israel"'s traits present a problem, frame a case, supply the details of a riddle. But the generative principles that conflict and so create the problem, the mooted issues expressed in a case, and the eccentricities of the system that pose the riddle derive not from the traits of an "Israel" but from other sources altogether. And it is to illustrate the intersection of those conflicted principles that the (adventitious) case of the "Israel" or of the "woman" happens to be introduced.[2]

The Mishnah's system reveals the systemically inert character of "Israel" in two ways. First, the system expresses its interest in the topic by illustrating the way(s) in which the category at hand comes to definition and serves to supply important facts. Second, by its silences, specifically by its failure to frame "Israel" as a categorical component (e.g., the topic of a tractate, the subject of a division), the system has its say as well. In the Mishnah's authorship's thought "Israel" serves as a taxonomic indicator, just as "woman" does. As we shall see time and again, "Israel"'s traits dictate relationships or derive from relationships. "Israel" exists therefore in relationship, not on its own, as an entity bearing its own weight and establishing its own presence. "Israel" is important in dictating the outcome of relationships, not subjected, in its own absolute terms, to description and analysis. This judgment that the social component of the Judaic system of the dual Torah in its initial statement, "Israel," takes a subordinated part in the composition of the whole, will take on far more compelling force when we come to the second stage in the unfolding of the documentary heritage of the Judaism of the dual Torah. There, as we shall see in Part II, "Israel" and its intransitive traits – its definition, its standing, its function in the system, its fate – form the center and dictate systemic teleology: the center of concern in the here and now, the purpose and direction of the whole in the determinate future. But the contrast alone does not serve to make the case.

The character of the definition of "Israel" in the Mishnah and associated writings indicates the importance accorded to the category. That definition, as we shall now see, proves negative, transitive, and merely relational, rarely positive and almost never substantive. At great length, and with a certain measure of tedium, we shall now prove a simple fact. The word and category "Israel" reach definition in relationship to other species of its genus, if nation, then Israel/not-gentile, if caste, then Israel/not-priest. These definitions viewed in this-worldly terms self-evidently tell us much about what "Israel" is when compared with (other) nations or (other) castes, but nothing about what "Israel" is. That is what I mean by "Israel" as transitive and not intransitive. And when, in the literature produced in the aftermath of the advent of Christianity, we find ample answers to the question, "Who is Israel? What is Israel?" and remarkable concentration on those answers as the categorically central components of the documents in which they occur, we shall in the contrast perceive how little "Israel" has served, and how abstract has been the account of "Israel," in the first stage in the formation of the ultimate system of the Judaism of the dual Torah.

For "Israel" in the first stage draws upon metaphors of a hierarchical character such as nation and caste, while "Israel" at the second stage gains analogical definition in metaphors of a concrete and societal character or of family, or it is represented as utterly other and sui generis. Both metaphorical constructs demand substantive definition, for example, in family genealogy or in those unique laws of national history and society that govern the unique social entity at hand. When, by contrast, we ask where and how the authorship of the Mishnah and its successor documents, Abot, Tosefta, Sifra, and the two Sifrés, focus upon the category "Israel," we shall see a quite different picture. For when that set of authorships selects and organizes facts to lay down important principles realized through the category "Israel," the answers prove to be one-dimensional and systemically of limited weight. There is a literary consequence to the choice of metaphors involving hierarchy and relationship. The metaphors of the first stage do not draw in their wake stories about Israel/non-Israel or Israel/priest; they serve, as I said, for purposes of philosophical classification and hierarchy, not historical theology, and consequently come to expression without a rich narrative statement. The metaphors of the second stage prove virtually inaccessible outside of the framework of narrative or, at least, parable.

ii.   "Israel" in the System of the Mishnah

A survey of the topics important to the framers of the Mishnah provides facts of fundamental importance in describing the social metaphors of the Judaism that appeals to the Mishnah as part of the Torah of Moses at Sinai. For all subsequent documents beyond the Mishnah refer either to Scripture or to the Mishnah and propose to elucidate its rules. So far as the Mishnah forms the center of interest for the Tosefta, Sifra, the two Sifrés, and the two Talmuds, its topical program constitutes a definitive statement. When we wish to know what to anticipate in a repertoire of metaphors for "Israel," we do well to start with the components and constituents of society – of "Israel" – important in the Mishnah itself. To accomplish such a survey, we will briefly review the topical program of the document, for the topics themselves guide us toward the component elements of society important to the framers of the Mishnaic system, and then probe a few suggestive chapters.

The basic and on-going theme of the Mishnah is sanctification. So far as it focuses as a document upon the holiness of Israel in its land, the Mishnah expresses that conception of sanctification and theory of its modes that will have been shaped among the priests' caste – those to whom the temple and its technology of joining heaven and holy land through the sacred place defined the heart of life. So far as the Mishnah takes up within its thematic repertoire the way in which transactions are conducted among ordinary folk and takes the position that transactions are embodied and expressed both on earth and in heaven through documents, the Mishnah expresses a view self-evidently valid to the scribal profession. The building block of Mishnaic discourse, the circumstance invoked and addressed whenever issues of concrete society and material transactions are taken up, is the householder and his context.

For the Mishnah's authorship the center and focus of social interest lie in the village, which is made up of households, each imagined to be a unit of production in agriculture. Although these are concrete facts of everyday life, the household in the Mishnah attains abstraction in an ideal definition. The households are constructed by and around the householder, father of an extended family, including his sons and their wives and children, his servants, men and bondwomen. Alongside are the craftsmen to whom he entrusts tasks he does not choose to do. The concerns of the householders are in transactions in land. Their measurement of value is expressed in acreage of top, middle, and bottom grade. Through real estate critical transactions are worked out. The marriage settlement depends upon real property. Civil penalties are exacted through payment in real property. Principal transactions are those of the householder who owns beasts that do damage or suffer it; who harvests his crops and sets aside and sanctifies a portion for use by the scheduled castes; who uses and sells his crops and feeds his family; and who will acquire more land. To these householders the Mishnah is addressed: They form the pivot of society and its bulwark, the units of which the village is composed, the corporate component of the society of Israel within the limits of village and holy land. The householder is the building block of the house of Israel, of its economy in the classic sense of the word. Among the constituent parts of Israel, the community or people in its land, then, are a caste, the priesthood; a profession, the scribes; and the socioeconomic group, the householders, who form the basic

productive unit around which other economic activities are understood to function.

Now the question, how do all these groups add up to "Israel," and
what an Israel is, for the moment is set aside for two reasons. First,
the premise of all discourse is that the entirety of the Jews' society is
"Israel." Second, the active issue of most discourse rarely requires the
specification of that fact. What we need to know about an "Israel," we
know; what we need to find out is the consequence of those fixed
facts. That characteristic of the category at hand marks the category as
systemically neutral and not a source of the energy that makes the
system work.

The first thing we shall learn about "Israel" in the system of the
Mishnah is that the word bears no autonomous meaning everywhere
in play. Quite to the contrary, "Israel" for the Mishnah and related
writings ordinarily finds definition in its opposite, whatever the
antonym is. It is in the deepest sense a transitive category. The classifications of subsequent importance that do bear autonomous and
intransitive meaning play little or no role in the earlier phase in the
unfolding writings. Israel/not-gentile and Israel/not-priest prove remarkably common senses of the word. Strikingly, Israel as family and
Israel as sui generis, critical to the second phase in the matter, make
at best cameo appearances. "Israel" therefore serves, as I suggested
earlier, as a systemic classifier, which conforms to the larger purpose
of the Mishnah's authorship, with its powerful concern for giving
things their rightful name and placing them in their correct category
and subjecting them all, each to its own intrinsic rule.[3]

We learn, second, that the antonyms shift from context to context.
So the word is not only defined in relationship to other words and
not as an autonomous category, but it also takes on various meanings,
each relative to its context. An "Israel" does not serve, therefore, as
a categorically definitive matter, in the way that Sabbath, writ of
divorce, the goring ox, the priestly ration ("heave offering"), the act
of exchanging a beast for one designated for use in the cult, or a pot
constitute definitive categories, each with a fixed and permanent
meaning. That is to say, while the meaning of Sabbath or goring ox
does not change from setting to setting, the sense imputed to "Israel"
undergoes remarkable shifts and changes.[4] Consequently, the word
finds meaning solely in relation to other words, in ways in which the
names of the structural categories of the Mishnah's system do not. By
contrast, the sense of "Israel" as family or as sui generis, which we
shall encounter later on, is fixed and intransitive. The metaphor of
"Israel" in the first stage is so abstract as scarcely to refer to a real
group of people, a concrete social entity, whereas in the second it

becomes concrete and palpable. Then "Israel" speaks of real people
(who see one another as family, for instance) and not only of a
transitive abstraction.

Apart from these two approaches to the sense of words, we have
no other entry into the way in which the Mishnah's authorship
thought about the matter. The Mishnah in all of its more than five
hundred chapters, comprising sixty-two tractates (excluding Abot,
with which we deal in a moment) scarcely defines "Israel," or even
"*an* Israel," in autonomous terms. That is because the classifier is not a
category; in more concrete terms, the document as a whole has no
division or even tractate devoted to "Israel," meaning, in its context,
who is an Israelite and who is not, what may one do or not do
because he or she is an Israelite, or how does (an) "Israel" function in
any of the settings so lovingly described in rich detail by the
jurisprudential philosophers of the Mishnah. Information on all
of these questions will prove abundant – but episodic and epiphenomenal. Nonetheless, through the use of the inestimable concordances of the great Kasovskys, father and son, we may describe
with little uncertainty the doctrine of "Israel" as a social entity,
explaining through masses of exemplary detail what the Mishnah does
tell us about its authorship's definition of an "Israel" and understanding of "Israel."

In short, an "Israel" may be one of two things. "Israel" may refer to
either a social entity, a social group defined by shared norms and
traits, imputed and expressed, in contradistinction to all other social
entities of the same genus (the point at which we began in Chapter 1)
– that is, a (unique) species of a common genus, people or nation,
Israel as against non-Israel. Or "Israel" may refer to a caste, a kind of
class defined by genealogy and endowed with economic and social
traits of differentiation, in contradistinction to all other castes of the
same genus – that is, a unique species of a common genus, one level
within the hierarchy of the social group, expressed as Israel as against
priest, Levite, proselyte, and the like, but, most commonly, Israel(ite
in caste), not priest(ly caste). The classification, of course, pertains to
the individual or to the group, without distinction. "Israel" within the
people stands for a caste, and "Israel" among the nations stands for a
nation; these meanings yield essentially the same thing, the one within
the borders of society, the other outside. In both cases "Israel"
constitutes a mode of hierarchization, and that within a system that, at
its foundations, constitutes a massive exercise in hierarchization.

Thus, when "Israel" stands alone, not as a qualifier or partitive, in
the Mishnah and successor writings, it ordinarily functions as a
contrastive, that is, Israel *and not* – either *not an outsider* or *not a*

higher caste. These are the two meanings associated with "Israel" in the principal document that came to closure before the end of the third century. Consequently, the best way to find out what meanings attach to the word "Israel" is to investigate the antonyms, in context, yielded by diverse usages. In the aggregate, therefore, we find two of fundamental categorical importance. Hearing "Israel," the authorship of the Mishnah might think of the opposite as gentile (or Samaritan, heretic); or he might think of "priest, Levite." All senses of the word "Israel" in the Mishnah fall within one or the other classification. For example, "Israel as nation," whether a political or a supernatural entity; Israel, not Samaritan; Israel as individual Israelite – all of these senses draw to begin with upon "Israel" as "not gentile." "Israel" as a caste within Israel the people forms a population of examples in the Mishnah equivalent in number to all the counterpart uses combined. Only when we reach the second stage in the formation of the Judaism of the dual Torah will the facts at hand prove to constitute significant choices, exclusions as much as inclusions.

iii. The Repertoire of Candidates: Toward an Inductive Survey of the Mishnah, Tractate Abot, the Tosefta, Sifra, Sifré to Numbers, Sifré to Deuteronomy, and Related Writings

For purposes of both internal and also external organization of the social world, "Israel" served to classify social entities of the frontier beyond and of the castes within. The precise modes of thought about "Israel" and, consequently, the shape and structure of the Mishnah's authorship's doctrine of Israel emerge in two ways. First, with the help of concordances, we survey how the word "Israel" is used, the meanings imputed to it implicitly in diverse contexts. That information, surveyed in the remainder of this chapter, identifies for us the sorts of topics and information it regarded as pertinent in any consideration of the subject, "Israel." Second, in Chapter 4 we undertake a probe of a sample of the literature and see how, in suggestive texts, the word takes on concrete meanings. In these two ways we gain entry into the systemic treatment of the word and, through the word, of the social entity for which, in the mind of the authorship at hand, the word stands.

Scripture presented a broad range of candidates for meanings to be imputed to "Israel." But Scripture provided mere information, not the criteria for selection, among available facts, of what would provide truth. All Judaisms found in Scripture what they sought. Judaic systems took shape around an urgent question that was given, in the system's way of life and worldview and identification of an "Israel," an ineluctable answer. Scripture's authoritative facts were many; those useful to a given system, a Judaism, few. Proof of that simple fact derives from the wide variety of choices, among available facts of Scripture, made by the diverse Judaisms of the history of Judaism. Were we to ask Scripture to define the meanings of "Israel" available to system builders later on, we would gain more facts than we can use. For the system builders first built their system and – once they knew what they wished to find out – quite naturally found in Scripture the facts they needed to serve that system. A survey of "Israel" in Scripture would prove monumentally irrelevant. When, moreover, we reach the understanding of "Israel" characteristic of writings of the second stage of the formation of the Judaism of the dual Torah, we shall see ample evidence of how a fresh set of concerns shaped a new focus and point of emphasis in scriptural study. Then Scripture would contribute a fresh repertoire of important facts and meanings, which, in the earlier phase, do not appear to have made a correspondingly deep impression. The contrast once again will underline the importance of what we do not find, as much as what we do uncover, in the Mishnah's picture. If we wish to understand the structure of a system and of important components thereof, we therefore commence with the system, not its sources, which were sorted out only after the fact. Surveying meanings available in concordance lists of the principal documents of the first stage of the Judaism under study provides the first set of candidates; reading important statements on our topic then allows us to see how these candidates take their places in the hierarchy of meanings imputed to the critical systemic component, the social one.

Kasovsky's Tosefta concordance gives us a rough-and-ready sense of the proportions of the two usages: Israel as a social entity as distinct from the gentiles, and Israel as a caste as distinct from priests and Levites. The former sense fills up something on the order of thirteen columns, the latter, three. The proportion in the Mishnah is somewhat closer to half and half. As between these two roughly assessed populations, I should regard the latter as the more likely figure, because many senses of the word Israel other than "Israel as against gentile" are included in the examples of "Israel" listed in the former columns.

As the adjectival predicate and not contrastive or partitive, "Israel" further serves in such clauses as "Land of . . . ," "house of . . . ," "son of . . . ," "daughter of . . . ," and so on as in the cases of laws of Israel, offspring of Israel, elders of Israel, seed of Israel, wisdom of Israel, congregation of Israel, strength of Israel, myriads of Israel, firstborn of Israel, virgin of Israel, redeemer of Israel, border of Israel, great ones of Israel, fields belonging to Israelites, mountains of Israel, camp of Israel, community of Israel, dead of Israel, tribes of Israel, youths of Israel, vengeance of Israel, princes of Israel, sight of Israel, sustainers of Israel, army of Israel, needs of Israel, shepherds of Israel, remnant of Israel, tribes of Israel, guardian of Israel, and on and on. All of these usages are the same as in "king of Israel." They bear the simple sense of "belonging to the social entity, Israel." For example, "daughter of Israel" means simply a Jewish woman, though it can bear the sense of a woman of the Israelite, not the priestly caste; and "sons of Israel" means simply, "Jews." I find the adjectival usage neutral and not categorical. In all of these adjectival usages "Israel" enjoys an implicit meaning, which derives from the contexts in which the word is given one or the other meanings deriving from relationship. My impression is that nearly all adjectival uses of ". . . of Israel" bear the sense of the particular people, *Israel and not non-Israel.*

There is one exception: "Land of Israel." I see no conception that any district may become ". . . of Israel" merely because Jews live there, though "villages of Israel" clearly bears the sense "villages in which most of the inhabitants are Jews." But that exception bears consequences for the issue of the Land, which is different from all other lands, and may be set aside here. The Land is sui generis, and, when we have "of Israel" attached to Land, the sense is the Land that is sui generis associated with – and I think, by reason of the residence of – the people that is sui generis. Let us now rapidly review the facts that yield the foregoing generalizations.

iv. "Israel" as Sui Generis

We begin with essentially negative items, for which senses of the word "Israel" the Mishnah provides few, if any, important examples. I do not find in the Mishnah or related documents common use of "Israel" as sui generis, that is, to refer to a group utterly incomparable in genus to other social entities. True, the Mishnah's authorship supplies numerous laws that apply to Israel, not to gentiles. Israel is therefore different from, and assuredly holier than, gentiles, who cannot become holy at all. But viewed as a group, "Israel" in the Mishnah rarely emerges as sui generis. Nor can I point to a single passage in the Tosefta, Sifra, or the two Sifrés that treats "Israel" as wholly a category by itself. The reason is clear. It derives from the character of the metaphor at hand, which generates no comparison whatsoever. Once the Mishnah's authorship understands by "Israel" an entity that stands in transitive relationships and is defined by contrast with, and in relationship to, some other social entity, the sense of "Israel" as sui generis can no longer come into play. For referring to what is sui generis would violate the Mishnah's rules of intellectual syntax. Therefore also the Mishnah's consequent language rules, for the item at issue, would be offended. For both syntactic regularities in this context of comparison and contrast, hierarchization and classification, require the item to constitute a category defined only by adjacent boundaries or limits – the unlike and the like.

This judgment that Israel sui generis occurs only seldom in the Mishnah will be qualified when in Chapter 4 we turn to the one Mishnah text that actually does address in autonomous and not comparative terms the issue of who is Israel. That text answers the question not in relationship to "Israel, not . . . ," but in very concrete and specific terms, and these terms clearly indicate that Israel is sui generis. The arena for discourse, however, proves startling; it is the supernatural, and not natural, principle of taxonomy that defines Israel as sui generis. Nothing in the rest of the Mishnah conforms. By contrast, the documents of the second phase find ample occasion to take up discourse on "Israel" as sui generis, spelling out the special laws that apply only to "Israel," for example. The present result is only one instance among many in which the character of the social metaphor affects the processes of thought about the social entity at hand.

v.   "Israel" as an Extended Family

While one influential scriptural myth of Israel, important both to the Priestly Code and to the Yahwist–Elohist source of the Pentateuch, treats the social entity as an extended family, the Mishnah's authorship rarely makes use of that sense of the category. Like Israel sui generis, the meaning of "Israel" as family when it does occur always bears supernatural, not narrowly familial or genealogical, meaning or occurs in a liturgical context, which is the same thing. When "fathers" or "ancestors" is joined to the noun "Israel," a supernatural sense intrudes; for example, "God of the fathers of Israel" (M. Bik. 1:4), "All Israelites are sons of princes" (which is ordinarily understood to allude to their being children of Abraham) (M. Shab. 14:4) – this for purposes of ritual classification. Not every genealogical reference demands the sense of "family" at all; for example, "the children of Israel" (M. Neg. 2:1) is simply synonymous with "Israel" the social entity, pure and simple. These usages are not commonplace and play no role in the formulation of the law, to which the bulk of the Mishnah is devoted.

The notion of Israel as family later on would be closely tied to the concept of merit.[5] This concept in the sense of an inherited stock of heavenly favor appears in the Mishnah only at M. Sot. 3:4,5. There, however, we do not locate the concomitant sense of merit inherited from Abraham, Isaac, Jacob, Sarah, Rebecca, Leah, and Rachel, which, appearing commonly in the documents of the Judaism of the dual Torah in its second formulation, infuses the notion of merit with profound meaning. The sense in the Mishnah is reason for suspending punishment inflicted by heaven:

> If the woman had any merit, this suspends the punishment that is coming to her.
>
> M. Sot. 3:4

> Ben Azzai says, "A man should teach Torah to his daughter, so that if she has to drink the bitter water, she may know that it is merit that may suspend the punishment that is coming to her."

> R. Simeon says, "Merit will not suspend the punishment that comes in drinking the bitter water, for if you say that merit does suspend the punishment, you will make the water of no effect for whoever drinks it, for people will say, 'They really were defiled but merit suspended the punishment.'"

> Rabbi says, "Merit will suspend the punishment, but the woman will not bear children or retain her looks. She will waste away by degrees."

> M. Sot. 3:5

Here the clear sense is that the woman enjoys the protection of merit. What is important for our inquiry is that the source of that protection is not specified. It may be her own deeds (e.g., in study of the Torah) or the deeds of her ancestors. The possibility that the woman has gained merit on her own, in Torah study, is made explicit both in what follows in context and also in exegetical treatment of the passage at hand. More important, before us is the sole point in the writings of the Mishnah and its circle at which the concept of *zekhut* in the sense of protective merit, capable of intervening in a situation extrinsic to the source of the merit, is invoked at all. It must follow that, while the idea of *zekhut*, or merit, circulates, the sense of the category is not spelled out, nor is the concept amply used in the larger program of the document. The reason that this fact bears heavy consequence will become clear in Part II.

A qualification on the notion of merit is required for the sake of completeness, though it does not change the picture relevant to our inquiry. The word for merit, *zekhut,* does occur very commonly in another sense altogether. That second and distinct meaning is grounds for acquittal or reason for imputing innocence, and that sense occurs at M. San. 4:1, 5:4,5, 6:1. The usage of the word seems to me quite separate from the foregoing, because at issue here is testimony to be given in court and not an unspecified source of protection from penalty. That legal sense has no bearing upon the definition of the social entity at hand, as the conception of *zekhut* would later on contribute to that definition. In the aggregate, we cannot regard as commonplace or systemically critical for the Mishnah the conception of Israel as an extended family.

A further sense of the word at hand also is not helpful to us. *Zekhut* in the meaning of "acquire possession of," a commonplace in the Mishnah, recurs throughout. Tosefta knows the conception of merit, in the sense of "on account of the merit accruing to Israel," at T. M.S. 5:27,29, and T. Sot. 11:10. The mixture of the legal and the theological senses may be discerned at T. B.B. 7:9, which speaks of sons inherited on account of the *zekhut* of the fathers of their fathers and of the mothers of their mothers – a legal context that can generate a theological connotation. The meanings familiar from M. Sanhedrin recur in T. Sanhedrin (e.g., at T. San. 3:3, 6:2, 7:3). The one important example of *zekhut* in the sense of an ongoing inheritance of a family is at T. Sot. 11:10: "Three good providers arose for Israel, Moses, Aaron, and Miriam, and on account of the merit attained by them, to Israel were given three good gifts." This constitutes the clearest statement of the notion of a continuing heritage handed on through a familiar relationship.

The same range of meanings occurs in Sifra, serving Leviticus – that is, to be found worthy, to gain as one's possession, to be acquitted in a court case. The other sense – legal power to acquire possession of something, extended to the notion of a right of possession imputed through inheritance – occurs in both the legal sense and the more subtle one. As to the former, we find, "A person cannot transfer by inheritance the right of possession of his daughter to his sons" (Sifra Behar 6:5); the latter seems to me the implication of the statement, "It was the *zekhut*/merit accruing to Israel that brought it about at Mount Sinai, for all of them were stated from Sinai" (Sifra Behuqotai 13:8). The two Sifrés for their part present no surprises. As before, when the root occurs as a verb, it bears the legal meanings now familiar: acquire right of possession of something; or win acquittal in a court case. Examples with the sense of "acquire merit through a deed" are not uncommon: Joseph acquired merit through taking care of the bones of his father (Sifré Numbers 106). The more narrowly legal sense of "acquire possession or advantage" is familiar: Amram had the merit of having a tribe called by his name (Sifré Numbers 116). The other sense occurs, as expected, in dealing with the passage of the accused wife (Sifré Numbers 8). In the aggregate, I see no substantial difference either in the repertoire of meanings or in the proportions of instances of the several meanings.

In all, we look in vain in the Mishnah, Tosefta, Sifra, and the two Sifrés for an extensive development of the conception of Israel as an extended family, heir in the latter days to the merit piled up in heaven by Abraham, Isaac, Jacob, Sarah, Rebecca, Leah, and Rachel. My sense is that an essentially legal category of the Mishnah and related writings later on was transformed in a figurative way; the legal contexts require the meaning of, first, enjoy a right, which yields, impart a right, endow with a right, and that generates the figurative sense of "create a heritage of advantage." From that third layer of meaning it is easy to develop the notion of a heritage, in heaven, of divine favor, created by the patriarchs and matriarchs, and left by them for the advantage of their children and grandchildren, and onward through the generations. But – to state with emphasis the simple result of this component of the inquiry – that more profound sense of Israel as family and therefore heir of the merit of the patriarchs and matriarchs *simply does not occur,* so far as I can tell, in the literature of the Mishnah and its nearest colleagues.

vi.   "Israel" as People or Nation

The Supernatural Dimension

When the framers of the Mishnah use the word "Israel," they may well mean the people of God, your people, and the like. In that usage, "Israel" refers to a supernatural social entity, one that stands in a special relationship with God and addresses God on distinctive terms.[6] Like the reference to "Israel" as sui generis, such (nongeneric) usages, as I have already suggested, most commonly occur in liturgical settings, for example, "Save, O Lord, your people, the remnant of Israel" (M. Ber. 4:4), "Let us bless the Lord, our God, the God of Israel" (M. Ber. 7:3). In relationship to God, "Israel" always bears a supernatural dimension, for example, "So too, the Holy One, blessed be he, purifies Israel" (M. Yoma 8:9), "The Holy One, blessed be he, found as a utensil to hold a blessing for Israel only peace" (M. Uqs. 3:12). But I do not know how people can have said "us," as in "save us, a social group," other than using the name they invoked, also in secular circumstances, for their group. "Israel" in liturgy does not function in a way different from the way "Israel" serves in a sentence on how one Israelite's cow gored another Israelite's cow.

That is why these merely episodic occurrences of Israel in a supernatural sense do not bear deep significance in the metaphorical treatment of an abstract entity. Rightly understood, the supernatural dimensions and considerations pertinent to this "Israel" indeed encompass the bulk of the rules of the Mishnah, even where "Israel" does not occur in so many words. And where "Israel" serves as antonym for gentile, the sense, even when neutral, bears subterranean meaning of a supernatural order, for example, "An Israelite may not raise pigs in any location" (M. San. 7:7), a rule that bears the sense, "but a gentile may do so," carries no explicit explanation. But the implicit sense, that the gentile is not subject to those rules of heaven that make Israel what it is, everywhere prevails. Along these same lines, "An Israelite may lend at usury the capital of a gentile with the gentile's knowledge and consent" (M. B.M. 5:6) stands for a more than merely ethnic difference.

The sense of Israel as a people in close relationship to God occurs in Tosefta as in the Mishnah, in liturgical contexts most commonly: "Listen to the sound of the prayer of your people, Israel" (T. Ber. 3:7). Israel's "father in heaven" occurs at T. Shab. 14:5, Sifra Qedoshim 10:8: ". . . which bring peace between Israel and their father in heaven." The inclusion of "Israel" in all liturgies bears this same supernatural connotation, as in, ". . . who sanctifies the Sabbath, Israel, and the seasons" (T. Ber. 3:13). Explicit statements on the supernatural status of Israel include the following: "Beloved are Israel, for even though they are unclean, the Presence of God is yet among them" (Sifré to Numbers 1); "Then the Israelites will say, 'If he who brought us out of Egypt and did the wonders and mighty deeds for us does not enter . . .'" (Sifré to Numbers 78). When we see what the Mishnah's authorship did do with "Israel," we shall appreciate more vividly the opportunities they did not choose to exploit. Then the contrast just now drawn will register.

The Political and Historical Dimension

From these sideshows we come to the main event. The single most common antonym for "Israel" is "non-Israel," that is, gentile. The first and most important fact is that that usage need not evoke invidious comparisons, which is why the ubiquitous premise of "Israel" as unique and holy in my judgment makes so slight a contribution to our understanding of the Mishnah's definition and utilization of the social metaphor at hand. Far more commonly than otherwise, "Israel" is the name of the social group, pure and simple. "Israel" may refer to the people without bearing any supernatural sense, for example, "So that the poor people of Israel may rely upon it in the Seventh Year" (M. Yad. 4:3), ". . . so that the last of Israel may reach the Euphrates" (M. Ta. 1:3), "He who sees a place in which miracles were done for Israel" (M. Ber. 9:1). When one wishes to speak of the distinct social entity, the Jews, the word "Israel" serves in a perfectly routine and neutral way, not Israel-by-contrast-to-gentiles any more than Israel-by-contrast-to-priests. For example, M. Sot. 1:8 refers to "the heart of Israel," meaning the people at large. "The stoning of the felon is done by all Israel" (M. San. 6:4) means simply everybody present. "For from there Torah goes forth to all Israel" (M. San. 11:2) again means the entirety of the nation.

If one wishes to impute the sense of every individual Israelite, the essentially secular and ordinary meaning does not shift. "Israel" may refer to the people, without bearing a supererogatory sense, at M. Sheq. 2:4, "When Israel came up from the exile," meaning "the Israelites" in general. So too, "So as not to frighten Israel," "Happy are you O Israel," (M. Yoma 5:1, 8:9), "Even though Israel requires his services" (M. Mak. 2:7), "Even the general of the army of Israel such as Joab" (M. Mak. 2:7) – all refer to Israelites as a social entity. In public worship, "Israel" may refer equally to the community at large or to the caste, the Israelites, in particular. Examples of the former include "the Israelites answered Moses, 'Amen'" (M. Sot. 5:4) and "until the Israelites went up from Jerusalem to the temple mount" (M. R.H. 3:8), meaning everybody, the entire group, the community at large; so too, "The court goes . . . and all Israel after them" (M. Sheb. 2:2). That particular usage bears no sense of exclusion, that is, "the Israelites alone, but not . . . ," then "the gentiles," "the Samaritans," "the priests," and the like, though in other contexts, it assuredly does. Israelite women are invariably called, "daughters of Israel" (e.g., M. Ned. 9:10), meaning simply Jewish women (also M. Yeb. 13:1), and that usage too bears no exclusionary sense, except now for gentiles. When a geographical usage involving "Israel" occurs, the sense is of a place populated by Israelites, as in "in all the towns of Israel" (M. Zeb. 14:7), meaning in all towns in which Israelites make up the inhabitants or the majority thereof.

To return to an important aside, there is no geographical sense of the word "Israel." "Israel" without qualification never refers to territory; when the framers of the Mishnah wish to speak of Israelite territory, they call it "Land of Israel," with Israel meaning people or nation. Villages in which Israelites live, wherever those villages are located, even in Syria or beyond, may be called "villages of Israel," meaning simply Jewish villages. Israel the people can *be* somewhere, for example, "When the Israelites were in the wilderness" (M. Men.

4:3), but no *place* can be "Israel." For instance, no reference to "in/into Israel" bears a geographical sense. All such references use "Israel" to mean, "the social entity," as at M. Yeb. 7:5, "If they are not fit to enter into Israel," meaning to marry Jews (so too M. Yeb. 12:6, Ket. 3:5).

While "Israel" therefore is the name of the social entity to which the Mishnah's authorship addresses its system, the fact remains that for the authorship of the Mishnah "Israel" does resonate as a differentiating category, with "non-Israel," gentile, the one routine antonym. Such a usage of "Israel" as a social entity very commonly occurs when someone wants for neutral purposes to distinguish Israelite from gentile, thus, "If a majority is Israelite . . . , if a majority is gentile . . ." (M. Mak. 2:5, 7). "Israelite" in contradistinction to gentile occurs in such ways as these: "A gentile who gave an Israelite . . ." (M. Hal. 3:5), "He who sells to a gentile in the Land [of Israel] or to an Israelite outside of the Land . . ." (M. Sheb. 5:7), "He who receives a field from an Israelite, a gentile, or a Samaritan . . ." (M. Dem. 6:1), "He who sells his field to a gentile, and an Israelite went and bought it from him . . ." (M. Git. 4:9), "The ox of a gentile that gored the ox of an Israelite . . ." and vice versa (M. B.Q. 4:3), "An Israelite woman ['daughter'] should not serve as midwife to a gentile . . ." (M. A.Z. 2:1), and so throughout that tractate. These usages treat the gentile as one classification, an outsider, one not subject to the laws of the Torah – for example, in connection with land ownership and the application of Seventh Year taboos – and the Israelite as another classification in that same connection. Genealogical origin with an Israelite, not a gentile, mother occurs at M. Bik. 1:4, Qid. 4:7. M. Ned. 3:11 treats gentile as the antonym of Israelite: "He who by vow prohibits himself from deriving benefit from an Israelite" may derive benefit from a gentile. Along these same lines, Israelite as antonym for gentile occurs at M. Git. 9:8, "What Israelites tell you"; M. Mak. 2:5 (also M. A.Z. 4:11), "A village in which Israelites and gentiles dwell . . ."; and the like. The distinctions made in these usages, however, are not narrowly political. In many instances, the antonymic difference yields cultic results: "A gentile who separated heave offering for produce belonging to an Israelite. . ." (M. Ter. 1:1). If on the Sabbath a gentile performs an action for his own purposes, an Israelite may derive benefit from that action (M. Shab. 16:8, 23:4). In connection with the prohibition of leaven on Passover, what belongs to a gentile is not subject to the taboo (M. Pes. 2:3). "The uncircumcised" is taken to be a synonym for "gentile," and "the circumcised" for Israelite male, so that if one takes a vow not to derive benefit from "the uncircumcised," the sense is understood not literally but figuratively – that is, circumcised gentiles are included in the vow, uncircumcised Israelites are excluded from it. Certain descriptive statements distinguish "Israelite women" from "gentile women" (M. Nid. 2:1).

The Tosefta's supplement to the Mishnah does not change the picture in any material way. "When Israel are engaged in the Torah . . ." (T. Suk. 2:6) uses the word Israel to refer to the group as a collectivity, one of the two common meanings of the word in the Tosefta, as in the Mishnah. The other sense, the contrastive, comes in its wake: "When Israel is enmeshed in trouble, and the nations of the world in prosperity . . ." (T. Sot. 13:9). "Israel" stands for the name of the group in a simple sense: "A king of Israel," "A court of Israel," "Israelite sinners" (T. San. 4:2, 9:8, 13:2,4); or "in accord with the law of Moses and Israel" (T. Ket. 4:9). So too, "because Israel [= the Israelites] was sent into exile to Babylonia" (T. Ar. 5:16). "Israel" stands for the group, not the territory, and such an expression as "the towns of Israel" (T. Ar. 5:18) refers to towns in which the majority of the people are Israel. The sense of Israel as antonym for gentile, Samaritan, or proselyte is a commonplace for Tosefta as well. Israel is referred to as a social entity in a simple sense, as in the following: "So it is for Israel: the later troubles make them forget the earlier ones" (T. Ber. 1:11). The contrast is drawn in the following: "When those in Israel became many who accepted philanthropy from gentiles, the gentiles began to wax and Israel to wane" (T. Sot. 14:10). The distinction of Israel/gentile makes its appearance at passages corresponding to those of the Mishnah that make the same point: T. Ber. 6:7; an Israelite and a gentile who were partners in a vineyard (T. T. Peah 3:12); and on and on. Israel reckons the calendar by the moon, the gentiles by the sun (T. Suk. 2:6). The Israel/Samaritan distinction occurs as well, for instance, an Israelite priest takes a share with a Samaritan priest (T. Dem. 1:23). Whether for a given purpose the Samaritan falls into the category of Israel or gentile comes under discussion (T. Ter. 4:12, T. Pes. 1:15).

Sifra's repertoire for "Israel" covers the same ground in the same proportions. Israel stands for the group, both on its own and as distinct from gentiles: "Does not Israel require atonement" (Shemini 40:3), "the Israelites said before Moses" (Shemini 40:4), "When Israel completed the work of making the tabernacle" (Sifra Shemini 40:15). The antonymic relationship with the gentiles is explicit: "Did not he who created Israel create the nations?" (Aharé 13:4). Sifré to Numbers 8 goes over the same familiar ground, for example, "Israel[ites] are not suspect in regard to . . . ." Equivalent usages in Sifré to Deuteronomy are abundant. Thus, Israel is the name of the social entity, sometimes perceived as a political agency as well, and Israel furthermore carries the implicit sense of contrast to outsider. Some minor variations on this indicative sense of the word underline the main result.

vii. "Israel" as Not-Samaritan, Not-Heretic

A subdivision of the usage Israel/not-gentile quite reasonably encompasses the marginal groups, Samaritans and heretics. The Samaritan is perceived as sufficiently close to an Israelite to participate in Israelite rites, therefore related. Thus, "One may recite, 'Amen,' after an Israelite who says a blessing, but not after a Samaritan, unless, in the case of the Samaritan, one hears the entire wording of the blessing" (M. Ber. 8:8). The Samaritan is not a gentile, but also not an Israelite, as at M. Dem. 5:9, "of that belonging to gentiles for that belonging to an Israelite . . . of that belonging to an Israelite for that belonging to a Samaritan." Sanitary napkins deriving from Israelites are distinguished from those that derive from Samaritans (M. Nid. 7:3). Along these same lines, "daughters of the Sadducees" stand in contrast to "the ways of Israel," meaning the holy people (M. Nid. 4:2). But this example is somewhat odd; we should not have expected Sadducees to fall into the same interstitial category as Samaritans. Because the word "Israel" means "we" or "us," a variety of others may be introduced by contrast.

viii. "Israel" as Israelite

"We" encompasses many "I"s. When the authorship of the Mishnah wishes to refer to an individual Jew, not surprisingly it speaks of "Israel," meaning an Israelite, occasionally in context not a gentile, but commonly as a simple fact: "we speak of an individual, one of us in general." As soon as we encountered "Israel" as the name of the group, we became aware of this further important sense of the name. The occurrences are typified by these: "An Israelite who married a *mamzer*-woman . . ." (M. Qid. 9:2);, "He who undertakes to sharecrop a field belonging to an Israelite, a gentile, a Samaritan . . ." (M. Dem. 6:1), meaning an individual person in the category of Israel, a Jew; "And let not a single soul of Israel be handed over to them" (M. Ter. 8:12), a similar sense; "people do not accept for sharecropping a field handed over on terms of 'iron flock' from an Israel[ite] [since it smacks of usury]" (M. B.M. 5:6); "Whoever saves . . . , whoever destroys a single life of Israel" (M. San. 4:5), meaning a Jew. A simpler usage of "Israel" for individual Jew occurs at M. Ned. 3:11: If someone says, "Forbidden . . . that an Israelite derive benefit from me," he may impart benefit to a non-Jew, and numerous equivalent passages.

Where the word "Israel" occurs in the plural, "Israelites," it always refers to two or more individual Jews: "Unless two Israelites prohibit one another" (M. Er. 6:1), "In a city in which gentiles and Israelites are located, it is permitted" (M. A.Z. 4:11). "Israel" may stand not for a person of Jewish identity, but an Israelite, and not a priest – as at M. Yoma 6:3: "And he was an Israelite" – but the difference and intent are readily determined in context. The usages in Tosefta and the later writings do not differ. "Israel" in the sense of an individual Jew, not in contradistinction to a gentile, occurs at T. Dem. 7:6: "an Israelite who took a field for sharecropping from his fellow, intending to cut the grain . . . ." This usage is as common in the Tosefta as in the Mishnah. Sifra knows "Israel" as both the people and any member of the people, and the same is so for the two Sifrés. In all, "Israel" as "we" marks off the insider from the outsider. But there is a second, quite contradictory sense of the word, having nothing to do with inside and outside "Israel" at all.

ix. "Israel" as a Caste within "Israel" the People

We now reach the second of the two very common usages, namely, Israel/not-priest, that is, Israel in contradiction to *kohen* (priest) or, less commonly, Levite. Israelite society was deemed divided into castes: priests, Levites, Israel, and on downward. "Israel" in the sense of the caste yields Israel as common folk, always defined in contradiction to Levites and *kohanim* or priests, occurs throughout – for example, Yoma 7:1: "For Israel unto itself . . . , for the priests unto themselves." The temple had its courtyard into which Israelites were permitted to enter, with inner spaces open to priests but closed to Israelites (e.g., M. Suk. 5:4). Related distinctions separate Israel from Nazirites, those who have taken the oath specified at Num. 6, *mamzerim,* offspring of a couple that can never legally marry (M. M.S. 5:4), or other special cultic categories.

This usage is not difficult to distinguish from the other contrastive meaning of the word. Wherever we find "priest" or "Levite," the word Israel bears the sense of a distinct caste within the larger nation or people. A sample of such usage is as follows: "An Israelite who received from a priest or a Levite . . ." (M. Dem. 6:4,5); "The daughter of an Israelite who consumed food in the status of priestly rations and afterward married a priest" (M. Ter. 6:2); and the like. "The ox belonging to an Israelite that gored an ox belonging to the sanctuary" (M. B.Q. 4:3) is of the same order. Two of Kasovky's Mishnah concordance's nine columns of entries under "Israel" without further qualifying language are taken up with examples of this usage. Such a statement as, "For they imposed upon themselves a strict rule, but an easy rule upon Israel" (M. Bes. 2:6, Ed. 3:10) treats "Israel" as the ordinary folk, in contradistinction to some higher caste or entity.

To be sure, the caste usage is not always pertinent. We find the contrast between "the court" and "all Israel" at M. R.H. 3:1. "Israel" as the people at large would then contrast to "the court." But "Israel" in the following sentence means the entire nation: "So long as Israel looks upward, toward heaven" (M. R.H. 3:8). Every usage of "Israel" in the sense of a particular group has a counterpart in "Israel" in the sense of a distinct caste within the group, Israel: "and an Israelite," "to an Israelite," "Israelites," and the like – all bear both senses; the concordance lists leave no doubt that the meanings are equally commonplace and mutually exclusive.

The Tosefta's use of Israel as a caste in contradistinction to Levites and priests not surprisingly corresponds to that of the Mishnah. For example, "In the case of a herd belonging to a priest that was grazing near a herd belonging to an Israelite" (T. Ter. 10:9); "A priest may anoint himself with oil in the status of priestly rations and take the son of his daughter, in the status of an Israelite, . . ." (T. Ter. 10:10); ". . . an Israelite who sold his beast to a priest for slaughter" (T. Hul. 9:4); and the like. The following is explicit for this usage: "When the time of the watch of the priests and Levites came, they would go up to Jerusalem, and Israel [the caste, Israelites] in that watch . . ." (T. Ta. 4:3). Israel as distinct from "Aaron," that is, the priesthood, occurs at Sifra Shemini 40:3, "What did Israel bring more than Aaron?" "You and your sons [the priesthood] are liable to the death penalty, but Israel is not liable" (Sifra Shemini 1:6). "If Israel is admonished not to come to the tent of meeting when drunk, all the more so the sons of Aaron" (Sifra Shemini 1:7). A reference to "Israel" is explicitly to the caste, so it is made clear at a variety of passages: Ahari 10:1, 8:1, 11:1, Qedoshim 10:1, Emor 7:1, and so on. Sifré to Numbers 43 has: "So the the priests should not say, 'We shall bless Israel.'" For a parallel contrast with the Levites, we find at Sifré to Numbers 67: "Israel worshiped an idol and the tribe of Levi did not worship an idol." Along these same lines of caste distinction, we find, "Did proselytes go into the inner sanctum? Is it not the case that all Israel [not the proselytes alone] did not enter the inner sanctum" (Sifré to Numbers 78).

x.   From Words to Sentences

So much for "Israel" as catalogs of usages signify its meaning and referent. If we wish to ask representative texts to show us how, in concrete statements, these meanings of "Israel" occur, we could readily draw up long lists of sentences, but not many sizable and sustained paragraphs. That is to say, Israel/non-Israel and Israel/not-priest constitute facts but do not generate propositions that vastly clarify the sense of the transitive category "Israel." The contrast we shall confront later on, in Part II, will lend force to this observation. For there, in the documents of the second phase in the unfolding of the Judaism of the dual Torah, we find enormous accounts of "Israel as family," "the merit of the ancestors," "Israel" in the balance with "Rome"; "Israel" as sui generis comes to expression in extraordinarily extensive statements indeed. Still, because our interest is not merely in meanings, but uses, of categorical words, we turn to several texts to show us how, in concrete terms, the Mishnah, Tosefta, and tractate Abot refer to social entities such as "Israel." We now see in very rich detail what it means to authorships of documents as they compose a literature for a social entity to serve as a systemic classifier. With "Israel" as a social metaphor that tells who is in and who is out, who is up and who is down, pertinent sentences will draw upon the facts implicit in that "Israel" – without telling us a great deal about "Israel" at all. An abstraction, "Israel" functions in a vast out-there of relationships, making slight impact on the intimate in-here of everyday destiny. For "Israel" to move from the abstract to the concrete and so gain intrinsic traits and definition, the thinkers who framed the documents at hand will have to gain quite a different perspective on "Israel" from the one before us.

NOTES

1 In my *History of the Mishnah Law of Women* (Leiden: Brill, 1980), vol. V, I argue that women form a prime systemic indicator, telling us about traits of the system as a whole. It is that proposition that is spelled out here with reference to "Israel," which seems to me to conform to the principal trait of women, namely, the abstraction of the category. In these abstractions the Mishnaic system shows its profoundly philosophical character. As we see in the next phase in the unfolding of the Judaism of the dual Torah, discourse turned concrete, specific, and deeply theological, so that the final statement of that Judaism exhibited both philosophical and theological traits and modes of thought. But the characterization of systemic thought in its own terms leads us far afield.

2 And in this respect, "woman" takes a more influential role in the unfolding of the system than does "Israel." For "woman" forms a categorical imperative, and "Israel" does not.

3 In my *Messiah in Context: Israel's History and Destiny in Formative Judaism* (Philadelphia: Fortress Press, 1984) I found that, in the Mishnaic stratum, the Messiah theme also functioned as a mode of hierarchical classification. Interestingly, classified by Messiah was a kind of priest; hence, as in the present case, the hierarchical issue proved one of caste.

4 I am not entirely sure what this fact implies.

5 See A. Marmorstein, *The Doctrine of Merits in Old Rabbinical Literature* (London: Jews College Publication no. 7, 1920). Marmorstein collects and arranges the relevant sayings.

6 We recognize the explicitly supernatural character of the meaning of "Israel" as a social entity enjoying a special relationship to God; for example, when all Israelites are assigned a portion in the world to come, except for those who, for supernatural reasons, by perfidy exempt themselves (M. San. 10:1). We shall return to this passage in the next chapter.

CHAPTER 4

"Israel" in the Mishnah, the Tosefta, and Tractate Abot: A Probe

i. Explicit and Implicit Social Entities in the Mishnah and Tosefta

A survey of the way in which words are used presents a repertoire of mere possibilities. To see the way in which the Mishnah actually treats the category "Israel," we now ask how the document speaks of (an) "Israel." For this purpose we turn to suggestive selections, that first explicitly, then implicitly, testify to the social imagination at work in the consensus represented by the Mishnah's authorship – that is, how in the aggregate they portray that abstraction, "Israel," as a society all at once and all together. For the present purpose we want to find out both what that authorship has to say and also how it forms its opinions. Accordingly, we take an interest in the mode, as much as in the result, of thought.

The most important lesson before us is this: The symbolic transaction involving the system's social entity takes place in mind and imagination. Concrete data from the world out there play a remarkably slight role. A general theory of matters applies also to the specific issues of "Israel," whether nation, society, or caste. To begin with, Scripture had spoken of God through analogies – "in our image, after our likeness" – and once theological anthropology had undertaken to define the human person in God's image, theological sociology would follow suit. In this mode of analogical and contrastive thought, what carried preponderant weight was not the evidence of the streets and households but the generative problematic of the system as a whole. The concrete specificities of the topical program covered by the system played no role in the framing of systemic logic. It follows that, in the case at hand, for the Mishnaic phase of the Judaism of the dual Torah, when social entities came into view, what

60

was important about them would be their relationships to other social entities.

Social entities projected by a system can be implicit or explicit. An explicit social entity is one given its own name. According to the definitions offered in Chapter 1, "Israel" and its subdivisions fall into the category of a social group. When our authorship contemplates an "Israel," it everywhere assumes that under examination is a social entity that involves direct interaction and communication, actions to carry out a system of values. A social group may be a family, a village, or any other entity in which there is a concrete encounter among persons who perceive themselves to form such a group. It may comprise a social group identified by its function (e.g., scribes or judges), by its genealogy (e.g., the priesthood, the Levites), or by (real or made-up) political facts (e.g., the monarchy). Because of the nature of the documents before us, I have now to introduce a further distinction, between an explicit and an implicit social entity. An implicit social entity lacks a name of its own, but enjoys clear recognition in statements that refer to society and its components (e.g., the outsider, whether Samaritan, Roman, or gentile). Viewed by our authorship, such implicit social entities constituted a mere category of society, lacking important differentiating traits. An explicit social entity has a name of its own, whether as a class (e.g., householder or slave), a caste (e.g., priesthood), a profession (e.g., scribes). It may be what we should now call an institution, such as a temple with an ongoing cult that outlives a given generation and remains stable and a permanent fact of social life. The importance of the distinction will presently become self-evident. But first, we turn attention to the texts and their traits.

To generate our categories properly, we turn directly to our sources and ask them to tell us about the explicit and implicit social entities, categories and classifications by which they make statements concerning society and its composition. Once more we recall that the task of defining "Israel" formed an exercise in a larger taxonomic mode, particular to the Mishnah's system, of specifying what one meant by any classification. To understand the texts important in the examination of "Israel," we have therefore to adjust our vision to a different way of seeing abstract categories and classifications. For when sages in the Mishnah and related writings defined, they thought in personal terms, not in abstractions such as institutions. They spoke not of the high priesthood but of the person of the high priest, not of policy but of personality. When they wished to tell us what an individual is, they did so by describing the relationships into which that individual might enter. So the king, not the monarchy, let alone the government, was defined in terms of the personal rights and obligations of the monarch, and the social foundations of the monarchy were delimited by the relationships between the monarch and various other entities.

For their part, these other entities – exemplary of the implicit social entities I mentioned just now – were called up to testify not because of intrinsic traits of their own, but because they entered into relationship with the monarch. We are told, for example, about "the people," or "ordinary folk," but these are not differentiated or defined in concrete terms. Rather, the category takes on meaning in contradistinction to the monarch. The same mode of thought pertains to (an) "Israel." When we invoke the notion of thinking through metaphors, we realize that the metaphorical approach begins with the incipience of thought itself. Government, an abstraction, is compared to the king, the personalization of an abstraction, who is then compared to the person of the king: He says, he does, he wants. The working of the metaphorical definition yields the end products we shall now examine. We therefore look for our social entities, in the present probe, in terms of individuals who are deemed to stand for components of a larger society, "all Israel" for instance, and, as is clear, these individuals will find definition in their relationship to other such persons, themselves introduced on account of their relevance to the principal social entity or component subject to discussion – a rather complex and cumbersome mode of thought indeed.

Our initial probe brings us to Mishnah tractate Sanhedrin, which concerns the institutions of the governance of Israel, their components and their powers, because that document deals with social entities that are named and described. To adjust to the modes of discourse at hand, we begin with the definition of king and high priest, and only then turn to "Israel" – the important social entitites of the document that we might wish to translate as state, church, and population. All of these metaphors together make up that equally metaphorical "Israel," serving as those analogies and comparisons that permit us to speak of the abstractions at hand.[1] Because we recognize that social thought in our sources treats as individual and personal what we should today regard as institutional facts of society stated in the abstract (even in statistics!), we should not be surprised, as I said, to find "high priest" and "king" standing for high priesthood and monarchy, respectively. Once we have seen in an immediate way how this mode of discourse carries on its affairs, we shall come to "Israel."

Mishnah tractate Sanhedrin

A. A high priest judges, and [others] judge him;
B. gives testimony, and [others] give testimony about him;
C. performs the rite of removing the shoe [Deut. 25:7–9], and [others] perform the rite of removing the shoe with his wife.
D. [Others] enter levirate marriage with his wife, but he does not enter into levirate marriage,
E. because he is prohibited to marry a widow.
F. [If] he suffers a death [in his family], he does not follow the bier.
G. "But when [the bearers of the bier] are not visible, he is visible; when they are visible, he is not.
H. "And he goes with them to the city gate," the words of R. Meir.
I. R. Judah says, "He never leaves the sanctuary,
J. "since it says, 'Nor shall he go out of the sanctuary' (Lev. 21:12)."
K. And when he gives comfort to others
L. the accepted practice is for all the people to pass one after another, and the appointed [prefect of the priests] stands between him and the people.
M. And when he receives consolation from others,
N. all the people say to him, "Let us be your atonement."
O. And he says to them, "May you be blessed by Heaven."
P. And when they provide him with the funeral meal,
Q. all the people sit on the ground, while he sits on a stool.

M. San. 2:1

What is interesting is the way in which the social entity, the high priest(hood), is described. Now we see in a concrete way what it means to define a social entity principally in relationship to others. We are not told what the high priest does as high priest. What we are told, for the purposes of the present tractate, is how the high priest(hood) compares with other social entities. First, the high priest is set into relationship with "others," that is, everyone else. That is in respect to the judiciary. Then he is placed in hierarchical relationship with the family at those interstitial points at which the high priesthood intersects with rules important to the institution of the family. Third, he is given public dignity in regard to mourning rites – that is, defined in respect to his office in its own terms of dignity.

We now see that the same mode of definition of a social entity applies to the monarch(y), which, like the high priest(hood), is defined not by function but by relationship. When, in a moment, we examine a counterpart text on what is an "Israel[ite]," we shall find the silences still more compelling.

A. The king does not judge, and [others] do not judge him;
B. does not give testimony, and [others] do not give testimony about him;
C. does not perform the rite of removing the shoe, and others do not perform the rite of removing the shoe with his wife;
D. does not enter into levirate marriage, nor [does his brother] enter levirate marriage with his wife.
E. R. Judah says, "If he wanted to perform the rite of removing the shoe or to enter into levirate marriage, his memory is a blessing."
F. They said to him, "They pay no attention to him [if he expressed the wish to do so]."
G. [Others] do not marry his widow.
H. R. Judah says, "A king may marry the widow of a king.
I. "For so we find in the case of David, that he married the widow of Saul,
J. "For it is said, 'And I gave you your master's house and your master's wives into your embrace' (2 Sam. 12:8)."

M. San. 2:2

A. [If] [the king] suffers a death in his family, he does not leave the gate of his palace.
B. R. Judah says, "If he wants to go out after the bier, he goes out,
C. "for thus we find in the case of David, that he went out after the bier of Abner,
D. "since it is said, 'And King David followed the bier' (2 Sam. 3:31)."
E. They said to him, "This action was only to appease the people."
F. And when they provide him with the funeral meal, all the people sit on the ground, while he sits on a couch.

M. San. 2:3

The king is defined in relationship to the high priest, with the commonalities and contrasts most striking. But the relationship of the monarch(y) or the state to "the others" – that is, the people at large ("Israel"), in addition to the temple/high priesthood – is further specified, with reference to the power to make war and exercise eminent domain and, again, to public dignity, particularly as it affects sumptuary laws. Here too, the mode of social thought follows two principles.

First, we define in terms of persons. What that means for the completed survey of uses of "Israel" to mean "individual Jew" is simple. Wherever we speak of the individual, we define the smallest whole unit of the social entity – that is, the individual, not two or three or more. That fact takes on meaning when we enter into the theological realm of "Israel" as sui generis; there we require "two or three" and do not alight upon the individual to constitute "Israel."

Second, as before, definition takes the form of relationship, now in yet a richer sense. For to define one entity, we not only explain how that entity relates to some other, but we also – and especially – compare and contrast that entity to some other. On the basis of that fixed mode of thought I claim once more to be justified in conceiving of the appropriate mode of inquiry to be an examination of metaphors of social entities, hence, social metaphors. That is not to suggest that functions are not specified. Quite to the contrary, what the monarch(y) does now is made explicit. But here too the rights and role of "others" are specified, so the definition of functions remains part of an exercise in analysis of relationships.

A. [The king] calls out [the army to wage] a war fought by choice on the instructions of a court of seventy-one.

B. He [may exercise the right to] open a road for himself, and [others] may not stop him.

C. The royal road has no required measure.

D. All the people plunder and lay before him [what they have grabbed], and he takes the first portion.

M. San. 2:4

At the same time, the principal point of interest focuses upon the personal, on the one side, and the interrelationship, on the other. If we wish to say what the monarch(y) is, we point to matters of the dignity and personal standing that define the social presence of the monarch: his gravity, the honor owing to him.

E. "He should not multiply wives to himself" (Deut. 17:17) – only eighteen.

F. R. Judah says, "He may have as many as he wants, so long as they do not entice him [to abandon the Lord (Deut. 7:4)]."

G. R. Simeon says, "Even if there is only one who entices him [to abandon the Lord] – lo, this one should not marry her."

H. If so, why is it said, "He should not multiply wives to himself"?

I. Even though they should be like Abigail [1 Sam. 25:3].

J. "He should not multiply horses to himself" (Deut. 17:16) – only enough for his chariot.

K. "Neither shall he greatly multiply to himself silver and gold" (Deut. 17:16) – only enough to pay his army.

L. "And he writes out a scroll of the Torah for himself" (Deut. 17:17).

M. When he goes to war, he takes it out with him; when he comes back, he brings it back with him; when he is in session in court, it is with him; when he is reclining, it is before him,

N. as it is said, "And it shall be with him, and he shall read in it all the days of his life" (Deut. 17:19).

M. San. 2:4

A. [Others may] not ride on his horse, sit on his throne, handle his sceptre.

B.   And [others may] not watch him while he is getting a haircut, or while he is nude, or in the bath-house,

C.   since it is said, "You shall surely set him as king over you" (Deut. 17:15) – that reverence for him will be upon you.

M. San. 2:5

What has already been said suffices to draw from the foregoing the important points for our analysis. Let us proceed to the Tosefta.

As we recall, the Tosefta comprises complementary materials, which cite and then amplify – much in the form of a commentary – statements in the corresponding chapter of the Mishnah. The Tosefta further contains supplementary materials, pertinent to the theme and even the proposition of a Mishnah passage. These amplify the Mishnah as much as does material expressed in the form of a commentary consisting of citation and gloss. The Tosefta may further contain materials on the Mishnah's theme but autonomous of the Mishnah's propositions. These may go back to the same period as the formation of the Mishnah. In all, however, in the Tosefta we deal with a document of the period after the closure of the Mishnah, therefore the third or even fourth century. The Tosefta's complement to the foregoing introduces the social entity of the patriarch(ate), which the Mishnah's account ignores. But the patriarch(ate) is given the same standing as the monarch(y).

Tosefta tractate Sanhedrin 4:3ff.

A.   Just as they make a burning for kings [who die], so they make a burning for patriarchs [who die].

B.   But they do not do so for ordinary people.

T. San. 4:3

The equivalence of monarch and patriarch is the important point, and this is made explicit. Further points of dignity, pertinent to the monarch and patriarch, are specified.

A.   Everybody stands, while he sits.

B.   And sitting was [permitted] in the temple courtyard only for kings of the house of David.

C.   All the people keep silent, when he is talking.

D.   He would call them, "My brothers" and "My people," as it is said, "Hear you, my brothers and my people" (1 Chron. 28:2).

E.   And they call him, "Our lord and our master,"

F.   as it is said, "But our Lord David, the King, has made Solomon king" (1 Kings 1:43).

T. San. 4:4

Tosefta's authorship stresses the relationship between monarch(y) and people, by noting, as we see, that the king may sit while others must stand, and then, by contrast, that the sumptuary limitations that apply to the king do not apply to everyone else: "But an ordinary person is permitted [to do] all of these things." So too:

> H. R. Yosé says, "Everything that is spelled out in the pericope of the king [Deut. 17:14] is [an ordinary person] permitted to do."
>
> T. San. 4:4

These passages lead us deep into the processes of imagination that yielded sages' categories and definitions. That is, they tell us how sages knew what they wanted to know, identified the data that required attention and explanation. That is the centerpiece of category formation, and it is outlined by the selected passages. Let me spell this out. Specifically, sages began within, in their imagination, and drew for detail upon their inner vision. We see that fact when we take a second look at the categories at hand: king, high priest. For, long before the destruction of the temple in 70 C.E., Israel, the people-nation, did not constitute a political entity governed by the bicameral institution of king and high priest. In reflecting on social facts, the authorship of the Mishnah recognized as categorical entities not the realities of the world round about, but the fantasy of a society governed by king and high priest, a condition that Israel, the nation, had not known for two centuries by the time of the closure of the Mishnah. We should, indeed, have to reach back to the time of the Maccabees, whose dynasty came to an end in the middle of the first century B.C.E., to locate a time at which such social facts pertained. Even then, we cannot say whether public life was conducted in the decorous way now portrayed in our passage, with two equal powers in charge. But we can say with certainty that to the framers of this passage, that possibility made little difference for composing the portrait of the political society of the "Israel" they proposed to construct. What we learn from a brief probe of the explicit social entities treated by the Mishnah's authorship is one fact. In the exercise of the imagination the social thought of the Mishnah's framers recognized no limits imposed by the facts of everyday life.

Our probe of how the Mishnah's authorship addresses explicit social entities has shown us the formal categories of "all Israel." But when taking up the workings of society, that is, concrete transactions among members of the social group at hand, matters become more subtle. We shall pursue a byway, a single instance in which our authorship considers the makeup of that larger abstraction, "Israel" as social entity, here, social group. Not proposing to describe subunits of the larger "Israel," but specifying the rules and procedures of a social interaction of members of that "Israel," the authorship of the Mishnah shows us how implicit entities come under definition, again, wholly in relationship to other entities, palpable and social, intangible and metaphysical alike. Recognizing these implicit entities helps us to grasp the mode of thought that comes to expression in processes of classification.

When we come to the implicit social entities, we find ourselves at a different stratum of society, on the one side, but also within what seems to me a more plausible picture of this-worldly social facts and relationships, on the other. Our probe carries us to the account of a meal, which I have chosen because the Mishnah's authorship treats this – in my view, intrinsically social – occasion in a highly particular way. They provide rules for the meal that have little to do with the act of eating, even with the act of eating in society. The meal, a social transaction, is made a symbolic occasion, in which extrinsic considerations intrude and transform the occasion into an expression, in society, of an implicit picture of society at large. The meal may therefore be compared with the occasion of a state funeral, just now surveyed. Once more we gain access to the way in which sages in the Mishnaic system express their conception of the social entity at hand.

Mishnah tractate Berakhot

A. These are the things which are between the House of Shammai and the House of Hillel in [regard to] the meal:

M. Ber.

The implicit social entities here are two. The "houses," we may stipulate without further ado, represent groups within the larger authorship understood as the authority of the Mishnah by the authorship of the Mishnah. More important are the participants in the occasion of a meal. Each participant is now described in terms applicable to all, which is to say, the rules govern conduct at the meal, with the implicit conception that all present conform to those rules and enter into the social entity by reason of that conformity. (So abstract a formulation helps us to understand the advantages of resorting, for definition, to the personal and concrete.) I give only a selection of the rules concerning the meal, to make the main point:

B. The House of Shammai say, "One blesses over the day, and afterward one blesses over the wine."

And the House of Hillel say, "One blesses over the wine, and afterward one blesses over the day."

M. Ber. 8:1

A.   The House of Shammai say, "They wash the hands and afterward mix the cup."
And the House of Hillel say, "They mix the cup and afterward wash the hands."

M. Ber. 8:2

A.   The House of Shammai say, "He dries his hands on the cloth and lays it on the table."
And the House of Hillel say, "On the pillow."

M. Ber. 8:3

A.   The House of Shammai say, "They clean the house, and afterward they wash the hands."
And the House of Hillel say, "They wash the hands, and afterward they clean the house."

M. Ber. 8:4

The social entity implicit in this passage engages in eating a meal, at which rites are conducted and (again, we stipulate) at which certain rules of commensality (washing hands, drying hands, location of cloth) are observed. We have then two social entities before us: first, authorities of opinion concerning rules now in the Mishnah; and, second, people who assemble for meals, but who are not necessarily members of a household or a family. A social entity therefore takes shape other than the natural modes of genealogy, on the one side, and everyday interaction in the home and family, the household unit, on the other. That, by definition, draws us outward to the abstract social entity comprising individuals who observe the same rules and – stretched outward to its farthest limit – yields an "Israel" defined by the same utter abstraction of conformity to a set of rules. But that available metaphor for "Israel," namely, all persons who keep the same rules, though possibly implicit through the Mishnah and its friends, in fact never serves; it is too abstract for personalization, except in the mode right before us.

Still, once we do enter into discourse on rules that define an abstract entity, we naturally move onward to the "nonentity," that is, "non-Israel." The same pericope draws attention to an "other," one that is specified: the gentile, the deceased, the idol, the Samaritan.

A.   They do not bless over the light or the spices of gentiles, nor the light or the spices of the dead, nor the light or the spices which are before an idol.

M. Ber. 8:6

C.   They respond Amen after an Israelite who blesses, and they do not respond Amen after a Samaritan who blesses, until hearing the entire blessing.

M. Ber. 8:8

Now we see the anticipated distinction between Israel and "other," the gentile. The implicit recognition of other social entities bears in its wake no important information. Whereas we learn much about the social entity that conducts a common meal, we are told nothing at all about the outsider, the gentile, except for his classification: one with the dead and the idol. The Samaritan is represented as a kind of Israelite, in that he says a blessing as does an Israelite, but the Samaritan is suspect as to the blessings that he says. There is one further social entity introduced in the matter by the Tosefta's amplification.

Tosefta Berakhot

A.   The House of Shammai say, "They clean the house, on account of the waste of food, and afterward they wash the hands."
B.   The House of Hillel say, "If the waiter was a disciple of a sage, he gathers the scraps which contain as much as an olive's bulk."

5:28 (Lieberman,[2] p. 30, ls. 65–68)

A.   The House of Shammai say, "He holds the cup of wine in his right hand and spiced oil in his left hand."
     "He blesses over the wine and afterward blesses over the oil."
B.   And the House of Hillel say, "He holds the sweet oil in his right hand and the cup of wine in his left hand."
C.   He blesses over the oil and smears it on the head of the waiter. If the waiter was a disciple of a sage, he [the diner] smears it on the wall, because it is not praiseworthy for a disciple of a sage to go forth perfumed.

5:29 (Lieberman, p. 30, ls. 68–72)

The implicit relationship between those who are eating and others is in two parts. First, the participants are assumed to be of a social class of sufficient means to afford servants, specifically, the waiter. Second, the waiter is assumed to have the right to belong to the social entity that conducts the meal. So the implicit social entity is defined not by means but by knowledge, as is made explicit, and the society at large is made up of social entities defined in accord with diverse traits, means being one, learning another. That conception of the social group (not merely social "entity") of course rests on premises as to sages' understanding of themselves and their group.

If we compare the shared materials of both documents at the relevant points, we note that it is the Tosefta's authorship that has introduced the category of the disciple of the sage, defined by knowledge learned (again, we stipulate) through discipleship, as well as the matter of the servant:

M. Ber.	T. Ber.
The House of Shammai say, "They clean the house and afterward wash the hands."	The House of Shammai say, "They clean the house *on account of the waste of food* and afterward wash the hands."
And the House of Hillel say, "They wash the hands and afterward clean the house." (8:4A)	The House of Hillel say, *"If the waiter was a disciple of a sage, he gathers the scraps which contain as much as an olive's bulk.* "They wash the hands and afterward clean the house." (5:28)
They respond Amen after an Israelite who blesses, and they do not respond Amen after a Samaritan who blesses, until one hears the entire blessing. (8:8C)	They answer Amen after *a blessing with the divine name recited by a gentile.* They do not answer Amen after a Samaritan who blesses *with the divine name* until they hear the entire blessing. (5:21 [Lieberman, p. 28, Is. 41-2])

Implicit in the discourse of the Mishnah's and Tosefta's authorships is a society made up of distinct social groups, of which at least two, the one framed by cultural considerations, the other by economic or class considerations, are to be discerned. The mode of definition for both explicit and implicit entities is constant. We deal with persons, not abstractions, and the social entities represented by persons find definition in the relationship between one person and the next.

The present probe has carried us somewhat far afield. Our interest in "Israel" left behind, we have entered into the more detailed issues of how, in concrete cases, the Mishnah's authorship thinks about the subdivisions and groups of the encompassing society. This has shown us a range of social entities within Israel, but that is not our primary purpose; it has also told us how sages carry on their processes of reflection and how they express the results of that expression. Let us now return to the main problem: Who, or what, is (an) Israel? The Mishnah's testimony proves explicit.

ii.   A Textual Probe of Israel as Sui Generis

When we ask the authorship of the Mishnah to tell us in explicit terms how they define (an) "Israel," they direct our attention to the one passage in which they systematically answer that question. It is framed, as a question of social definition must be, in terms of who is in and who is out. (An) "Israel" then is defined within the categories of inclusion and exclusion, which implicitly yields the definition that all who are out are out and all who are in are in, and, all together, the ones that are in (implicitly) constitute the social entity or social group. When the Mishnah's authorship wishes to define "Israel" by itself and on its own terms, rather than as a classification among other classifications in an enormous system of taxonomy, "Israel" may be set forth as an entity not only in its own terms but also sui generis. But, as we now expect, the context will be defined by supernatural considerations. For this-worldly purposes I should claim that that kind of definition, which by the nature of the unique is essentially beyond all metaphor, becomes possible only when we leave behind issues of classification altogether, which is why Israel as sui generis will predominate only in the second phase of the Judaism of the dual Torah, when issues other than those of classification prove paramount.

Definition through specification of relationships is possible only when all species belong to a single genus. When, by contrast, there are traits particular to a genus, when no other genus may be compared with that particular genus, then definition by traits and not by relationships becomes the required procedure of thought. According to that broad theory, we have "Israel" as sui generis only when we appeal to traits of a supernatural character to begin with.[3] Now, as we shall see, what characterizes the entity that is sui generis will be traits to begin with pertinent only to that entity, and, for the case at hand, the categories are defined in terms of belief: affirming a given doctrine, denying another. That fact bears in its wake the implication that Israel as a social entity, encompassing each of its members, is defined by reference to matters of correct doctrine. All "Israelites" – persons who hold the correct opinion – then constitute "Israel." I know of no passage of the Mishnah and related literature more concrete and explicit on who is in and who is out. But the "in" is not within this world at all. It is who enters or has a share of the world to come. Then all those "Israelites" who constitute in themselves the social entity, the group, "Israel," form a supernatural, not merely a social entity – and no wonder all metaphors fail.

The premise is that we speak only of Israel, and the result is the definition of Israel in terms we should not have anticipated at all: not

Israel as against non-Israel or gentile; not Israel as against non-Israel, the priest; but Israel as against those who deny convictions now deemed – explicitly – indicatively and normatively to form the characteristics of "Israel"[ite]. Here is an "Israel" that, at first glance, is defined not in relationships but intransitively and intrinsically, contrary to my allegations just some pages ago. But that impression will soon shift, for Israel now invokes non-Israel, just as it did earlier, but for a different purpose and in a separate context. What this means, therefore, is that Israel is not a social entity at all like other social entities, for the purposes of present discourse, but an entity that finds definition, as to genus and not species, elsewhere. To state the result simply: In what follows, Israel is implicitly sui generis.

Mishnah tractate Sanhedrin

A. All Israelites have a share in the world to come,
B. as it is said, "your people also shall be all righteous, they shall inherit the land forever; the branch of my planting, the work of my hands, that I may be glorified" (Is. 60:21).
C. And these are the ones who have no portion in the world to come:
D. He who says, the resurrection of the dead is a teaching which does not derive from the Torah, and the Torah does not come from Heaven; and an Epicurean.
E. R. Aqiba says, "Also: He who reads in heretical books,
F. "and he who whispers over a wound and says, 'I will put none of the diseases upon you which I have put on the Egyptians, for I am the Lord who heals you' (Ex. 15:26)."
G. Abba Saul says, "Also: He who pronounces the divine Name as it is spelled out."

M. San. 11:1

Israel is defined inclusively: To be "Israel" is to have a share in the world to come. "Israel" then is a social entity that is made up of those who share a common conviction, and that "Israel" therefore bears an other-worldly destiny. Other social entities are not so defined within the Mishnah – and that by definition! – and it must follow that (an) "Israel" in the conception of the authorship of the Mishnah is sui generis, in that other social entities do not find their definition within the range of supernatural facts pertinent to "Israel"; an "Israel" is a social group that endows its individual members with life in the world to come; an "Israel"[ite] is one who enjoys the world to come. Excluded from this "Israel" are "Israel"[ite]s who within the established criteria of social identification exclude themselves. The power to define by relationships does not run out, however, because in this supernatural context of an Israel that is sui generis, we still know who is "Israel" because we are told who is "non-Israel," now, specific nonbelievers or sinners. These are, as we should expect, persons who reject the stated belief.

A. Three kings and four ordinary folk have no portion in the world to come.
B. Three kings: Jeroboam, Ahab, and Manasseh.
C. R. Judah says, "Manasseh has a portion in the world to come,
D. "since it is said, 'And he prayed to him and he was entreated of him and heard his supplication and brought him again to Jerusalem into his kingdom' (2 Chron. 33:13)."
E. They said to him, "To his kingdom he brought him back, but to the life of the world to come he did not bring him back."
F. Four ordinary folk: Balaam, Doeg, Ahitophel, and Gehazi.

M. San. 11:2

Not only persons, but also classes of Israelites are specified, in all cases contributing to the definition of (an) Israel. The excluded classes of Israelites bear in common a supernatural fault, which is that they have sinned against God.

We begin with those excluded from the world to come who are not Israel, namely, the generations of the flood and of the dispersion. This somewhat complicates matters, because we should have thought that at issue in enjoying the world to come would be only (an) "Israel." It should follow that gentiles of whatever sort hardly require specification; they all are alike. But the focus of what follows – classes of excluded Israelites, who have sinned against God – leads to the supposition that the specified gentiles are included because of their place in the biblical narrative. The implication is not that all other gentiles enjoy the world to come except for these, and the focus of definition remains on Israel, pure and simple.

A. The generation of the flood has no share in the world to come,
B. and they shall not stand in the judgment,
C. since it is written, "My spirit shall not judge with man forever" (Gen. 6:3),
D. neither judgment nor spirit.
E. The generation of the dispersion has no share in the world to come,
F. since it is said, "So the Lord scattered them abroad from there upon the face of the whole earth" (Gen. 11:8).
G. "So the Lord scattered them abroad" – in this world,
H. "and the Lord scattered them from there" – in the world to come.
I. The men of Sodom have no portion in the world to come,
J. since it is said, "Now the men of Sodom were wicked and sinners against the Lord exceedingly" (Gen. 13:13).

K.   "Wicked" – in this world,
L.   "And sinners" – in the world to come.
M.   But they will stand in judgment.
N.   R. Nehemiah says, "Both these and those will not stand in judgment,
O.   "for it is said, 'Therefore the wicked shall not stand in judgment [108A], nor sinners in the congregation of the righteous' (Ps. 1:5).
P.   'Therefore the wicked shall not stand in judgment' – this refers to the generation of the flood.
Q.   'Nor sinners in the congregation of the righteous' – this refers to the men of Sodom."
R. · They said to him, "They will not stand in the congregation of the righteous, but they will stand in the congregation of the sinners."
S.   The spies have no portion in the world to come,
T.   as it is said, "Even those men who brought up an evil report of the land died by the plague before the Lord" (Num. 14:37).
U.   "Died" – in this world.
V.   "By the plague" – in the world to come.
W.   "The generation of the wilderness has no portion in the world to come and will not stand in judgment,
X.   "for it is written, 'In this wilderness they shall be consumed and there they shall die' (Num. 14:35)," the words of R. Aqiba.
Y.   R. Eliezer says, "Concerning them it says, 'Gather my saints together to me, those that have made a covenant with me by sacrifice' (Ps. 50:5)."
Z.   "The party of Korah is not destined to rise up,
AA.   "for it is written, 'And the earth closed upon them' – in this world.
BB.   "'And they perished from among the assembly' – in the world to come," the words of R. Aqiba.
CC.   And R. Eliezer says, "Concerning them it says, 'The Lord kills and resurrects, brings down to Sheol and brings up again' (1 Sam. 2:6)."
DD.   "The ten tribes are not destined to return,
EE.   "since it is said, 'And he cast them into another land, as on this day' (Deut. 29:28). Just as the day passes and does not return, so they have gone their way and will not return," the words of R. Aqiba.
FF.   R. Eliezer says, "Just as this day is dark and then grows light, so the ten tribes for whom it now is dark – thus in the future it is destined to grow light for them."

M. San. 11:3

A.   The townsfolk of an apostate town have no portion in the world to come,
B.   as it is said, "Certain base fellows [sons of Belial] have gone out from the midst of thee and have drawn away the inhabitants of their city" (Deut. 13:14).
C.   And they are not put to death unless those who misled the [town] come from that same town and from that same tribe,
D.   and unless the majority is misled,
E.   and unless men did the misleading.

F. [If] women or children misled them,
G. of if a minority of the town was misled,
H. or if those who misled the town came from outside of it,
I. lo, they are treated as individuals [and not as a whole town],
J. and they [thus] require [testimony against them] by two witnesses, and a statement of warning, for each and every one of them.
K. This rule is more strict for individuals than for the community:
L. for individuals are put to death by stoning.
M. Therefore their property is saved.
N. But the community is put to death by the sword,
O. Therefore their property is lost.

M. San. 11:4

The catalog leaves us no doubt that the candidates for inclusion or exclusion are presented by the biblical narrative. Hence I see no implicit assumption that all gentiles except those specified have a share in the world to come. That seems to me a proposition altogether beyond the imagination of our authorship. Tosefta Sanhedrin for its part does not suggest that some gentiles enjoy the world to come.

Tosefta Sanhedrin

A. The Israelites who sinned with their bodies and gentiles who sinned with their bodies go down to Gehenna and are judged there for twelve months.
B. And after twelve months their souls perish, their bodies are burned, Gehenna absorbs them, and they are turned into dirt.
C. And the wind blows them and scatters them under the feet of the righteous,
D. as it is written, "And you shall tread down the wicked, for they shall be dust under the soles of the feet of the righteous in the day that I do this, says the Lord of Hosts" (Mal. 4:3).

T. San. 13:4

A. But heretics, apostates, traitors, Epicureans, those who deny the Torah, those who separate from the ways of the community, those who deny the resurrection of the dead, and whoever both sinned and caused the public to sin –
B. for example, Jeroboam and Ahab,
C. and those who sent their arrows against the land of the living and stretched out their hands against the "lofty habitation" [the temple],
D. Gehenna is locked behind them, and they are judged therein for all generations,
E. since it is said, "And they shall go forth and look at the corpses of the men who were transgressors against me. For their worm dies not, and

their fire is not quenched. And they shall be an abhorring unto all flesh" (Is. 66:24).

F. Sheol will waste away, but they will not waste away,

G. for it is written, ". . . and their form shall cause Sheol to waste away" (Ps. 49:14).

H. What made this happen to them? Because they stretched out their hand against the "lofty habitation,"

I. as it is said, Because of his lofty habitation, and lofty habitation refers only to the temple, as it is said, "I have surely built you as a lofty habitation, a place for you to dwell in forever" (I Kings 8:13).

T. San. 13:5

The implicit principle of T. San. 13:5 is clearly that we deal only with Israelites, not with gentiles. Accordingly, the authorship of the Tosefta seems to take for granted that Israel is a supernatural entity, and a person's separation from Israel is brought about by supernatural considerations. Thus, when Israel is sui generis, it is because the context of definition speaks of supernatural and not this-worldly matters. When we come to the second phase of the unfolding of the writings of the Judaism of the dual Torah, we shall find a far more elaborate statement of the traits of that social entity that is sui generis. But the main point – that we deal with an entity that is supernatural and not subject to the rules of this world – defines matters throughout.

iii. Israel and Social Metaphors in Tractate Abot

The Mishnah's first and most systematic apologetic, tractate Abot, brought to closure a generation beyond the Mishnah, in ca. 250 C.E., presents us with the only truly general statement, in the form of aphorisms to be sure, of the Mishnah's system, its Judaism. We turn to Abot for a picture of two matters, first, meanings imputed to "Israel," and, second and much more interesting, where and how the category "Israel" plays a role in the comprehensive statement of a systematic character that is attempted by the authorship at hand. Tractate Abot is in three distinct parts. Chapters 1 and 2 are composed of three lists of sequential authorities, from Sinai through the second century C.E. The first list, 1:1–15, carries us from Moses at Sinai down through authorities who flourished to the destruction of the temple in 70 C.E. The list has a brief appendix, 1:16–18. Then chapter 2 is made up of two lists that continue the one of chapter 1, the first serving the patriarchate, the other, the sages: The one list specifies aphorisms assigned to names otherwise associated with the patriarchal administration, the other, names associated with the important sage authorities. There are then some appended sayings of authorities of the same time. Chapters 3 and 4 string together, in no clear order, sayings attributed to authorities of the second century C.E., most of whom also appear in the Mishnah. Chapter 5 is made up of compositions stated mostly anonymously and constructed on the basis of mnemonic patterns formed of numbers.

The former of the two catalogs, Abot 2:1–7, lists Rabbi, meaning, Judah the Patriarch, sponsor of the Mishnah, of ca. 200 C.E., and his successors ("sons" in a genealogical and political sense). The latter of the two, 2:8–12, has as the counterpart Yohanan ben Zakkai, founder of the academy of Yavneh that, after 70 C.E., carried forward the chain of the transmission of the Torah described in the present document as the ancestry of the Mishnah, and his disciples ("sons" in a supernatural sense). The net effect is to claim that the two pillars on which the Mishnah's authority rested – the political pillar of the Jews' administration and the scribal pillar of the Jews' legal and theological traditions – form the foundation of the document as a whole. But the values of the scribes predominate; the important point, beginning, middle, and end, stresses study of the Torah. That fact bears heavy consequences for treatment of the social entity, "Israel," as we shall see in a moment. We find two pertinent sayings within the chains of tradition of chapters 1 and 2. One refers to the government, an entity out there, the other, to the community, treated in equally indeterminate terms. The point of the former is that governments are not to be trusted, of the latter that one is to preserve ties to the community:

> [Judah, son of R. Judah the Patriarch:] "Be wary of the government, for they get friendly with a person only for their own convenience. They look like friends when it is to their benefit, but they do not stand by a person when he is in need."
>
> Abot 2:3

> . . . Hillel says: "Do not walk out on the community."
>
> Abot 2:4

In neither saying do I find profound thought on the social entity "Israel." What we have falls into the category of good advice on wise conduct, nothing more. "Israel" does not form a topic that receives sustained attention. Sayings that, from a systemic perspective, are equivalently neutral, include the following:

A.   R. Hananiah, Prefect of the Priests, says, "Pray for the welfare of the government. For if it were not for fear of it, one man would swallow his fellow alive."

Abot 3:2

These sayings do not contribute to a pattern of inquiry into the social entity, Israel. They add up to good advice.

That is not to suggest that thought about the meaning of a social entity defined by shared traits and norms does not enter into the program of the document. Quite to the contrary, from a gathering of two persons on upward, the framers of Abot explicitly identify what they mean by a social entity, a social group within the definition given in chapter 1, and, it follows, how they distinguish one such entity from another. But this entity they do not call an "Israel." They have another socially definitive category in mind:

B. R. Hananiah b. Teradion says, "[If] two sit together and between them do not pass teachings of the Torah, lo, this is a seat of the scornful, as it is said, 'Nor sits in the seat of the scornful' (Ps. 1:1).

"But two who are sitting, and words of the Torah do pass between them – the Presence is with them, as it is said, 'Then they that feared the Lord spoke with one another, and the Lord hearkened and heard, and a book of remembrance was written before him, for them that feared the Lord and gave thought to his name' (Mal. 3:16)."

"I know that this applies to two. How do I know that even if a single person sits and works on the Torah, the Holy One, blessed be He, set aside a reward for him? As it is said, 'Let him sit alone and keep silent, because he has laid it upon him' (Lam. 3:28)."

Abot 3:2

R. Simeon says, "Three who ate at a single table and did not talk about teachings of the Torah while at that table are as though they ate from dead sacrifices (Ps. 106:28), as it is said, 'For all tables are full of vomit and filthiness [if they are] without God' (Ps. 106:28).

"But three who ate at a single table and did talk about teachings of the Torah while at that table are as if they ate at the table of the Omnipresent, blessed is he, as it is said, 'And he said to me, This is the table that is before the Lord' (Ez. 41:22)."

Abot 3:3

R. Halafta of Kefar Hananiah says, "Among ten who sit and work hard on the Torah the Presence comes to rest, as it is said, 'God stands in the congregation of God' (Ps. 82:1).

"And how do we know that the same is so even of five? For it is said, 'And he has founded his group upon the earth' (Amos 9:6).

"And how do we know that this is so even of three? Since it is said, 'And he judges among the judges' (Ps. 82:1).

"And how do we know that this is so even of two? Because it is said, 'Then they that feared the Lord spoke with one another, and the Lord hearkened and heard' (Mal. 3:16).

"And how do we know that this is so even of one? Since it is said, 'In every place where I record my name I will come to you and I will bless you' (Ex. 20:24)."

Abot 3:6

The concluding saying, concerning "even . . . one," alerts us to the fact that our definitions correspond to those in M. San. 10:1ff. "Israel" is made up of "Israelites" – even one individual constituting an "Israel" when such a person engages in Torah study. We may then generalize as we did before. A social entity, a social group in particular – yet not called an "Israel"! – takes shape in one of two ways: either because people do exchange Torah teachings, or because they do not do so. The one type of entity is differentiated from the other by that sole indicator, which conforms to the larger system at hand. Here we have another social entity that is sui generis, though it is not called (an) Israel.

Along these same lines, the individual and "Israel" serve as examples of the same thing, namely, God's love, which is all the greater because the person and the social entity are informed of that love. Like "Israel" in the Mishnah, here too "Israel" is inert, not generating a proposition but contributing to the statement of one. The proposition has to do with God's love, illustrated, by the way, in the condition of Israel too. So we see how a systemically neutral "Israel" plays its part in making the points important to the system, and how the traits of "Israel" fail to generate distinctive propositions:

A. He would say, "Precious is the human being, who was created in the image [of God]. It was an act of still greater love that it was made known to him that he was created in the image [of God], as it is said, 'For in the image of God he made man' (Gen. 9:6)."

B Precious is Israel [that is, are Israelites], who are called children to the Omnipresent. It was an act of still greater love that it was made known to them that they were called children to the Omnipresent, as it is said, "You are the children of the Lord your God" (Deut. 14:1).

C Precious are Israelites, to whom was given the precious thing. It was an act of still greater love that it was made known to them that to them was given that precious thing with which the world was made, as it is said, "For I give you a good doctrine. Do not forsake my Torah" (Prov. 4:2).

Abot 3:14

Once more we observe an "Israel" that is sui generis, beginning with a simple fact. "Israel" here means "Israelite," not the social entity viewed as a collectivity, but those who belong to the entity – and therefore constitute that entity, even one by one. These are the children of the Lord, as Scripture says; "Israel[ites]" are shown to be beloved because the Torah was given to them and because that fact was made known to them. In making these statements, the central issue is the Torah, not Israel. What is celebrated is the gift of the Torah, the information therein.

We cannot point to these sayings as evidence of an unfolding social metaphor, fully exposed, richly exploited. That would come much later, and, in the contrast, we shall see how flat and one-dimensional is the use of "Israel" in the present passage, aimed as it is not at "Israel" but at celebration of the Torah. What that tells us is a simple fact. Tractate Abot spins out the inner logic of Torah study; that is what forms out of the sayings a cogent statement – and not the issue of "Israel." Then "Israel" serves as a minor detail, helping to make the points that the authorship of Abot wishes to make about Torah study. When we speak of categorical imperatives and categorically tangential entities, here is a case of what is at stake.

Proof of the inconsequentiality of the category "Israel" in the context of tractate Abot derives from one simple fact. Among the scores of sayings of which the document is composed, all of those concerning a social entity in general, and Israel in particular, make an appearance only as part of a larger case concerning the centrality of the Torah in the salvific process of individual life. The social entity is peripheral to that salvific process, as it is to the teleology of the Mishnah as defined by tractate Abot.[4] The social entity, Israel, makes no contribution on its own and, more consequentially, receives no sustained attention in its own right. That, sum and substance, constitutes the thought I can locate in tractate Abot, on issues of the social entity in general and on Israel in particular. That doctrine conforms to the prevailing emphasis within tractate Abot on Torah study, which is its principal theme. The point of the whole, of course, is that God revealed the Torah to Moses, who handed it on through a chain of tradition to the present. Within that context, social thought in general takes a decidedly subordinated role.

Now to account for the entire picture of an "Israel" defined in relationships among abstractions (however personalized), with "Israel" as sui generis a category of the supernatural. For the problem before us is simple. Where is that "Israel" in the middle range, that is, a social group possessing traits of its own, defined intransitively, within its own terms and not always in a transitive relationship? And why do we not deal in the writings of the Mishnah and its continuators with an "Israel" possessed of a social tangibility, a facticity in the here and now? These traits, which presently appear to be noteworthy by their absence, will take on substance when we move on to the second phase of the literature, which represents "Israel" on its own terms and with its own traits, an "Israel" that is sui generis but also substantive and immediate, not solely an aspect of the supernatural. When we account for the shape and character of the social metaphors before us, we shall also set our path toward the next passage, with its metaphors that yield a quite palpable and real "Israel."

NOTES

1 What about God? If we cannot speak of the concrete and tangible social world except in analogy and metaphor, we likewise cannot expect to describe God except in the same way – hence my forthcoming study concerning the personality of God: *The Incarnation of God: The Character of Divinity in Formative Judaism* (Philadelphia: Fortress Press, 1988). It could as well have been called "'In our image, after our likeness': Judaism and its theological metaphors." Once we understand how the authorships before us work out their symbolic transactions and give them concrete expression in speech and writing, we shall follow their thought and speech on other topics too. And the order – first society, then divinity – is required by the nature of things. But, as I have already stated quite bluntly, what we actually follow is first theological anthropology, then theological sociology. I remain troubled by how to define and express the third component of the system, that concerning "way of life." For worldview or ethos and social entity find ready expression in "God" and "Israel," respectively. But of what do we speak when we talk about that generality, "way of life"? That is a separate set of questions, to which I shall turn when the time is ripe.

2 Saul Lieberman, *Tosefta Zeraim* (New York: Jewish Theological Seminary, 1954). Hereafter cited as Lieberman.

3 Whether or not that theory of the matter is right I cannot say; it emerges from the particular case of "Israel."

4 I have dealt with this matter in *Messiah in Context. Israel's History and Destiny in Formative Judaism* (Philadelphia: Fortress Press, 1983). It will play a considerable role in Part II, below.

CHAPTER 5

The First Phase of the Judaism of the Dual Torah and Its Social Metaphors

i. "Israel" as Chosen Metaphor

The most surprising metaphor operative in the Mishnah and related writings as they take up the social entity, the social group they have chosen to discuss, has not yet received notice. But it is scattered across the surface of all of the writings, the simple allusion to "Israel" when speaking of the "us" of Jewry today. When sages spoke of "Israel," the word bore two identical meanings: the "Israel" of the Jews now and here, but also the "Israel" of which Scripture – the Torah – spoke. That word choice, which applies to both individual and social group, comes prior to all definitions of who and what (an) "Israel" is. And the word dictates for the system all of the metaphors, both in the first and in the second phases of the documents. What "Israel" accomplishes therefore is the simple but astonishing comparison of the Jews of the here and now to that "Israel" of which Scripture speaks.

That metaphor, flowing from the metaphorization of the group to begin with, constituted no given. Nothing imposed upon sages the comparison of the defeated people of the villages and households with the social entity of which Scripture tells. Treating the group within the perspective of a metaphor is not unique to sages. But deeming the given group to constitute "Israel" of which Scripture had spoken formed a remarkable choice. We know that that reading of "Israel" required a choice because we can identify a repertoire of possibilities. By consequence, sages' generative metaphor of "Israel," read as this social group, here and now, seen in the analogy of the "Israel" of the then and there of Scripture, was assuredly not the only possibility facing sages in reflecting on the social entity of the system that, in mind, they engaged in composing. Each Judaic system defined its particular "Israel," and the only one in the present context to encompass within its "Israel" pretty much all Jews is the one represented by the Mishnah and its friends.

The other Judaisms that are amply documented qualify matters in one way or another, for instance, identifying as "Israel" only the group at hand, or encompassing within "Israel" persons not exhibiting traits deemed indicative by Jews generally. The Essenes of Qumran took as their "Israel" only themselves; had the Mishnah's authorship done the same, its "Israel" would have been known individually and by name: Rabbi Judah, Rabbi Meir, and their colleagues. But sages did not represent themselves as "the true Israel" or see their estate as "the saving remnant," or, all the more so, the only remnant of scriptural "Israel." Paul took the latter way, identifying with the "Israel" of Scripture not only the Jews of his own day but also persons who, in the generality of opinion, did not belong within that category. It follows that that datum of the Judaism of the dual Torah, which identifies as "Israel" pretty much everyone all Jews (as does the Mishnah, we noted, when it calls "Israel" any individual Jew, and when it knows as "Israel" that social entity that constitutes "us" but not "them," the gentiles), represents a choice. It is the one that defined all other choices. Let me spell this matter out with some care. For the very notion that evoking the name "Israel" itself constitutes an act of metaphorization of the social group is hardly self-evident.

"Israel" in the first phase of the formation of Judaism finds definition in relationship to its opposite. We cannot fairly characterize as metaphors the notion of "Israel" as not-gentile or not-priest, nor does the reading of "Israel," though abstract, as "people" or "holy people" vastly change the picture. What we have is scarcely a process of transmuting into metaphor a mere abstraction, a perception of societal bonds among persons. The entire process of thought pursues philosophical lines, defining matters and sorting them out as do the scientists in natural philosophy, through comparison and contrast of traits. Only when the traits of mind shift, as they do in the second phase of the formation of Judaism portrayed in its canonical writings, and sages turn to categories of history – and therefore also to storytelling and other forms of narrative – does the poetry of metaphor and analogy come into play. Then we shall see those powerful metaphors that impart to the data at hand the color and life that, in the Judaism at hand, "Israel" has displayed from then to now.

And yet when sages engaged in a process of treating as concrete things that began as imaginary entities, that process drew them into what I think is a work of supererogatory imagination that we may justifiably call metaphor. For sages in the Mishnah did not merely describe a group; they portrayed it as they wished to. They did not assemble facts and then define the social entity, the social group, as a matter of mere description of the given. They imputed to the social group, Jews, the standing of the systemic entity, "Israel," and they assigned to that entity traits that, to begin with, form in the distant reaches of mind – for example, belief in the resurrection of the dead as a scriptural doctrine. For to call persons who did not after all see and know one another a holy people, and to identify those persons in the here and now with that "Israel" of which Scripture speaks are daring acts of metaphorization, the most remarkable ones that we shall witness in the formative processes of the Judaism of the dual Torah. And the powerful argumentation assigned to the metaphorization of the social group consisted of treating as fact what was a statement of imagination, poetry – always calling "Israel" the group, the individual, in the everyday world of mundane discourse of which the Mishnah is composed.

What made self-evident the identification of the persons or groups with a single group, what made obvious the connection between that single group and the "Israel" of received Scripture? To others within Jewry it was not at all self-evident that all Jews constituted one "Israel," and that that one "Israel" formed the direct and immediate continuation, in the here and now, with the "Israel" of holy writ and revelation. The Essene community at Qumran did not come to that conclusion, and the sense and meaning of "Israel" proposed by the authorships of the Mishnah and related writings did not strike Philo as the main point at all. Paul, for his part, reflected on "Israel" within categories not at all symmetrical with those of the Mishnah.

These three[1] represent a considerable alternative to the one chosen by the authorship of the Mishnah and found self-evident and compelling by the Judaism they inaugurated. We shall not understand that they made choices, let alone the enduring power of their selection of metaphor, if we take for granted that they did what was merely called for by the data. Nothing could be further from the truth. The identification of Jewry in the here and now with the "Israel" of Scripture constituted an act of metaphor, comparison, contrast, identification, and analogy and was that Judaism's most daring social metaphor. The fact that through the ages it has seemed self-evident, a given of the Jews' everyday circumstance, shows us the success of the Judaism of the dual Torah, as much as seeing that metaphor as a choice among alternatives shows us the reason for that success. Seeing Jews and calling them "Israel" – an act of imaginative daring indeed – forms the metaphor that gives the system its energy, and from that metaphor all else derived its momentum. No wonder, then, that when we first took up the initial statement of the Judaism of the dual Torah, we found fresh and unprecedented in context the doctrine of "Israel" as "all Israel." That doctrine, a statement of metaphor, now proves to be the key to the system as a whole.[2]

ii. Transitive "Israel"

To understand the meaning of "Israel" as the Mishnah and its friends sort matters out, we revert to the sense of gentile. To the authorship of the Mishnah gentiles represent an undifferentiated mass: Whether a gentile is a Roman or an Aramaean or a Syrian or a Briton does not matter (except, e.g., at M. Neg. 2:2, as to skin tone, an Ethiopian is different from a German). Also, in this relationship, "Israel" is not differentiated either. Just as "gentile" is an abstract category, so is "Israel." "*Kohen*" is a category, and so is "Israel." For the purposes for which Israel/priest are defined, no further differentiation is undertaken. That is where matters end. But, as we shall see, to the Judaic system represented by the Yerushalmi and its associated writings, "gentile" may be Roman or other-than-Roman, for instance, Babylonian, Median, or Greek. That act of further differentiation – we may call it "speciation" – makes a considerable difference in the appreciation of gentile.

When, therefore, we see "Israel" as a drastic act of the metaphorization of the social group at hand, we should not forget that "Israel" serves in a more immediate way as classifier and taxonomic category. In the Mishnah's authorship's "Israel," we confront an abstraction in a system of philosophy. Later on, the shift will carry us to an "Israel" that bears that socially vivid sense that the metaphor implicitly requires – a real social entity, with a story attached. Systemically, so too will the counterpart, Rome, gain that speciation that "the gentiles" lack.

The Mishnah's interest in "Israel" contains certain ambiguities. On the one side, as I have stressed, "Israel" forms the implicit locus of all discourse, its society the ubiquitous focus of sanctification. On the other, the particular traits of "Israel" when viewed in the this-worldly framework of most of the Mishnah's discussions emerge through a series of contrasts and comparisons, not as intrinsically important, systemically determinative facts. Because we know what "Israel" or "an Israel" is mainly when we can specify the antonym, the range of possibilities for the definition or specification of "Israel" is not fully explored in the Mishnah's framework. Can an "Israel" be only a not-gentile or only a not-priest? What then can we say of those many other "Israel"s important to Scripture, for instance, "Israel" as the extended family of one man, Abraham, and his wife, Sarah? Where is the "Israel" selected by God for special concern: "Only you have I known . . ."? The "Israel" of that heightened reality of Leviticus, living on an animate, enchanted land that is capable of discerning the moral condition of its inhabitants and, in total disgust, vomiting out the evil ones – I do not perceive that "Israel" in the rather philosophical and (in the nature of things) secular system of classification and categorization in which the Mishnah's "Israel" figures. When "Israel" forms a principle of taxonomy, "Israel" ceases to constitute an actor in a historical and supernatural drama. And that judgment also encompasses the "Israel" that is sui generis because of its affirmation or denial of the resurrection of the dead as a scriptural principle.

In the second stage in the formation of the Judaism of the dual Torah, the repertoire of meanings imputed to "Israel" vastly expands, and, more to the point, the issue of "Israel" proves programmatically definitive in at least two important documents and paramount in a third. In the contrast between the coming "Israel" and the one at hand, these facts concerning the place and importance imputed to "Israel" in the writings of the first stage in the formation of Judaism take on sharp meaning. We have therefore to ask ourselves why an essentially inert taxonomic category should become active and definitive. We shall want to know what has imparted to "Israel" in particular systemically definitive power and position. The answers to these questions derive from changes we discern in the world in which Jews lived, on the one side, and in which the authorships of the writings conducted their affairs, on the other. The proposed answers form a principal thesis of this book, so let me announce them now and commence the work of setting forth evidence and argumentation. Because we shall discern important differences in the "Israel"s of the first and the second sets of writings, we must ask what accounts for those differences. I see in the salient traits of the later time two facts not present in the earlier.

Between 200 and 300 C.E., the approximate and rough dates for the closure of the first statement of the Judaism of the dual Torah, and 400 and 500 C.E., the counterpart dates for the second, two decisive changes in the Jews' political life took place. One was in the political context of the world beyond, the other, the political circumstance of the world within, "Israel." The political control of the world at large in the fourth and fifth centuries, first, lay in Christian, not pagan, hands. Second, the picture we have of the position of sages in the fourth and fifth centuries points to a group of lawyer-philosophers who now exercised practical authority and carried out the everyday administration of the life of the communities in which they lived. Nothing in the

Mishnah and related writings portrays the authorships of those documents in a comparable position. Indeed, the very theoretical character of the Mishnah's political conceptions suggests that the sage as administrator lay beyond the imagination of the authorship of the Mishnah, with shifts in the perspective of the authorship(s) of the Tosefta suggesting incipient change in how the political world may be imagined.

iii.   Social Metaphors of Judaism without Christianity

Both matters will be amply spelled out in the context of the age of which they proved characteristic. Here it suffices to take note of the slight importance accorded in the program of the Mishnah and successor documents to issues critical to Christianity. To take up three that would later on engage the interest of the Judaic sages, we point to history, Messiah, and who is Israel. All three would require from sages a theory of an "Israel" part of palpable history, a teleology involving eschatology and therefore a Messiah, and of "Israel" as the true as against the false "Israel." All three requirements of a theory of "Israel" congruent to the challenge and crisis presented by Christianity's political triumph would characterize the social metaphors of the second phase of the documents of the Judaism of the dual Torah.

Christian theologians maintained that the advent of Jesus Christ marked a decisive change in the unfolding of the history of humanity. The meaning and direction of history therefore proved an important question, with the result that systemic teleology encompassed the issue of eschatology, in a way in which in the Mishnah (for one example) it did not – and did not have to. The Christian theologians of course assigned to Jesus the status of Christ, ordinarily meaning Messiah, and reflected deeply on Christology. Some of them carved out for Christians a place in "Israel," defining "Israel" in such terms as permitted them to do so. Later on Judaic sages would address precisely these issues.

But that was not in the Mishnah or in its successor writings. At no point, for example, can I discern in the Mishnah an interest in issues that differentiated the one "Israel" from the other, the old (after the flesh, so the new said) from the new (after the spirit). Later on, we shall see precisely that interest. More to the point, we already have looked in vain for appeal in the Mishnah, even in Sifra and the two Sifrés, to the meaning of being "Israel after the flesh," that is, Israel as the extended family of Abraham and Sarah. The substance of the heritage and succession, the concept of the inherited merit of the patriarchs and matriarchs, cannot be shown present at any point in the Mishnah, though the implications of the passage at Sotah permitted us to speculate that the notion of the merit of the ancestors can be invoked in the exegesis of one passage.

"Israel" as a category defined without attention to, or interest in, issues vital to the Christian opposition in the second and third centuries by contrast took on a form of its own. That form, imparted by the chosen *via negativa* of not-gentile, not-priest, discovered its repertoire of possibilities from the generative question of sanctification: Who is holy Israel? Not the gentile. What is the holiest caste, by contrast to Israel as non-Israel? The priest. These issues come to the fore when we take as our critical question the issue of sanctification, its outer limits, its interior degrees and gradations. That is why "Israel" in the Mishnah forms an issue defined in terms to which Christianity simply proves irrelevant. And that was, I need hardly add, because, into the sages' view of things, Christianity scarcely entered. Whether the reason was that Christians were not numerous or not threatening or for other reasons not to be taken seriously, I cannot say. All our evidence tells us as fact only that, in the view of the authorship of the Mishnah, other concerns than the challenge of Christianity and its reading of who is Israel predominated. That is the one fact beyond all question, emerging as it does from what the Mishnah's authorship selected for its program, which, by the way, tells us what that same authorship, not to mention its successors, neglected.

iv. Social Metaphors of Sages without Authority

The "Israel" of the Mishnah meant "anybody." The laconic, descriptive use of "Israel" for individual and "us" bore the implication that anyone any time, not merely sages, can do what is required and meet the norm. And that bore the potential for what was to develop. The other striking trait of the authorship of the writings of the late fourth and fifth century is their picture of writers in charge of their world and, therefore, of an "Israel" in their model. The authorships of the principal documents that reached closure in the late fourth and fifth century included in their writing a clear and protracted account of what they claimed that they did in the world they also described. Because they made public decisions of a practical sort, the authorships of the Yerushalmi, Genesis Rabbah, Leviticus Rabbah, and associated writings portray themselves as a social entity, a social group defined by clear-cut norms of a political, not solely intellectual or theological, character. They were people who wrote books and also made other people do, or refrain from doing, things those books said people should or should not do: authorities, not merely authors.

The authorship of the Mishnah never suggested that it saw itself in the same way. The Mishnah contains virtually no allegations that the sages whose opinions it records exercised concrete authority over the world. There are a few stories about how sages made rulings, and those we have prove striking not merely by their paucity but more especially by their triviality. At most sages decided neighborhood disputes. True enough, "sage" in tractate Abot commonly serves as a synonym for judge. And in the Tosefta we find a tendency to cite precedents alongside rulings. But most of these precedents concern what sages did in their own circles, not outside. More to the point, sages in the Mishnah and the Tosefta are rarely, if ever, portrayed as they are commonly presented in the Yerushalmi. That later portrait encompasses, for instance, sages' settling land disputes, carrying out acts of governance of the community at large, contending with other political authorities, and doing other public deeds. Within the same portrait, "all Israel" now emerges in the image and after the likeness of sages' own group. The Mishnah's resort to descriptive language of the ordinary hid the potentiality of this development of "Israel," the use of the metaphor "Israel" to stand for how things are – which is just as "we" both describe and dictate. Thus, the second important change in the world portrayed by the writings of the fifth as against the third century is the contrast between the portraits of the social authority and role of sages in the two documents, the Mishnah and the Yerushalmi. The authorship of the Mishnah does not indicate that it can imagine the social world of the Jews, including the sages' position in that world, as the authorships of the Yerushalmi and related writings portray it.

A social group thinking about a social group, sages of the Mishnah treat "Israel" as a rather theoretical category, while sages of the Yerushalmi and related writings represent "Israel" in a very concrete way, as a political entity on the one side and as a family on the other. The difference suggests to me that the one set of sages projected "Israel" as an extension of their own imagination and experience of being an "Israel" – and so too did the other. In my view, the system of the Mishnah in the aggregate hardly addresses a social world at all. An imaginary Israel in the first phase of the Judaism of the dual Torah scarcely is given a social definition. Instead we are handed a caste definition, Israel as not-priest, which I may characterize as the issue of sanctification writ small. As a substitute we are given a definition so deeply embedded in self-evidence, Israel as not-gentile, as to provide virtually no consequential information. For that Israel is not a gentile hardly serves as a definition of what (an) "Israel" is. It is a truism. Exclusion is no definition.

The reason, so I maintain, is that the Mishnah in its original composition did not derive from political classes but from philosophical ones. But within the "Israel" of Mishnaic metaphor is contained the extension and the expansion of that metaphor. And the Mishnah, for its part, almost immediately became a political document in the postpatriarchal period, and then it served, in the exegesis of the heirs and successors of the authorship of the Mishnah, as a document of "Israel." In the literature of sages "Israel" became an important political category – whether as family, whether as historic entity – when rabbis thought that they both constituted Israel and served as the model for Israel. And that came about when rabbis saw a community that they ran. Then they imagined an "Israel" not as abstraction and mode of classification, but as a concrete and vivid social reality. Consequently the category; "Israel," took on an importance, a systemic consequence as an explicitly definitive category, that we cannot discern in the literature of the first period in the formation of the Judaism of the dual Torah. These proposals concerning "Israel" in the first statement of Judaism clearly require testing by comparison with, and contrast to, the use and representation of "Israel" in the second statement, to which we now turn.

NOTES

---

1 We shall meet all three again in Chapter 11.

2 We shall return at the end to this notion that a system derives its logic from one overriding question. Enough has been said to show us that the metaphor "Israel" answers the urgent and acute question – the one concerning the enduring sanctification beyond the catastrophe – addressed by the authorships of the Mishnah and associated writings.

PART II

"Israel" in the Second Statement of Judaism, 300–600 C.E.

CHAPTER 6

"Israel" on Its Own Terms

i.   From the Mishnah to the Yerushalmi

The second statement of the Judaism of the dual Torah emerged in writings that came to closure between the time of Constantine, after ca. 300 C.E., and the rise of Islam in the Middle East, ca. 640 C.E. The first important document of that period was the Talmud of the Land of Israel or Yerushalmi, closed at ca. 400 C.E., and the last, the Talmud of Babylonia or Bavli, closed at ca. 600 C.E.[1]

Looking backward from the end of the fourth century to the end of the first, a generation beyond the destruction of the Jerusalem temple, the framers of the Yerushalmi surely perceived what need not have appeared obvious and unavoidable, namely, the definitive end, for here and now at any rate, of the old order of cultic sanctification. After a hundred years beyond the destruction of Jerusalem in 70 C.E., there may have been some doubt. After two centuries more, however, with the total fiasco of Julian's project of rebuilding the temple in 362–3 C.E. near at hand, there can have been little hope left for a near-term restoration. The two foreordained dates therefore had passed – three generations beyond the destruction yielding the disappointed hope invested in Bar Kokhba, three hundred years (more or less) the disgraceful failure of Julian's temple. The Roman emperor who, in his war with Christianity, would have made himself (from Israel's perspective) into the new Cyrus died in war with Iran, and the hope for a restored Jerusalem in the near term perished as well. The Mishnah had designed a world in which the temple stood at the center, a society in which the priests presided at the top, and a way of life in which the dominant issue was the sanctification of Israelite life. Whether the full realization of that world, society, and way of life was thought to come sooner or later, the system had been

95

meant only initially as a utopia, but in the end, from the time of its promulgation in ca. 200 C.E. as a plan and constitution for a material society here in the Land of Israel. But now, at best, that restored grace would come much later than anyone had ever anticipated.

The old order was cracking; the new order was not yet established. But, from the perspective of Israel, the waiting went on. The interim from temple to temple was not differentiated. Whether conditions were less favorable or more favorable hardly made a difference. History stretched backward, to a point of disaster, and forward, to an unseen and incalculable time of a restoration far beyond the near horizon. Short of supernatural events, salvation simply was not in sight. True, in theory at least, Israel for its part lived under its own government, framed within the rules of sanctification, and constituted a holy society. But when would salvation come, and how could people even now hasten its day? These issues, in the nature of things, proved more pressing as the decades rolled by, becoming first one century, then another, while none knew how many more, and how much more, must still be endured. Not only so, but the other stunning change hardly pointed in a promising direction. In the two hundred years from the closure of the Mishnah to the completion of the Yerushalmi, pagan rule had given way to the sovereignty of Christian emperors.

Sages worked out in the pages of the Yerushalmi and in the exegetical compilations of the age a Judaism intersecting with the Mishnah's but essentially asymmetrical with it. That Talmud presented a system of salvation, but one focused on the salvific power of the sanctification of the holy people. The first of the two Talmuds, the one closed at the end of the fourth century, set the compass and locked it into place. The Yerushalmi is not like the Mishnah, which provides a full and exhaustive account of its system and its viewpoint. Whatever we know about the Mishnah's system is in that book itself. Indeed the Yerushalmi and the Mishnah are really not comparable with one another. The Yerushalmi is continuous with the Mishnah. But the character of the document, therefore also the world to which its evidence pertains, presents us with a different picture of "Israel" from that of the Mishnah. The Mishnah, in ca. 200 C.E., described an orderly world, in which Israelite society is neatly divided among its castes, arranged in priority around the center that is the temple, systematically engaged in a life of sanctification remote from the disorderly events of the day. The world portrayed by the authorship of the Yerushalmi is disorderly and chaotic, not classical and proportioned. But it also attains to a reality and immediacy in a way that the Mishnah's idealizations do not permit.

While the Yerushalmi aims principally at the exegesis and amplification of the laws of the Mishnah, it also points toward a matrix beyond its text. One the one hand, the Yerushalmi's authorship's interest in the Mishnah's statements is purposeful. Transcending the Mishnah's facts, it expresses the speculative concerns of philosophical lawyers wholly within the framework of the Mishnah's modes of thought. But these same exegetes – both the ones who are named and the still more influential ones who speak through the Yerushalmi's single voice – speak implicitly within the framework of a larger worldview, not exhausted by the Mishnah. So they bring to the Mishnah a program defined outside of the Mishnah and expressing concerns of a segment of society beyond their own immediate circle. The Yerushalmi's discussions, to begin with, are not limited to the contents of the Mishnah. Discourse encompasses a world of institutions, authorities, and effective power, which predominate quite beyond the imagination of the Mishnah's framers. The Talmud's picture of that world, furthermore, essentially ignores the specifications for these same matters of the Mishnah's law.

To take one striking example, the Mishnah's government for Israel rests upon a high priest and a king, with administrative courts ascending upward to the authority of the temple mount. The Yerushalmi does not even pretend that such a world exists. Its authorship, rather, takes for granted the government of a set of small-claims courts and petty bureaus of state, over which rabbis, defined as judges, lawyers, and masters of disciples in the law, preside. At the head of it all is a patriarch, not a priest anointed for the purpose. That example provides an instance of the curious discontinuity between the Mishnah's view of the world and of the society of Israel, on the one side, and that of the Yerushalmi, continuous with the Mishnah and framed as little more than an exegesis of that code, on the other hand. When I speak of a second phase in the unfolding of the documents of the Judaism of the dual Torah, that discontinuity serves to clarify my meaning. Let me now spell out the shifts relevant to our case, the one involving the crisis of Christianity's political triumph, the other, the change in sages' political standing.

ii. The Challenge of Christianity

As I have already suggested, two factors account for the shift in the character of the agenda upon which sages did their work. Externally, Jews confronted the remarkable shift in the character of the Roman Empire that took place when the state first legalized, then established Christianity as most favored religion, and finally undertook to extirpate paganism and, by the way, to subordinate Judaism. Internally, sages for their part gained an active role in the government of the Jews of the Land of Israel, so revising their conception, from theoretical to actual, of that "Israel" of which they spoke. These two distinct and divergent factors imparted to "Israel" a sense and significance, in material reality, for which we look in vain in the earlier-redacted writings.

The legalization of Christianity by Constantine and the establishment of Christianity as the state religion by his heirs and successors began the slow and extended process by which Christianity became the religion of the Roman Empire and, in due course, of the West. After a spell of ferocious persecution of Christians under Diocletian, the succeeding emperor, Constantine, converted to Christianity. Thus, Christianity attained the status of a licit religion; however, Constantine did not convert the faith of the army, let alone of the Empire.[2] Yet during the following century, from 312 C.E. onward, the Roman Empire, its government and institutions, came under Christian domination. Writing nearly a century later, for example, Jerome, cited by Kelly, captures the astonishment that Christians felt – and from this we may infer the amazement that affected Jews as well:

> Every island, prison, and salt-mine was crowded with Christian captives in chains . . . with the present era when (such as the seemingly impossible transformations worked by God in his goodness) the selfsame imperial government which used to make a bonfire of Christian sacred books has them adorned sumptuously with gold, purple, and precious stones, and, instead of razing church buildings to the ground, pays for the construction of magnificent basilicas with gilded ceilings and marble-encrusted walls.[3]

Kelly states the simple fact:

> At the beginning of the century [the Church] had been reeling under a violent persecution. . . . Now it found itself showered with benefactions and privileges, invited to undertake responsibilities, and progressively given a directive role in society.[4]

So the age of Constantine presented even to contemporaries an era of dramatic change.

Constantine's sons took an active interest in the Church. The Christian empire undertook a long war against its pagan enemy, tearing down temples and ultimately curtailing pagans' rights of worship.[5] Constantine's sons and successors closed temples and destroyed idols, making ever more severe laws. Of greater consequence, the Christian emperors also assumed responsibility for the governance of the Church of Christ triumphant. At Nicaea in 325 C.E. Constantine called a council to settle the issues of Arianism that had vexed the Church. At issue was the nature of Christ in relationship to God. "Christ cannot have the identical nature of God; he is God, but he is distinct from God and can be described only in a distinctive way." But the matter remained subject to dispute for another century or more. The importance from our perspective is simple. The state now vigorously entered the life of the Church, and none could doubt that the empire had turned Christian. In addition, the head of state, from Constantine onward, not only favored Christianity but despised Judaism. Constantine, for example, saw the Jews as "a hostile people, a nation of parricides, who slew their Lord."[6] With the emperor Julian, Christianity faced a serious reverse, for Julian intended a revolution from above, to lead the state to paganism, reopening pagan temples and fostering pagan culture. But Julian's brief reign, 361–3 C.E., brought in its wake a ferocious counterrevolution, with the Christian state now suppressing the institutions of paganism, and Christian men in the streets of the towns and villages taking an active role on their own as well. Julian's successors persecuted pagan philosophy. Valentinian I (364–75) and Valens (364–78) took an active role in the campaign against Neoplatonism. In 380 C.E. the emperor Theodosius (379–95) decreed the end of paganism:

> It is our desire that all the various nations which are subject to
> our clemency and moderation should continue in the profession
> of that religion which was delivered to the Romans by the divine
> Apostle Peter.

Paganism found itself subjected to penalties. The state church, a principal indicator of the Christian civilization that the West was to know, now came into being. In 381 C.E. Theodosius forbade sacrifices and closed most temples. In 391–2 C.E. a new set of penalties imposed sanctions on paganism.

At the beginning of the fourth century Rome was pagan; at the end, Christian. In the beginning Jews in the Land of Israel administered their own affairs. In the end their institution of self-administration lost the recognition it had formerly enjoyed. In the beginning Judaism enjoyed entirely licit status, and the Jews, the protection of the state. In the end Judaism suffered abridgment of its former liberties, and the Jews of theirs. In the beginning, the Jews lived in the Land of Israel, and in some numbers. In the end they lived in Palestine, as a minority. Constantine and his mother built churches and shrines all over the country, but especially in Jerusalem, so the Land of Israel received yet another name, for another important group, now becoming the Holy Land. To turn to the broader perspective, from the beginning of the fourth century, we look backward over an uninterrupted procession of philosophers and emperors, Aristotle and Plato and Socrates and Alexander and Caesar upon Caesar. From the end of the fourth century we look forward to Constantinople, Kiev, and Moscow in the east, to Christian Rome, Paris and London, to cathedrals and saints, to an empire called Holy and Roman and a public life infused with Christian piety and Christian sanctity, to pope after pope after pope. Before Constantine's conversion in 312 C.E. Christianity scarcely imagined a politics; its collective life was lived mostly in private. Afterward Christianity undertook to govern, shaped the public and political institutions of empires and through popes and emperors alike defined the political history of the world for long centuries to come. From the viewpoint of the Jews, therefore, the shift signified by the conversion of Constantine marked a caesura in history.

The Mishnah, as I have argued, took as its critical issue the matter of whether, and how, "Israel" remained a holy people, because that issue proved acute in the period of the Mishnah's framers' systematic work, the mid-second century. The Mishnah therefore is a document worked out in a world in which Christianity made no impact, so far as Israel's sages were concerned. Their minds were elsewhere. When, we recall, in the aftermath of the destruction in 70 C.E., sages worked out a Judaism without a temple and a cult, they produced the Mishnah, a system of sanctification focused on the holiness of the priesthood, the cultic festivals, and the temple and its sacrifices, as well as on the rules for protecting that holiness from levitical uncleanness – four of the six divisions of the Mishnah on a single theme. The Mishnah's system stresses the issue of sanctification, pure and simple.

The Talmud of the Land of Israel, by contrast, reached closure approximately a century after the political triumph of Christianity. When, in the aftermath of the conversion of the Roman Empire to Christianity and the confirmation of the triumph of Christianity in the generation beyond Julian "the apostate," sages worked out, in the pages of the Talmud of the Land of Israel and in the exegetical compilations of the era, a Judaism intersecting with the Mishnah's but essentially asymmetrical with it, it was a system for salvation, but one focused on the salvific power of the sanctification of the holy people. Given the political changes of the age, with their implications for the meaning and end of history as Israel would experience it, the fresh emphasis on salvation, the introduction of the figure of the Messiah as a principal teleological force, and the statement of an eschatological teleology for the system as a whole all constitute answers to urgent questions. The questions were raised by Christian theologians, the answers provided by the Judaic sages. The former held that the Christian triumph confirmed the Christhood of Jesus, the rejection of Israel, and the end of Israel's hope for salvation at the end of time. The latter offered the Torah in its dual media, the affirmation of Israel as children of Abraham, Isaac, and Jacob, and the coming of the Messiah at the end of time. The questions and answers fit the challenge of the age.

The profound shift in characterization of "Israel" that took place in the documents of the late fourth and fifth centuries responded to the crisis presented by the political triumph of Christianity. Fundamental in character, those changes effected upon the received system marked dramatic shifts in the modes of symbolization of the canon, of the system as a whole, and of the purpose and goal of the system. Each of the important changes in the documents first redacted at the end of the fourth century dealt with a powerful challenge presented by the triumph of Christianity in Constantine's age. The Judaism of the dual Torah, in response to the issues defined by Christianity as it assumed control of the Roman Empire, provided as self-evidently valid answers a system deriving its power from the Torah, read by sages, embodied by sages, and exemplified by sages. Not surprisingly, the characterization of "Israel" and the meanings imputed to that category form part of a larger exercise in the re-visioning of the structure and vocabulary of the received faith. A rapid survey of the principal points in the political challenge of triumphant Christianity suffices.

The first change revealed in the unfolding of the sages' canon pertains to the use of Scripture. The change at hand specifically is in making books out of the collection of exegeses of Scripture. That represents an innovation because the Mishnah, and the exegetical literature that served the Mishnah, did not take shape around the order of biblical passages, even when relevant, let alone the explanation of verses of Scripture. The authorship of the Mishnah and its principal heirs followed their own program, arranging ideas by subject matter. But in the third and especially the later fourth centuries, other writings entering the canon took shape around the explanation of verses of Scripture, resulting in a second mode of organizing ideas besides the topical mode paramount for the Mishnah, the Tosefta, and the Yerushalmi (and the Bavli later on).

With Christianity addressing the world (including the Jews) with a systematic exegetical apologetic, beginning of course with Matthew's and the other Gospels' demonstration of how events in the life

of Jesus fulfilled, as a living exegesis, the prophecies of the shared
Scripture, a Judaic response took the form of a counterpart exegesis.
In the Mishnah, sages found unnecessary a systematic exegesis of
Scripture, because there was no reading contrary to theirs. But the
Christians did compose a powerful apologetic out of the systematic
exegesis of the shared Scripture, and, confronting that challenge
when Christianity made further indifference impolitic and impos-
sible, sages replied with their compositions.

By the fourth century the Church had reached a consensus on the
bulk of the New Testament canon, having earlier accepted as its own
the Old Testament. Accordingly, the issue of Scripture had come to
the fore, and in framing the question of Scripture, the Church focused
sages' attention on that larger matter of systematic exegesis. When,
for example, Jerome referred to the Jews' having a "second Torah,"
one that was not authoritative, and when a sequence of important
fathers of the Church produced exegeses, in profoundly Christo-
logical terms, of Scripture, the issue was raised. It would be joined
when sages speaking on their own and to their chosen audience went
through pretty much the same processes. This they did by explaining
the standing of that "second Torah," and by producing not merely
counterpart exegeses to those of the Christians but counterpart
compilations of such exegeses.

The generative symbol of the literary culture of the sages, the
Torah, stands for the system as a whole. From the Yerushalmi
onward, the symbol of the Torah took on the meaning that, when
Judaism had reached its final form at the end of this period, would
prove indicative. It was the doctrine that, when Moses received the
Torah at Mount Sinai, it came down with him in two media, written
and oral – the former now contained in the canon of Scripture, the
latter transmitted through the process of formulation for ease in
memorization, and then through memorization, from Moses and
Joshua to the most current generation. That doctrine of the dual
Torah, that is of the Torah in two media, came about in response to
the problem of explaining the standing and authority of the Mishnah.
But the broadening of the symbol of the Torah first took shape
around the figure of the sage. That symbolism accounted for the
sages' authority. Only later on, in the fourth century in the pages of
the Yerushalmi, did the doctrine of the dual Torah reach expression.
So in the unfolding of the documents of the canon of Judaism, the
generative symbol of Torah reveals a striking change. Beginning as a
rather generalized account of how sages' teachings relate to God's
will, the symbol of Torah gained concrete form in its application to
the dual Torah, written and oral, Scripture and Mishnah. Within the

unfolding of the canonical writings, such a shift represents a symbolic change of fundamental character.

When we speak of "torah," in rabbinic literature of late antiquity, we no longer denote a particular book, or the contents of such a book. Instead, we connote a broad range of clearly distinct categories of noun and verb, concrete fact and abstract relationship alike. "Torah" stands for a kind of human being. It connotes a social status and a sort of social group. It refers to a type of social relationship. It further denotes a legal status and differentiates things and persons, actions and status, points of social differentiation and legal and normative standing, as well as "revealed truth." In all, the main points of insistence of the whole of Israel's life and history come to full symbolic expression in that single word. If people wanted to explain how they would be saved, they would use the word Torah. If they wished to sort out their parlous relationships with gentiles, they would use the word Torah. Torah stood for salvation and accounted for Israel's this-worldly condition and the hope, for both individual and nation alike, of life in the world to come. For the kind of Judaism under discussion, therefore, the word Torah stood for everything. The Torah symbolized the whole, at once and entire.

The ultimate position, then, was that the Torah reached Israel in two forms or media: one [Torah] in writing, the other [Torah] handed on orally, that is, in memory. This final step, fully revealed in the Yerushalmi, brought the conception of Torah to its logical conclusion. Torah came in several media, written, oral, incarnate. So what the sage said was in the status of the Torah, was Torah, because the sage was Torah incarnate. The abstract symbol now had become concrete and material once more. We recognize the many, diverse ways in which the Talmud stated that conviction. Every passage in which knowledge of the Torah yields power over this world and the next, capacity to coerce to the sage's will the natural and supernatural worlds alike, rests upon the same viewpoint. The Yerushalmi's theory of the Torah thus carries us through several stages in the processes of the symbolization of the word Torah. First transformed from something material and concrete into something abstract and beyond all metaphor (the opposite of the process affecting "Israel"), the word Torah finally emerged once more in a concrete aspect, now as the encompassing and universal mode of stating the whole doctrine, all at once, of Judaism in its formative age.

The teleology of a system answers the question of purpose and goal. It explains why someone should do what the system requires. It may also spell out what will happen if someone does or does not do what the system demands. As I pointed out earlier, the Mishnah and its successor documents, Abot and the Tosefta, present one picture of the purpose of the system as a whole, a teleology without eschatological focus. The two Talmuds, along with some intermediate documents, later laid forth a different picture, specifically, an eschatological teleology. The documents do cohere. The Talmuds, beginning with the Yerushalmi, the former of the two, to be sure carried forward not only the exegesis of the Mishnah but also the basic values of the Mishnah's system. But they did present substantial changes too, and that is the main point for our purpose.

The philosophers of the Mishnah did not make use of the Messiah myth in the construction of a teleology for their system. They found it possible to present a statement of goals for their projected life of Israel that was entirely separate from appeals to history and eschatology. Because they certainly knew, and even alluded to, long-standing and widely held convictions on eschatological subjects, beginning with those in Scripture, the framers thereby testified that, knowing the larger repertoire, they made choices different from others before and after them. Their document accurately and ubiquitously expresses these choices, both affirmative and negative. The appearance in the Talmuds of a messianic eschatology fully consonant with the larger characteristic of the rabbinic system – with its stress on the viewpoints and proof texts of Scripture, its interest in what was happening to Israel, its focus upon the national-historical dimension of the life of the group – indicates that the encompassing rabbinic system stands essentially autonomous of the prior, Mishnaic system. True, what had gone before was absorbed and fully assimilated. But the talmudic system, expressed in part in each of the non-Mishnaic segments of the canon, and fully spelled out in all of them, is different in the aggregate from the Mishnaic system.

The Mishnah had presented an ahistorical and, in the nature of things, noneschatological teleology, and did not make use of the messiah theme to express its teleology. By contrast, the Talmuds provide an eschatological and therefore a messiah-centered teleology for their system. Theirs is the more familiar teleology of Judaism, which, from the Talmud of the Land of Israel onward, commonly explains the end and meaning of the system by referring to the end of time and the coming of the Messiah. The teleology of Judaism as it was expressed in the Talmuds of both the Land of Israel and Babylonia thus takes an eschatological shape, in its appeal to the end of history. Once people speak of the end of time – the eschaton – moreover, they commonly invoke the figure of a messiah, or The Messiah, who will bring on the end and preside over what happens then. The Judaism that emerged from late antiquity therefore took shape as a profoundly eschatological and messianic statement.

The Mishnah's authorship constructed a system of Judaism in which the entire teleological dimension reached full exposure while hardly invoking the person or functions of a messianic figure of any kind. The Mishnah's noneschatological teleology would then present a striking contrast to that of the Yerushalmi, which framed the teleological doctrine around the person of the Messiah. The issue of eschatology, framed in mythic terms, further draws in its wake the issue of how history comes to full conceptual expression. For by "history" people understand not anything that happens, but only selected events, to which deep meaning is imputed. That meaning may be expressed in diverse ways. One of them is to translate the selected event into a symbol, for example, the abstraction "war" as a particular animal or god. Another is to translate through the interpretation of the symbol as history, that is, theology. The Mishnah's framers presented no elaborate theory of events, a fact fully consonant with their systematic points of insistence and encompassing concern. One by one events do not matter. The philosopher-lawyers exhibited no theory of history either. Their conception of Israel's destiny in no way called upon historical categories of either narrative or didactic explanation to describe and account for the future. The small importance attributed to the figure of the Messiah as a historical-eschatological figure, therefore, fully accords with the larger traits of the system as a whole. Let me speak with emphasis: If, as in the Mishnah, what is important in Israel's existence was *sanctification,* an ongoing process, and *not salvation,* understood as a one-time event at the end, then *no one would find reason to narrate history*.

Few then would form the obsession about the Messiah so characteristic of Judaism in its later, rabbinic mode. The figure of the Messiah looms large in both documents. The teleology of the system portrayed in them rests upon the premise of the coming of the Messiah. If one does so and so, the Messiah will come, and if not, the Messiah will tarry. So the compilers and authors of the two Talmuds laid enormous emphasis upon the sin of Israel and the capacity of Israel through repentance both to overcome sin and to bring the Messiah. "The attribute of justice" delays the Messiah's coming. The Messiah will come this very day, if Israel deserves. The Messiah will come when there are no more arrogant ("conceited") Israelites, when judges and officers disappear, when the haughty judges cease to exist, "Today, if you will obey" (Ps. 95:7). The importance, for our understanding of the social metaphors affecting "Israel," of these shifts, from the first to the second phase in the unfolding of the documents of the Judaism of the Torah, will become amply clear in a moment. Let us first consider the other salient factor, the characterization of the authorships of the writings at hand, as that characterization shifted from the Mishnah to the Yerushalmi.

iii Sages from the Mishnah to the Yerushalmi

The Yerushalmi, in ca. 400 C.E., portrayed the chaos of Jews living among gentiles, governed by a diversity of authorities, lacking all order and arrangement, awaiting a time of salvation for which, through sanctification, they make themselves ready. That social fact of Israel's life, as distinct from the political setting of that life, did not change between 200 and 400 C.E. People lived more or less as they had before Constantine. But the representation of the social realities did change, and that different perspective on matters requires us to ask why what one authorship ignored another found absolutely self-evident. The reason, I maintain, is that – as evidenced by its own portrait of Israel's social life – the former authorship, that of the Mishnah, did not confront the material social reality of a community out there, because it had little to do with the concrete governance of that community. And the latter authorship represented itself as fully in charge of the everyday life of the community, hence in constant touch with a real "Israel" consisting of a social group living a palpable everyday life.

We may compare the former authorship to legal philosophers, in abstract terms thinking about logic and order. The latter authorship, the one of the Yerushalmi, encompassed men deeply involved in the administration of the concrete social group, "Israel" as a real-life community. We may see that authorship as analogous to judges, lawyers, bureaucrats, heads of local governments, not philosophers alone but men of affairs. When they represented "Israel," they drew upon concrete knowledge of, engagement in, a very real social world indeed. The facts portrayed by this second authorship, as we shall see later on, draw upon experience entirely beyond the world portrayed in the imagination of the first one, and it is in the contrast between the two representations of the everyday, the Mishnah's and the Yerushalmi's, that we shall find ample reason for this theory of the change in the perspective upon "Israel" that permeates the writings of the late fourth and fifth centuries surveyed presently.

The Mishnah's Israel in imagination is governed by an Israelite king, high priest, and sanhedrin – a political world that for two centuries had existed, if at all, only in imagination or aspiration. The Talmud's portrait of Israel represents Jews who lived under both rabbis near at hand, settling everyday disputes of streets and households, and also distant archons of a nameless state, to be manipulated and placated on earth as in heaven. The Mishnah's Judaism breathes the pure air of public piazza and stoa, the Talmud's, the ripe stench of private alleyway and courtyard. The image of the Mishnah's Judaism is evoked by the majestic Parthenon, perfect in all its proportions, conceived in a single moment of pure rationality. The Talmud's Judaism is a scarcely choate cathedral in process, the labor of many generations, each of its parts the conception of diverse moments of devotion, all of them the culmination of an ongoing and evolving process of revelation in the here and now.

When we study the Mishnah, we contemplate a fine conception of nowhere in particular, addressed to whom it may concern, a utopian vision in an exact sense of the word.[7] When we turn to the Talmud, we see a familiar world, as we have known it from the Talmud's day to our own. It is a locative perspective upon the here and the now, so far as the Yerushalmi portrays that concrete present. In literary terms, in the transition from the Mishnah to the Talmud of the Land of Israel, we leave behind the strict and formal classicism of the Mishnah, like Plato's *Republic* describing for no one in particular an ideal society never, in its day, to be seen. We come, rather, to focus upon the disorderly detail of the workaday world, taking the utopian Mishnah along with us. If Aristotle's *Politics* had been written as a gloss to Plato's *Republic,* amplifying and extending piece by piece the once whole but no longer cogent writing of Plato, we should have a rough analogy to what the Yerushalmi has done with the Mishnah of Judah the Patriarch. If, further, many philosophers took up the fantastic account of the Republic and out of its materials, and other writings, worked out new *Republics*, so bringing diversity to what had been a single conception and book, we should find a possible precedent for what happened from 200 to 400 C.E. in the move, in Judaism, from the theoretical to the practical, the monothetic to the polythetic, the uniform to the diverse, the cogent to the chaotic, and from system to tradition. The relevance of these larger literary–philosophical contrasts is transparent.[8]

What is important in the inquiry into the way in which people imagined "Israel" is a simple fact. The Yerushalmi for its part testifies to the existence of a coherent worldview and way of life embodied in a distinct and distinctive society or estate of Jews: the rabbis – masters and disciples – of the third and fourth centuries in the Land of Israel. As we shall see, the authorship of the Yerushalmi devotes ample attention to these sages and their practical and everyday government, a portrait with no counterpart in the Mishnah and related writings. These masters and disciples, deeply engaged with the life of the ordinary people, thought about an "Israel" in a strikingly different way from their predecessors. We have first to survey the portrait of Israel in the more important documents, and then, at the end, to account for it by referring to the documentary portrait of sages as a social entity in relationship to, and forming a consensus concerning, a still larger and equally palpable entity that the Yerushalmi presents to us.[9]

iv. The Judaism of Sanctification and Salvation in the Yerushalmi, Genesis Rabbah, Leviticus Rabbah, and Related Writings

The original metaphorization of the Jews' social groups by identification with Scripture's "Israel" contained within itself the potential for what now took place, the interpretation of "Israel" not in relationship to other entities but on its own. If "Israel" now formed that entity of which Scripture spoke, then that "Israel" constituted not merely a category compared with other categories, but an entity unto itself. The metaphor promised as much, even though the Mishnaic system, in taking over the metaphorization of the group as it did, did not make use of the metaphor "Israel" in such a concrete way. In the second phrase in the formation of the Judaism of the dual Torah, by contrast, "Israel" found definition on its own terms, and not principally in relationship to "non-Israel," whatever that, in context, may have meant. "Israel" now bore an absolute, not a relative meaning, with concrete, not abstract valence. The documents that carried forward and continued the Mishnah exhibit striking changes, in particular within those writings brought to closure at the end of the fourth century and in the hundred years thereafter, and the representation of "Israel" followed suit. These writings, overall, present us with a Judaic system interested in sanctification in the here and now and also in salvation at the end of time, a system in which the teleology bore in its wake an eschatological doctrine of a salvific character. "Israel" for its part became a historical entity, with traits that were intrinsic, not merely aspects of a relationship of comparison and contrast. And, it follows, "Israel" served not only as a classification but also as the hero of stories, the subject of sustained (if episodic) narratives. So too other important systemic categories, such as the "gentile," also acquired definition and nuance, as an exercise in differentiation affected diverse components of the whole. We shall have to explain for ourselves both the specific changes

affecting our "Israel," and also the more general shifts in the representation of the system as a whole, on the one side, and the
everyday world, on the other, that characterize the writings of the late
fourth and fifth centuries. A different way of approaching the documents is now required, to match the fresh problem before us.

When we contemplated the meanings imputed to "Israel" in the
Mishnah and related writings, we found sufficient a survey of data in
concordances, and our inquiry into discrete passages showed us why.
"Israel" bore heavy meaning in relationship to "non-Israel," whether
nation or caste, but slight sense in the concrete representation of
social reality. Now we should be ill-served by a survey of meanings
imputed to a word. As to the available repertoire of meanings, moreover, those that we shall find do not vastly shift from what they had
been. But we require far more extensive inquiry into the account of
"Israel" provided by a variety of authorships, and for diverse purposes. For "Israel" in the writings redacted in the late fourth and fifth
centuries gains flesh and substance, becoming not merely a category
to be set into relationship with other categories, but the name of a
palpable social group, living out a concrete historical existence in a
world of material reality, about which people told important stories
and made weighty comments – a different "Israel" altogether.

Consequently, we shall have to survey principal documents not
merely for their use of words but to ask about their treatment of
concrete issues. We shall see that in treating "Israel" on its own terms,
our several authorships make detailed and important statements, not
merely allusions or references to a given taxonomic classifier. My
attention to the larger statement made by a document's authorship,
rather than merely word usages, therefore forms part of my larger
thesis that, in the second stage, what is said about "Israel" is as
important as the classification pertinent to "Israel." I of course do not
suggest that the selected documents alone supply important testimony. Quite to the contrary, I should maintain that a survey of other
writings of the same period and place – the late fourth and fifth
centuries, in the Land of Israel – should yield further full and systematic statements concerning "Israel" viewed as a social entity, a
group, fully defined concretely and autonomously and not only as an
abstraction.

We therefore shall concentrate, among the documents of the
second stage in the formation of the Judaism of the dual Torah, upon
two types of writings, one presenting a system as an exegesis of
the Mishnah, the other deriving a system from addressing Scripture.[10] How these authorships address "Israel" – the meanings
implicitly imputed to the category, the uses made of it – provides

the focus of our inquiry. Three themes of "Israel" occupy our attention, Israel as an extended family, in the theory of merit, in the practice of appeal to the matriarchs and patriarchs as family models; Israel as people or nation in confrontation with other peoples or nations; and Israel as sui generis. This third item carries forward the familiar fact that when Israel is sui generis, it is because of supernatural intervention into Israel's life as a group: God makes "Israel" different from all other social entities. The first of the three themes reaches rich expression in Genesis Rabbah, the second in both Leviticus Rabbah and Genesis Rabbah, the third in Leviticus Rabbah and the Yerushalmi. To display the treatment of these themes, I provide ample abstracts out of the designated documents. The reader may then compare the character and substance of these abstracts with the results of our survey, through concordances, of nearly the entirety of the prior stage in the unfolding of the literature. Obviously, these same themes come to expression in all of the three documents surveyed here, and attention to other documents of the age would yield ample instances for the facts to be displayed out of the resources of the ones we consider. But what we find in the principal documents suffices to show the striking differences between the "Israel"s of the Mishnah and related writings and the "Israel"s paramount in the documents of the second stage in the unfolding of the Judaism of the dual Torah.

NOTES

1 All these dates are rough guesses but conform to the opinion expressed in conventional encyclopedia articles.
2 Ramsay MacMullen, *Christianizing the Roman Empire* (New Haven: Yale University Press, 1984), p. 456.
3 J. N. D. Kelly, *Jerome: His Life, Writings, and Controversies* (New York: Harper & Row, 1975), p. 295.
4 Ibid., pp. 1–2.
5 Jacob Burckhardt, *The Age of Constantine the Great* (New York: Doubleday Anchor Books, 1958), trans. Moses Hadas (p. 293 for Constantine).
6 W. F. C. Frend, *The Rise of Christianity* (Philadelphia: Fortress Press, 1984), p. 499.
7 In time to come I plan to work on how the Mishnah's system presents a counterpart to Plato's *Republic* and Aristotle's *Politics*.
8 On the issue of system versus tradition, see my *The Bavli and its Sources: The Question of Tradition in the Case of Tractate Sukkah* (Atlanta: Scholars Press for Brown Judaic Studies, 1987) and *The Formation of the Jewish*

Intellect: Making Connections and Drawing Conclusions in the Traditional System of Judaism, in press.

9 Once more I represent the Yerushalmi's authorship as a social group thinking about a social group, while I see the Mishnah's as a social group reflecting upon abstract relationships among abstract entities. The distinction is not critical to my argument but seems to me worth drawing.

10 I could have chosen other documents of the same phase in the unfolding of the Judaism at hand. But these are given the earliest dates of the lot. I have worked systematically not only on the ones we survey but also on such later items as Pesiqta deRab Kahana, The Fathers According to Rabbi Nathan, and the Talmud of Babylonia. But the first statements to emerge, the ones accomplished by the authorships of the Yerushalmi, Genesis Rabbah, and Leviticus Rabbah, strike me as the most cogent. I do not mean to suggest I cover all canonical documents, nor do I wish to imply that other documents do not have important contributions to make to our inquiry. Let us get this far.

CHAPTER 7

"Israel" as Family

i.   The Metaphor of the Family, "Israel"

When sages wished to know what (an) "Israel" was, in the fourth century they reread the story of the origins of Scripture's "Israel" for the answer. To begin with, as Scripture told them the story, "Israel" was a man, Jacob, and his children are "the children of Jacob." That man's name was also "Israel," and, it followed, "the children of Israel" composed the extended family of that man. By extension, "Israel" formed the family of Abraham and Sarah, Isaac and Rebecca, Jacob and Leah and Rachel. "Israel" therefore invoked the metaphor of genealogy to explain the bonds that linked persons unseen into a single social entity; the shared traits were imputed, not empirical. That social metaphor of "Israel" – a simple one, really, and easily grasped – bore consequences in two ways. First, children in general are admonished to follow the good example of their parents. The deeds of the patriarchs and matriarchs therefore taught lessons on how the children were to act. Of greater interest in an account of "Israel" as a social metaphor, "Israel" lived twice, once in the patriarchs and matriarchs, a second time in the life of the heirs as the descendants relived those earlier lives. The stories of the family were carefully reread to provide a picture of the meaning of the latterday events of the descendants of that same family. Accordingly, the lives of the patriarchs signaled the history of Israel.

The polemical purpose of the claim that that abstraction "Israel" was to be compared to the family of the mythic ancestor lies right at the surface. With another "Israel," the Christian Church, now claiming to constitute the true one, Jews found it possible to confront that claim and to turn it against the other side. "You claim to form 'Israel after the spirit.' Fine, and *we* are Israel after the flesh – and genealogy forms the link, that alone." (Converts did not present an anomaly, of course, because they were held to be children of Abraham and Sarah, who had "made souls," that is, converts, in Haran, a point repeated in the documents of the period.) That fleshly continuity formed of all of "us" a single family, rendering spurious the notion that "Israel" could be other than genealogically defined. But that polemic seems to me adventitious and not primary. At the same time the metaphor provided a quite separate component to sages' larger system.

ii. A Social Metaphor and a Field Theory of Society: "Israel" and the Social Contract

The metaphor of Israel as family supplied an encompassing theory of society, accounting for that sense of constituting a corporate social entity that clearly infused the documents of the Judaism of the dual Torah from the very outset. Such a theory explained not only who "Israel" as a whole was. It also set forth the responsibilities of Israel's social entity, its society; it defined the character of that entity; it explained who owes what to whom and why; and it accounted for the inner structure and interplay of relationship within the community, here and now, constituted by Jews in their villages and neighborhoods of towns. Accordingly, "Israel" as family bridged the gap between an account of the entirety of the social group, "Israel," and a picture of the components of that social group as they lived out their lives in their households and villages. An encompassing theory of society, covering all components from least to greatest, holding the whole together in correct order and proportion, derived from "Israel" viewed as extended family.[1]

Can we say that the Mishnaic phase had presented an encompassing theory of society as a whole? In general terms, yes, but in specifics, no. Invoking the metaphor "Israel" for a group subjected to metaphor and so identified with the biblical "Israel," the Mishnah accounted for the whole. And as to the parts, the here and the now of household and village, the Mishnah's "Israel" accomplished a suitable explanation. But the space in between the large and theoretical and the mundane was left vacant. The Mishnah's system had explained by "Israel" the identification of that large entity, the entirety of the social group, with biblical "Israel" and, in its extraordinary exegesis of the everyday as modality of the sacred, had also infused in the parts that sense that the whole was meant to make. But the parts remained just that: details of a larger whole that derived place and proportion only in that whole. That abstraction of "Israel" as not "non-Israel," holy and not gentile people, left the middle-range components of society unaccounted for.

The Mishnah could explain village and "all Israel," just as its system used the word "Israel" for individual and entire social entity. But the region and its counterparts, the "we" composed of regions, the corporate society of the Jews of a given country, language group, and the like, the real-life world of communities – these did not constitute subdivisions of the "Israel" that knew all and each, but nothing in between. The omitted entity, I see, was the family itself, which played no important role in the Mishnah's system, except as one of the taxonomic indicators. By contrast "Israel" as family imparted to the details an autonomy and a meaning of their own, so that each complex component of the whole formed a microcosm of the whole: family to village to "Israel" as one large family.

The village then constituted "Israel," as much as did the region, the neighborhood, the corporate society people could empirically identify, the theoretical social entity they could only imagine. All formed "all Israel," viewed under the aspect of Heaven, and, of still greater consequence, each household – that is, each building block of the village community – constituted in itself a model of, the model for, "Israel." The utter abstraction of the Mishnah had left "Israel" as individual or as "all Israel," thus without articulated linkage to the concrete middle range of the Jews' everyday social life. Dealing with exquisite detail and the intangible whole, the Mishnah's system had left that realm of the society of Jews in the workaday household and village outside the metaphorical frame of "Israel," and "Israel" viewed in the image of family made up that omitted middle range.

That theory of "Israel" as a society made up of persons who because they constituted a family stood in a clear relationship of obligation and responsibility to one another corresponded to what people much later would call the social contract, a kind of compact that in palpable ways told families and households how in the aggregate they formed something larger and tangible. The web of interaction spun out of concrete interchange now was spun out of not the gossamer thread of abstraction and theory but the tough hemp of family ties. "Israel" formed a society because "Israel" was compared to an extended family. That, sum and substance, supplied to the Jews in their households (themselves a made-up category that, in the end, transformed the relationship of the nuclear family into an abstraction capable of holding together quite unrelated persons) an account of the tie from household to household, from village to village, encompassing ultimately "all Israel."

Now if we ask the authorship of the Mishnah to point to its encompassing theory of "Israel" as an ongoing society, where will they lead us? If they tell us that "Israel" forms a society because it is not "non-Israel," they evade the question altogether. For "non-Israel" formed an undifferentiated other. It did not constitute a society, but only a category. And for the same reason "Israel" as caste contained no elements that could be spun out into a theory of interpersonal relationships that would account for the ongoing life of households in community, villages, towns, and upward. The theory of society that infuses the Mishnaic system forms part of a larger abstract program: "Israel" constitutes a holy people, a people apart, a people different from all other peoples; "Israel" constitutes a caste. But how everyday "Israel" forms a community, how in the aggregate everyday relationships are composed and held together, and how to account for the corresponding middle-range aggregates of "non-Israel" – these are not questions answered by the Mishnah's metaphors for "Israel." But they are questions that the Mishnah's authorship does answer. And this point is critical to my argument.

Obviously, as I have underscored already, the Mishnah's system answers these questions in exquisite detail. We certainly know how everyday relationships are to be ordered, whether involving a gored ox or a bereaved king. We may tease out of these threads and strands a fabric of community at large. But what is the connection between the solution to the problem of the gored ox or the bereaved king and the social theory, the theory of the entity "Israel" that the framers of the Mishnah have formed for themselves? I have not got the slightest idea. Indeed, faced by the requirement to state the connection between "Israel" at large and that social theory, that theory of society that is expressed in these details, we have nothing to say. For no one in the Mishnaic system draws the connection, and the available metaphors do not suggest that there was one (though there assuredly is). The contrast, then, to the power of the metaphor of "Israel" as family hardly requires specification. If "we" form a family, then we know full well what links us, the common ancestry, the obligations imposed by common ancestry upon the cousins who make up the family today. The link between the commonplace interactions and relationships that make "us" into a community, on the one side, and that encompassing entity, "Israel," "all Israel," now is drawn. The large comprehends the little, the abstraction of "us" overall ("the circumcised," for instance) gains concrete reality in the "us" of the here and now of home and village, all together, all forming a "family." In that fundamental way, the metaphor of "Israel" as family therefore provided the field theory of "Israel" linking the most abstract component, the entirety of the social group, to the most mundane, the specificity of the household. One theory, framed in that metaphor of such surpassing simplicity, now held the whole together. That is what I mean when I propose that the metaphor of family provided an encompassing theory of society, an account of the social contract encompassing all social entities, Jews' and gentiles' as well, that, so far as I can see, no other metaphor accomplished.

iii.   The Patriarchs and Matriarchs and the Family of Israel in Genesis Rabbah

Were we to picture the ethnic composition of the Land of Israel/ Palestine with different colored dots, the country would look like a speckled panther. The metaphor of "Israel" as family served a very distinctive and critical function. The metaphor of "Israel = family" linked villages of Jewish coloration into a hide of a single hue. And onward and upward, "family" allowed Jews to relate their own social entity to those other entities, the political presence of which they chose to take account. That fact underlines the metaphorical nature of the concept of "Israel" as family. Accordingly, we survey how "Israel" as family comes to expression in the document that makes the most sustained and systematic statement of the matter, Genesis Rabbah. In this theory we should not miss the extraordinary polemic utility, of which, in passing, we have already taken note. "Israel" as family also understood itself to form a nation or people. That nation-people held a land, a rather peculiar (enchanted or holy) Land at that, one that, in its imputed traits, was as sui generis, in the metaphorical thought of the system at hand, as Israel was. Competing for the same territory, Israel's claim to what it called the Land of Israel – thus, *of Israel* in particular – now rested on right of inheritance such as a family enjoyed, and this was made explicit. The passage shows how high the stakes were in the claim to constitute the genealogical descendant of the ancestors.

A.   "But to the sons of his concubines, Abraham gave gifts, and while he was still living, he sent them away from his son Isaac, eastward to the east country" (Gen. 25:6):

B.   In the time of Alexander of Macedonia the sons of Ishmael came to dispute with Israel about the birthright, and with them came two wicked families, the Canaanites and the Egyptians.

C.   They said, "Who will go and engage in a disputation with them."

D.   Gebiah b. Qosem [the enchanter] said, "I shall go and engage in a disputation with them."

E.   They said to him, "Be careful not to let the Land of Israel fall into their possession."

F. He said to them, "I shall go and engage in a disputation with them. If I win over them, well and good. And if not, you may say, 'Who is this hunchback to represent us?'"

G. He went and engaged in a disputation with them. Said to them Alexander of Macedonia, "Who lays claim against whom?"

H. The Ishmaelites said, "We lay claim, and we bring our evidence from their own Torah: 'But he shall acknowledge the firstborn, the son of the hated' (Deut. 21;17). Now Ishmael was the firstborn. [We therefore claim the land as heirs of the firstborn of Abraham.]"

I. Said to him Gebiah b. Qosem, "My royal lord, does a man not do whatever he likes with his sons?"

J. He said to him, "Indeed so."

K. "And lo, it is written, 'Abraham gave all that he had to Isaac' (Gen. 25:2)."

L. [Alexander asked,] "Then where is the deed of gift to the other sons?"

M. He said to him, "'But to the sons of his concubines, Abraham gave gifts, [and while he was still living, he sent them away from his son Isaac, eastward to the east country]' (Gen. 25:6)."

N. [The Ishmaelites had no claim on the land.] They abandoned the field in shame.

Gen. R. LXI:VII.1

The metaphor now shifts, and the notion of Israel today as the family of Abraham, as against the Ishmaelites, also of the same family, gives way. But the theme of family records persists. Canaan has no claim, for Canaan was also a family, comparable with Israel – but descended from a slave. The power of the metaphor of family is that it can explain not only the social entity formed by Jews, but the social entities confronted by them. All fell into the same genus, making up diverse species. The theory of society before us – that is, the theory of "Israel" – thus accounts for the existence, also, of all societies, and, as we shall see when we deal with Rome, the theory of "Israel" does so with extraordinary force.

O. The Canaanites said, "We lay claim, and we bring our evidence from their own Torah. Throughout their Torah it is written, 'the land of Canaan.' So let them give us back our land."

P. Said to him Gebiah b. Qosem, "My royal lord, does a man not do whatever he likes with his slave?"

Q. He said to him, "Indeed so."

R. He said to him, "And lo, it is written, 'A slave of slaves shall Canaan be to his brothers' (Gen. 9:25). So they are really our slaves."

S. [The Cannanites had no claim to the land and in fact should be serving Israel.] They abandoned the field in shame.

Gen. R. LXI:VII.1

The same metaphor serves both "Israel" and "Canaan." Each formed the latterday heir of the earliest family, and both lived out the original paradigm. The mode of thought at hand imputes the same genus to both social entities, and then makes it possible to distinguish among the two species at hand. We shall see the same mode of thought – the family, but which wing of the family – when we consider the confrontation with Christianity and with Rome, in each case conceived in the same personal way. The metaphor applies to both and yields its own meanings for each. The final claim in the passage before us moves away from the metaphor of family. But the notion of a continuous, physical descent is implicit here as well. "Israel" has inherited the wealth of Egypt. Since the notion of inheritance forms a component of the metaphor of family (a conception critical, as we shall see in the next section, in the supernatural patrimony of the "children of Israel" in the merit of the ancestors), we survey the conclusion of the passage.

T.   The Egyptians said, "We lay claim, and we bring our evidence from their own Torah. Six hundred thousand of them left us, taking away our silver and gold utensils: 'They despoiled the Egyptians' (Ex. 12:36). Let them give them back to us."

U.   Gebiah b. Qosem said, "My royal lord, six hundred thousand men worked for them for two hundred and ten years, some as silversmiths and some as goldsmiths. Let them pay us our salary at the rate of a *denar* a day."

V.   The mathematicians went and added up what was owing, and they had not reached the sum covering a century before the Egyptians had to forfeit what they had claimed. They abandoned the field in shame. [Alexander] wanted to go up to Jerusalem. The Samaritans said to him, "Be careful. They will not permit you to enter their most holy sanctuary."

W.   When Gebiah b. Qosem found out about this, he went and made for himself two felt shoes, with two precious stones worth twenty thousand pieces of silver set in them. When he got to the mountain of the house [of the Temple], he said to him, "My royal lord, take off your shoes and put on these two felt slippers, for the floor is slippery, and you should not slip and fall."

X.   When they came to the most holy sanctuary, he said to him, "Up to this point, we have the right to enter. From this point onward, we do not have the right to enter."

Y.   He said to him, "When we get out of here, I'm going to even out your hump."

Z.   He said to him, "You will be called a great surgeon and get a big fee."

Gen. R. LXI:VII.1

The Ishmaelites, Abraham's children, deprived as they were of their inheritance, fall into the same genus as does Israel. So too, as I said, did Canaan. As to the Egyptians, that is a different matter. Now "Israel" is that same "Israel" of which Scripture spoke. The social metaphor shifts within the story, though the story, of course, is not affected.

Families inherited the estate of the founders, and "Israel" was a family with a sizable heritage and inheritance. Thinking not in terms of abstractions but in personal and concrete ways, sages personalized but, through the invented personalities, were able to make perfectly clear statements for themselves. Along these same lines, when the Church theologian-historians faced the task of explaining the connection between diverse nations or peoples and the Church, they worked out relationships between the king of a country and Jesus, as in the case of the correspondence between Jesus and Abgar, which accounted for the place of the Church of Edessa within the family of Christianity. Because the Church understood that not only Jesus' blood relatives, but also his disciples, standing in a supernatural relationship with him, entered into the original communion, the invented discipleship of kings made a place, within a larger social theory of the Church, for the new and diverse groups. When, in the fourth century, a principal world ruler did convert, the Church had an understanding of the role of persons and personalities in the history of salvation. The mode of thought before us, therefore, finds ample place in a larger scheme of thinking about society and the relationships of its components.

Families have histories, and "Israel" as family found in the record of its family history those points of coherence that transformed events into meaningful patterns, that is, the history of the social unit, the nation-family, as a whole. This matter is simply expressed by the common wisdom – like parent, like child; the apple does not fall far from the tree; and the like. Whether true or false, that folk wisdom surely accounts for the commonsense quality of sages' search, in the deeds of the patriarchs and matriarchs, for messages concerning the future history of the children. But sages assuredly were not common folk. They were philosophers, and their inquiry constituted a chapter in the history of what used to be called natural philosophy, and what today we know as social science. Specifically, sages looked at the facts of history for the laws of history. They proposed to generalize, and, out of generalization, to explain their own particular circumstance. That is why we may compare them to social scientists or social philosophers, trying to turn anecdotes into insight and to demonstrate how we may know the difference between impressions and truths. Genesis provided facts concerning the family. Careful sifting of those facts will yield the laws that dictated why to that family things happened one way rather than some other.

Among these social laws of the family history, one took priority, the laws that explained the movement of empires upward and downward and pointed toward the ultimate end of it all. Scripture provided the model for the ages of empires, yielding a picture of four monarchies, to be followed by Israel as the fifth. Sages repeated this familiar viewpoint (one we shall rehearse when we consider "Israel" as sui generis, now for quite other reasons). In reading Genesis, in particular, they found that time and again events in the lives of the patriarchs prefigured the four monarchies, among which, of course, the fourth, last, and most intolerable was Rome. Israel's history falls under God's dominion. Whatever will happen carries out God's plan, and that plan for the future has been laid out in the account of the origins supplied by Genesis. The fourth kingdom, Rome, is part of that plan, which we can discover by carefully studying Abraham's life and God's word to him.

A. "Then the Lord said to Abram, 'Know of a surety [that your descendants will be sojourners in a land that is not theirs, and they will be slaves there, and they will be oppressed for four hundred years; but I will bring judgment on the nation which they serve, and afterward they shall come out with great possessions']" (Gen. 15:13–14):

B. "Know" that I shall scatter them.

C. "Of a certainty" that I shall bring them back together again.

D. "Know" that I shall put them out as a pledge [in expiation of their sins].

E. "Of a certainty" that I shall redeem them.

F. "Know" that I shall make them slaves.

G. "Of a certainty" that I shall free them.

Gen. R. XLIV:XVIII.1

No. 1 parses the cited verse and joins within its simple formula the entire history of Israel, punishment and forgiveness alike. Not only the patriarchs, but also the matriarchs, so acted as to shape the future life of the family, Israel. One extended statement of the matter suffices. Here is how sages take up the detail of Abraham's provision of a bit of water, showing what that act had to do with the history of Israel later on. The intricate working out of the whole, involving the merit of the patriarchs, the way in which the deeds of the patriarchs provide a sign for proper conduct for their children, and the history and salvation of Israel, shows how, within a single metaphor, the entire system of the Judaism of the dual Torah could reach concrete expression.

A. "Let a little water be brought" (Gen. 18:4):
B. Said to him the Holy One, blessed be he, "You have said, 'Let a little water be brought' (Gen. 18:4). By your life, I shall pay your descendants back for this: 'Then sang Israel this song, "spring up O well, sing you to it"' (Num. 21:7)."
C. That recompense took place in the wilderness. Where do we find that it took place in the Land of Israel as well?
D. "A land of brooks of water" (Deut. 8:7).
E. And where do we find that it will take place in the age to come?
F. "And it shall come to pass in that day that living waters shall go out of Jerusalem" (Zech. 14:8).
G. ["And wash your feet" (Gen. 18:4)]: [Said to him the Holy One, blessed be he,] "You have said, 'And wash your feet.' By your life, I shall pay your descendants back for this: 'Then I washed you in water' (Ez. 16:9)."
H. That recompense took place in the wilderness. Where do we find that it took place in the Land of Israel as well?
I. "Wash you, make you clean" (Is. 1:16).
J. And where do we find that it will take place in the age to come?
K. "When the Lord will have washed away the filth of the daughters of Zion" (Is. 4:4).
L. [Said to him the Holy One, blessed be he,] "You have said, 'And rest yourselves under the tree' (Gen. 18:4). By your life, I shall pay your descendants back for this: 'He spread a cloud for a screen' (Ps. 105:39)."
M. That recompense took place in the wilderness. Where do we find that it took place in the Land of Israel as well?
N. "You shall dwell in booths for seven days" (Lev. 23:42).
O. And where do we find that it will take place in the age to come?
P. "And there shall be a pavilion for a shadow in the day-time from the heat" (Is. 4:6).
Q. [Said to him the Holy One, blessed be he,] "You have said, 'While I fetch a morsel of bread that you may refresh yourself' (Gen. 18:5). By your life, I shall pay your descendants back for this: 'Behold I will cause to rain bread from heaven for you' (Ex. 16:45)"
R. That recompense took place in the wilderness. Where do we find that it took place in the Land of Israel as well?
S. "A land of wheat and barley" (Deut. 8:8).
T. And where do we find that it will take place in the age to come?
U. "He will be as a rich cornfield in the land" (Ps. 82:16).
V. [Said to him the Holy One, blessed be he,] "You ran after the herd ['And Abraham ran to the herd' (Gen. 18:7)]. By your life, I shall pay your descendants back for this: 'And there went forth a wind from the Lord and brought across quails from the sea' (Num. 11:27)."

W.   That recompense took place in the wilderness. Where do we find that it took place in the Land of Israel as well?

X.   "Now the children of Reuben and the children of Gad had a very great multitude of cattle" (Num. 32:1).

Y.   And where do we find that it will take place in the age to come?

Z.   "And it will come to pass in that day that a man shall rear a young cow and two sheep" (Is. 7:21).

AA.   [Said to him the Holy One, blessed be he,] "You stood by them: 'And he stood by them under the tree while they ate' (Gen. 18:8). By your life, I shall pay your descendants back for this: 'And the Lord went before them' (Ex. 13:21)."

BB.   That recompense took place in the wilderness. Where do we find that it took place in the Land of Israel as well?

CC.   "God stands in the congregation of God" (Ps. 82:1).

DD.   And where do we find that it will take place in the age to come?

EE.   "The breaker is gone up before them . . . and the Lord at the head of them" (Mic. 2:13).

Gen. R. XLVIII:X.2

Everything that Abraham did brought a reward to his descendants. The enormous emphasis on the way in which Abraham's deeds pre-figured the history of Israel, in the wilderness, in the Land, and finally in the age to come, provokes us to wonder who held that there were other children of Abraham, besides this "Israel." The answer – the triumphant Christians in particular, who right from the beginning, with Paul and the evangelists, imputed it to the earliest generations and said it in so many words – then is clear. We note that there are five statements of the same proposition, each drawing upon a clause in the base verse. The extended statement moreover serves as a sustained introduction to the treatment of the individual clauses that now follow, item by item. Obviously, it is the merit of the ancestors that connects the living Israel to the lives of the patriarchs and matriarchs of old.

Precisely what lessons about history or social rules of Judaism did the sages derive for the descendants of Abraham and Sarah? Clearly, the lessons concern God's conduct with Israel, then and now. One important example concerns God's threats to punish Israel. In the polemic of the age, with the Christians accusing Israel of having sinned and citing the prophets for evidence, the following can have provided a striking response. God can change the plan originally conceived. None of the prophetic warnings lay beyond God's power of re-vision, should Israel's repentance warrant.

A.   "For ever, O Lord, your word stands fast in heaven" (Ps. 119:89):

B.   But does God's word not stand fast on earth?

C. But what you said to Abraham in heaven, "At this season I shall return to you" (Gen. 18:14) [was carried out:]
D. "The Lord remembered Sarah as he had said and the Lord did to Sarah as he had promised" (Gen. 21:1).

Gen. R. LIII:IV.1

A. R. Menahamah and R. Nahman of Jaffa in the name of R. Jacob of Caesarea opened discourse by citing the following verse: "'O God of hosts, return, we beseech you' (Ps. 80:15).
B. "'Return and carry out what you promised to Abraham: "Look from heaven and behold" (Ps. 80:15). "Look now toward heaven and count the stars"' (Gen. 15:5).
C. "'And be mindful of this vine' (Ps. 80:15). 'The Lord remembered Sarah as he had said and the Lord did to Sarah as he had promised' (Gen. 21:1)."

Gen. R. LIII:IV.2

A. R. Samuel bar Nahman opened discourse with this verse: "God is not a man, that he should lie" (Num. 23:19).
B. Said R. Samuel bar Nahman, "The beginning of this verse does not correspond to its end, and the end does not correspond to its beginning.
C. "'God is not a man that he should lie' (Num. 23:18), but the verse ends, 'When he has said, he will not do it, and when he has spoken, he will not make it good' (Num. 23:18).
D. "[That obviously is impossible. Hence:] When the Holy One, blessed be he, makes a decree to bring good to the world: 'God is not a man that he should lie' (Num. 23:18).
E. "But when he makes a decree to bring evil on the world: 'When he has said, he [nonetheless] will not do it, and when he has spoken, he will not make it good' (Num. 23:18).
F. "When he said to Abraham, 'For through Isaac shall your descendants be named,' 'God is not a man that he should lie' (Num. 23:18).
G. "When he said to him, 'Take your son, your only son' (Gen. 22:2), 'When he has said, he will not do it, and when he has spoken, he will not make it good' (Num. 23:18).
H. "When the Holy One, blessed be he, said to Moses, 'I have surely remembered you' (Ex. 3:16), 'God is not a man that he should lie' (Num. 23:18).
I. "When he said to him, 'Let me alone, that I may destroy them' (Deut. 9:14), 'When he has said, he will not do it, and when he has spoken, he will not make it good' (Num. 23:18).
J. "When he said to Abraham, 'And also that nation whom they shall serve will I judge' (Gen. 15:14), 'God is not a man that he should lie' (Num. 23:18).
K. "When he said to him, 'And they shall serve them and they shall afflict them for four hundred years' (Gen. 15:13), 'When he has said, he will

not do it, and when he has spoken, he will not make it good' (Num.
23:18).

L.   "When God said to him, 'I will certainly return to you' (Gen. 18:10),
'God is not a man that he should lie' (Num. 23:18).

M.   "'The Lord remembered Sarah as he had said and the Lord did to Sarah
as he had promised' (Gen. 21:1)."

Gen. R. LIII:IV.3

The main point is that God will always carry out his word when it
has to do with a blessing, but God may well go back on his word
when it has to do with punishment. The later events in the history of
Israel are drawn together to make this important point. The single
most important paradigm for history therefore emerged from the
binding of Isaac, the deed at Moriah, portrayed on synagogue mosaics
(e.g., at Beth Alpha) and reflected upon as the source for knowledge
of the laws of the history of Israel, heirs and continuators of Abraham
and Isaac. Sages drew one specific lesson. Future Israel would live
from the model and merit of that moment.

A.   "On the third day Abraham lifted up his eyes and saw the place afar
off" (Gen. 22:4):

B.   "After two days he will revive us, on the third day he will raise us up,
that we may live in his presence" (Hos. 16:2).

C.   On the third day of the tribes: "And Joseph said to them on the third
day, 'This do and live'" (Gen. 42:18).

D.   On the third day of the giving of the Torah: "And it came to pass on
the third day when it was morning" (Ex. 19:16).

E.   On the third day of the spies: "And hide yourselves there for three
days" (Josh 2:16).

F.   On the third day of Jonah: "And Jonah was in the belly of the fish three
days and three nights" (Jonah 2:1).

G.   On the third day of the return from the Exile: "And we abode there
three days" (Ezra 8:32).

H.   On the third day of the resurrection of the dead: "After two days he
will revive us, on the third day he will raise us up, that we may live in
his presence" (Hos. 16:2).

I.   On the third day of Esther: "Now it came to pass on the third day that
Esther put on her royal apparel" (Est. 5:1).

J.   She put on the monarchy of the house of her fathers.

K.   On account of what sort of merit?

L.   Rabbis say, "On account of the third day of the giving of the Torah."

M.   R. Levi said, "It is on account of the merit of the third day of Abraham:
'On the third day Abraham lifted up his eyes and saw the place afar
off' (Gen. 22:4)."

Gen. R. LVI:I.1

A. " . . . lifted up his eyes and saw the place afar off" (Gen. 22:4):
B. What did he see? He saw a cloud attached to the mountain. He said, "It would appear that that is the place concerning which the Holy One, blessed be he, told me to offer up my son."

Gen. R. LVI:I.2

The third day marks the fulfillment of the promise, at the end of time of the resurrection of the dead and, at appropriate moments, of Israel's redemption. The reference to the third day at Gen. 22:2 then invokes the entire panoply of Israel's history. The relevance of the composition emerges at the end. Prior to the concluding segment, the passage forms a kind of litany and falls into the category of a liturgy. Still, the recurrent hermeneutic that teaches that the stories of the patriarchs prefigure the history of Israel certainly makes its appearance.

Whereas Abraham founded Israel, Isaac and Jacob carried forth the birthright and the blessing. This they did through the process of selection, ending in the assignment of the birthright to Jacob alone. The importance of that fact for the definition of "Israel" hardly requires explication. The lives of all three patriarchs flowed together, each being identified with the other as a single long life. This immediately produced the proposition that the historical life of Israel, the nation, continued the individual lives of the patriarchs. The theory of who is Israel, therefore, is seen once more to have rested on genealogy: Israel is one extended family, all being children of the same fathers and mothers, the patriarchs and matriarchs of Genesis. This theory of Israelite society, and of the Jewish people in the time of the sages of Genesis Rabbah, made of the people a family and of genealogy a kind of ecclesiology. The importance of that proposition in countering the Christian claim to be a new Israel cannot escape notice. Israel, sages maintained, is Israel after the flesh, and that in a most literal sense. But the basic claim, for its part, depended upon the facts of Scripture, not upon the logical requirements of theological dispute. Here is how those facts emerged in the case of Isaac.

A. "These are the descendants of Isaac, Abraham's son: Abraham was the father of Isaac" (Gen. 25:19):
B. Abram was called Abraham: "Abram, the same is Abraham" (1 Chron. 1:27).
C. Isaac was called Abraham: "These are the descendants of Isaac, Abraham's son, Abraham."
D. Jacob was called Israel, as it is written, "Your name shall be called no more Jacob but Israel" (Gen. 32:29).

E. Isaac also was called Israel: "And these are the names of the children of Israel, who came into Egypt, Jacob and his" (Gen. 46:8).

F. Abraham was called Israel as well.

G. R. Nathan said, "This matter is deep: 'Now the time that the children of Israel dwelt in Egypt' (Ex. 12:40), and in the land of Canaan and in the land of Goshen 'was four hundred and thirty years' (Ex. 12:40)." [Freedman,[2] p. 557, n. 6: They were in Egypt for only 210 years. Hence their sojourn in Canaan and Goshen must be added, which means, from the birth of Isaac. Hence the children of Israel commence with Isaac. And since he was Abraham's son, it follows that Abraham was called Israel.]

Gen. R. LXIII:III.1

The polemic at hand, linking the patriarchs to the history of Israel, claiming that all of the patriarchs bear the same names, derives proof in part from the base verse. But the composition in no way rests upon the exegesis of the base verse. Its syllogism transcends the case at hand. The importance of Isaac in particular derived from his relationship to the two nations that would engage in struggle, Jacob, who was and is Israel, and Esau, who stood for Rome. By himself, as a symbol for Israel's history Isaac remained a shadowy figure. Still, Isaac plays his role in setting forth the laws of Israel's history. In sages' typology, Esau always stands for Rome, and later we shall see that the representation of Esau as sibling, brother, and enemy distinguishes Esau–Rome from all other nations. Esau is not an outsider, not a gentile, but also not Israel, legitimate heir. We once more recall the power of the social theory to hold all together all of the middle-range components of society: all nations within a single theory. The genealogical metaphor here displays that remarkable capacity.

A. "[He said, 'Behold I am old; I do not know the day of my death.] Now then take your weapons, [your quiver and your bow, and go out to the field and hunt game for me, and prepare for me savory food, such as I love, and bring it to me that I may eat; that I may bless you before I die']" (Gen. 27:2–4):

B. "Sharpen your hunting gear, so that you will not feed me carrion or an animal that was improperly slaughtered.

C. "Take your *own* hunting gear, so that you will not feed me meat that has been stolen or grabbed."

Gen. R. LXV:XIII.1

Isaac's first point is that Esau does not ordinarily observe the food laws, such as those concerning humane slaughter of animals. He furthermore steals, whereas, by inference, Jacob takes only what he has lawfully acquired. This prepares the way for the main point:

A. "Your quiver":
B. [Since the word for "quiver" and the word for "held in suspense" share the same consonants, we interpret the statement as follows:] he said to him, "Lo, the blessings [that I am about to give] are held in suspense. For the one who is worthy of a blessing, there will be a blessing."

Gen. R. LXV:XIII.2

A. Another matter: "Now then take your weapons, your quiver and your bow and go out to the field":
B. "Weapons" refers to Babylonia, as it is said, "And the weapons he brought to the treasure house of his god" (Gen. 2:2).
C. "Your quiver" speaks of Media, as it says, "So they suspended Haman on the gallows" (Est. 7:10). [The play on the words is the same as at No. 2.]
D. "And your bow" addresses Greece: "For I bend Judah for me, I fill the bow with Ephraim and I will store up your sons, O Zion, against your sons, O Javan [Greece]" (Zech. 9:13).
E. "and go out to the field" means Edom: "Unto the land of Seir, the field of Edom" (Gen. 32:4).

Gen. R. LXV:XIII.3

Once more the patriarchs lay out the future history of their family and, in dealing with their own affairs, prefigure what is to come. The power of the metaphor of family is not exhausted in its capacity to link household to household; quite to the contrary, as with any really successful metaphor, it draws everything into one thing and makes sense of the whole all together and all at once. Here the households that are joined are today's to yesterday's to those of the entirety of past and future.

A. "And Rebecca was listening when Isaac spoke to his son Esau. So when Esau went to the field to hunt for game and bring it . . ." (Gen. 27:5):
B. If he found it, well and good.
C. And if not, ". . . to bring it" even by theft or violence.

Gen. R. LXV:XIII.5

The matter of the blessing is represented as more conditional than the narrative suggests. Isaac now is not sure who will get the blessing; his sense is that it will go to whoever deserves it. No. 3 then moves from the moral to the national, making the statement a clear reference to the history of Israel (as though, by this point, it were not obvious). What the author of the item at hand contributes, then, is the specific details. What the compositor does is move the reader's mind from the philological to the moral to the national dimension of exegesis of the statements at hand. Esau steals, but Jacob takes only what is lawful. Now we see, not surprisingly, how Isaac foresaw the entire history of Israel.

A. ["See the smell of my son is as the smell of a field which the Lord has blessed" (Gen. 27:27):] Another matter: this teaches that the Holy One, blessed be he, showed him the house of the sanctuary as it was built, wiped out, and built once more.

B. "See the smell of my son": This refers to the Temple in all its beauty, in line with this verse: "A sweet smell to me shall you observe" (Num. 28:2).

C. ". . . is as the smell of a field": This refers to the Temple as it was wiped out, thus: "Zion shall be ploughed as a field" (Mic. 3:12).

D. ". . . which the Lord has blessed": This speaks of the Temple as it was restored once more in the age to come, as it is said, "For there the Lord commanded the blessing, even life for ever" (Ps. 133:3).

Gen. R. LXVI:XXIII.1

The conclusion explicitly links the blessing of Jacob to the temple throughout its history. The concluding proof text presumably justifies the entire identification of the blessing at hand with what was to come. Whatever future history finds adumbration in the life of Jacob derives from the struggle with Esau. Israel and Rome – these two contend for the world. Still, Isaac plays his part in the matter. Rome does have a legitimate claim, and that claim demands recognition – an amazing, if grudging concession on the part of sages that Christian Rome at least is Esau – different from the gentiles, but also not Israel.

Jacob's contribution to knowledge of the meaning and end of Israel's history, as sages uncovered it, is exemplified in the following:

A. ". . . so that I come again to my father's house in peace, then the Lord shall be my God" (Gen. 28:20–22):

B. R. Joshua of Sikhnin in the name of R. Levi: "The Holy One, blessed be he, took the language used by the patriarchs and turned it into a key to the redemption of their descendants.

C. "Said the Holy One, blessed be he, to Jacob, 'You have said, "Then the Lord shall be my God." By your life, all of the acts of goodness, blessing, and consolation which I am going to carry out for your descendants I shall bestow only by using the same language:

D. ""Then in that day, living waters shall go out from Jerusalem" (Zech. 14:8). "Then in that day a man shall rear a young cow and two sheep" (Is. 7:21). "Then, in that day, the Lord will set his hand again the second time to recover the remnant of his people" (Is. 11:11). "Then, in that day, the mountains shall drop down sweet wine" (Joel 4:18). "Then, in that day, a great horn shall be blown and they shall come who were lost in the land of Assyria" (Is. 27:13).'"

Gen. R. LXX:VI:1

The union of Jacob's biography and Israel's history yields the passage at hand. It is important only because it makes the statement that we have now heard throughout our survey of Genesis Rabbah as explicit as one can imagine. Now the history of the redemption of Israel is located in the colloquy between Jacob and Laban's sons.

A. "Now Laban had two daughters, the name of the older was Leah, and the name of the younger was Rachel" (Gen. 29:16):
B. They were like two beams running from one end of the world to the other.
C. This one produced captains and that one produced captains, this one produced kings and that one produced kings, this one produced lion tamers and that one produced lion tamers, this one produced conquerors of nations and that one produced conquerors of nations, this one produced those who divided countries and that one produced dividers of countries.
D. The offering brought by the son of this one overrode the prohibitions of the Sabbath, and the offering brought by the son of that one overrode the prohibitions of the Sabbath.
E. The war fought by this one overrode the prohibitions of the Sabbath, and the war fought by that one overrode the prohibitions of the Sabbath.
F. To this one were given two nights, and to that one were given two nights.
G. The night of Pharaoh and the night of Sennacherib were for Leah, and the night of Gideon was for Rachel, and the night of Mordecai was for Rachel, as it is said, "On that night the king could not sleep" (Est. 6:1).

Gen. R. LXX:XV.1

The metaphor encompasses not only "Israel" but also "Rome." It makes sense of all the important social entities, for in this metaphor, "Israel" is consubstantial with other social entities, which relate to "Israel" just as "Israel" as a society relates to itself, present and past. Accordingly, "Rome" is a family just as is "Israel," and, more to the point, "Rome" enters into "Israel's" life in an intelligible way precisely because "Rome" too is a part of that same family that is constituted by "Israel." That is a stunning claim, working itself out time after time so smoothly, with such self-evidence, as to conceal its daring. Again we see how the metaphor that joins past to present, household to household to "all Israel," in fact encompasses the other noteworthy social entity and takes it into full account – a powerful, successful field theory indeed. The contrast to the taxonomic metaphor is clear. "Non-Israel" accommodates, it classifies, but it does not explain. Then, ironically, neither does "Israel." Here we have explanation, which, after all, is the purpose of natural philosophy in its social aspect.

It is no surprise, therefore, that much that Jacob said serves to illuminate Israel's future history.

A. "[Then Esau said, 'Let us journey on our way, and I will go before you.'] But Jacob said to him, 'My lord knows [that the children are frail, and that the flocks and herds giving suck are a care to me; and if they are overdriven for one day, all the flocks will die. Let my lord pass on before his servant, and I will lead on slowly, according to the pace of the cattle which are before me and according to the pace of the children, until I come to my lord in Seir']" (Gen. 33:12–14):

B. Said R. Berekhiah, "'My lord knows that the children are frail' refers to Moses and Aaron.

C. ". . . and that the 'flocks and herds giving suck are a care to me' speaks of Israel: 'And you, my flock, the flock of my pasture, are men' (Ez. 34:31)."

D. R. Huna in the name of R. Aha: "If it were not for the tender mercies of the Holy One, blessed be he, 'and if they are overdriven for one day, all the flocks will die' in the time of Hadrian."

E. R. Berekhiah in the name of R. Levi: "'My lord knows that the children are frail' speaks of David and Solomon.

F. "'. . . the flocks and herds' refers to Israel: 'And you, my flock, the flock of my pasture, are men' (Ez. 34:31).

G. Said R. Huna in the name of R. Aha, "If it were not for the tender mercies of the Holy One, blessed be he, 'and if they are overdriven for one day, all the flocks will die' in the time of Haman."

Gen. R. LXXVIII:XIII.1

The event at hand now is identified with other moments in the history of Israel. The metaphor of family makes a place for women as much as men, matriarchs as much as patriarchs, in a way in which the gender neutral, but in fact masculine, metaphors of the Mishnaic system do not. The metaphorical role of the matriarchs, imputed in the case of Rachel, is as follows:

A. "So Rachel died and she was buried on the way to Ephrath, [that is, Bethlehem, and Jacob set up a pillar upon her grave; it is the pillar of Rachel's tomb, which is there to this day. Israel journeyed on and pitched his tent beyond the tower of Eder]" (Gen. 35:16–21):

B. Why did Jacob bury Rachel on the way to Ephrath?

C. Jacob foresaw that the exiles would pass by there [en route to Babylonia].

D. Therefore he buried her there, so that she should seek mercy for them: "A voice is heard in Ramah . . . Rachel weeping for her children. . . . Thus says the Lord, 'Keep your voice from weeping . . . and there is hope for your future'" (Jer. 31:15–16).

Gen. R. LXXXII:X.1

We see no differentiation between matriarch and patriarch; both components of the family accomplish the same purpose, which is to link the whole together, providing for the descendants. The deeds of the patriarchs and matriarchs aim at the needs of Israel later on. The link between the lives of the patriarchs and the history of Israel forms a major theme in the exegetical repertoire before us. These propositions really laid down a single judgment for both the individual and the family in the form of the community and the nation. Every detail of the narrative of Genesis therefore served to prefigure what was to be, and "Israel" as extended family found itself, time and again, in the revealed facts of the family record of Abraham, Isaac, and Israel. A survey of how sages read Genesis has brought us time and again to a clear perception of sages' thinking about "Israel." We see how they thought and therefore understand the positions they reached. Imagining the group to constitute a family, they organized the entire social world – Israel's part, the nations' share – within the single metaphor at hand. That mode of thought gave them a rich resource for interpreting in the context of world politics the everyday history of Israel and also explaining the future to be anticipated for Israel.

iv. Merit in Genesis Rabbah

The ancestors not only set an example for their descendants and signaled in advance what would happen to them. In the second stage in the formation of the Judaism of the dual Torah, the doctrine of merit joined with the notion of "Israel" as "children of Israel" to give concrete substance to the explanation of what and who Israel was. Within the metaphor invoked also by the notion of the *zekhut avot,* the merit of the ancestors, Israel was a family, the children of Abraham, Isaac, and Jacob, or children of Israel, in a concrete and genealogical sense. Israel hence fell into the genus family as the particular species of family generated by Abraham and Sarah. The distinguishing trait of that species was that it possessed the inheritance, or heritage, of the patriarchs and matriarchs, and that inheritance, consisting of merit, served the descendants and heirs as protection and support.

The metaphor of family thus worked itself out within its own logic, generating secondary analogies and comparisons. The single most important of these involved the analogy of spiritual and material estates, a theory that took up that rather general notion of "merit," which surely existed as a potentiality in the Mishnah, and gave it flesh and form. Now "merit" was joined to the metaphor of the genealogy of patriarchs and matriarchs and served to form the missing link, explaining how the inheritance and heritage were transmitted from them to their heirs. Consequently, the family "Israel" could draw upon the family estate, consisting of the inherited merit of matriarchs and patriarchs in such a way as to benefit today from the heritage of yesterday. This notion involved very concrete problems. If "Israel, the family" sinned, it could call upon the "merit" accumulated by Abraham and Isaac at the binding of Isaac (Gen. 22) to win forgiveness for that sin. True, "fathers will not die on account of the sin of the sons," but the children may benefit from the merit of the forebears. That concrete expression of the larger metaphor imparted to the metaphor a practical consequence, moral and theological, that was not at all neglected.

The Hebrew for the notion of the merit of the ancestors is *zekhut abot*. The use of *zekhut* (merit) in the Mishnah, we recall, bears a clear and simple meaning. If something good happened to someone, the cause ordinarily derived from the merit that that person had attained for some reason or other. We are not told the source of the merit when the matter of merit is invoked. In the writings of the second phase in the formation of Judaism, by contrast, that merit might accrue not only because of one's own character or deeds, but because someone else, related to that person, had handed it on. So if a woman became pregnant, always deemed the greatest blessing God could bestow, the immediate question is, On account of what sort of merit or on account of whose merit? It could be her own or an ancestor's merit. But if something good happened, that demanded of the exegete an account of the cause. How then would one attain merit? That question finds its answer in stories explaining the matter of the source of merit, on the one side, and its beneficial result, on the other. The doctrine of merit in the writings at hand was therefore framed in a way that would link merit to ancestry, hence, as *zekhut abot,* the merit of the ancestors.

This specific and denotative sense of merit proves inseparable from the general and connotative sense familiar from M. Sotah and its continuators. The doctrine of the merit of the ancestors served as a component of the powerful polemic concerning Israel. Specifically, that concrete, historical Israel, meaning for Christian theologians "Israel after the flesh," in the literature before us manifestly and explicitly claimed fleshly origin in Abraham and Sarah. The extended family indeed constituted precisely what the Christian theologians said: an Israel after the flesh, a family linked by genealogy. The heritage then became an inheritance, and what was inherited from the ancestors was a heavenly store, a treasure of merit, which protected the descendants when their own merit proved insufficient. A survey of Genesis Rabbah proves indicative of the character and use of the doctrine of merit, because that systematic reading of the book of Genesis dealt with the founders of the family and made explicit the definition of Israel as family. What we shall see is that merit draws in its wake the notion of the inheritance of an ongoing family, that of Abraham and Sarah, and merit worked itself out in the moments of crisis of that family in its larger affairs.

In the first example we see a definition of merit and how it is attained. It may be personal or inherited. Here it is personal. Specifically, Jacob reflects on the power that Esau's merit had gained for Esau. He had gained that merit by living in the land of Israel and also by paying honor and respect to Isaac. Jacob then feared that, because of the merit gained by Esau, he, Jacob, would not be able to overcome him. So merit worked on its own; it was a credit gained by proper action, which went to the credit of the person who had done that action.

A. "Then Jacob was greatly afraid and distressed" (Gen. 32:7): [This is Jacob's soliloquy:] "Because of all those years that Esau was living in the Land of Israel, perhaps he may come against me with the power of the merit he has now attained by dwelling in the Land of Israel.

B. "Because of all those years of paying honor to his father, perhaps he may come against me with the power of the merit he attained by honoring his father.

C. "So he said: 'Let the days of mourning for my father be at hand, then I will slay my brother Jacob' (Gen. 27:41).

D. "Now the old man is dead."

E. Said R. Judah bar Simon, "This is what the Holy One, blessed be he, had said to him, 'Return to the land of your fathers and to your kindred' (Gen. 31:3). [Supplying a further soliloquy for Jacob:] 'Perhaps the stipulations [of protection by God] applied only up to this point [at which I enter the land].'"

Gen. R. LXXVI:II.2

We see that merit is not only inherited but attained, and the source of the merit may be dwelling in the Land of Israel itself. Then the very physical location of a human being within the Land infuses that person with merit, of which the Land, as much as the ancestors, is a generative source. But from our perspective, Israel as family makes the patriarchs and matriarchs the key to merit. Another important side of the conception of merit attributes to the ancestors that store of merit upon which the descendants draw. So the Israelites later on enjoy enormous merit through the deeds of the patriarchs and matriarchs. That conception comes to expression in what follows:

A. ". . . for with only my staff I crossed this Jordan, and now I have become two companies":

B. R. Judah bar Simon in the name of R. Yohanan: "In the Torah, in the Prophets, and in the Writings we find proof that the Israelites were able to cross the Jordan only on account of the merit achieved by Jacob:

C. "In the Torah: '. . . for with only my staff I crossed this Jordan, and now I have become two companies.'

D. "In the prophets: 'Then you shall let your children know, saying, "Israel came over this Jordan on dry land"' (Josh. 4:22), meaning our father, Israel.

E. "In the Writings: 'What ails you, O you sea, that you flee? You Jordan, that you burn backward? At the presence of the God of Jacob' (Ps. 114:5ff.)."

F. Said R. Levi, "There is a place, where [Freedman:] the Jordan falls with a roar into the hot springs of Tiberias.

G. "In his fear Jacob hid in there and locked Esau out. But the Holy One, blessed be he, dug a hole for him at another spot 'When you pass through the waters, I will be with you, and through the rivers, and they shall not overflow you, when you walk through the fire, you shall not be burned' (Is. 43:2)."

Gen. R. LXXVI:V.2

Jacob did not only leave merit as an estate to his heirs. The process is reciprocal and ongoing. Merit deriving from the ancestors had helped Jacob himself:

A. "When the man saw that he did not prevail against Jacob, [he touched the hollow of his thigh, and Jacob's thigh was put out of joint as he wrestled with him]" (Gen. 32:25):

B. Said R. Hinena bar Isaac, "[God said to the angel,] 'He is coming against you with five "amulets" hung on his neck, that is, his own merit, the merit of his father and of his mother and of his grandfather and of his grandmother.

C. "'Check yourself out, can you stand up against even his own merit [let alone the merit of his parents and grandparents]?'

D. "The matter may be compared to a king who had a savage dog and a tame lion. The king would take his son and sick him against the lion, and if the dog came to have a fight with the son, he would say to the dog, 'The lion cannot have a fight with him, are you going to make out in a fight with him?'

E. "So if the nations come to have a fight with Israel, the Holy One, blessed be he, says to them, 'Your angelic prince could not stand up to Israel, and as to you, how much the more so!'"

Gen. R. LXXVII:III.3

And the reciprocity of the process extended in all directions. Merit might project not only backward, deriving from an ancestor and serving a descendant, but forward as well. Thus Joseph accrued so much merit that the generations that came before him were credited with his merit:

A. "These are the generations of the family of Jacob. Joseph [being seventeen years old, was shepherding the flock with his brothers]" (Gen. 37:2):

B. These generations came along only on account of the merit of Joseph.

C. Did Jacob go to Laban for any reason other than for Rachel?

D. These generations thus waited until Joseph was born, in line with this verse: "And when Rachel had borne Joseph, Jacob said to Laban, 'Send me away'" (Gen. 30:215).

E. Who brought them down to Egypt? It was Joseph.

F. Who supported them in Egypt? It was Joseph.

G. The sea split open only on account of the merit of Joseph: "The waters saw you, O God" (Ps. 77:17). "You have with your arm redeemed your people, the sons of Jacob and Joseph" (Ps. 77:16).

H. R. Yudan said, "Also the Jordan was divided only on account of the merit of Joseph."

Gen. R. LXXXIV:V.2

The passage at hand asks why only Joseph is mentioned as the family of Jacob. The inner polemic is that the merit of Jacob and Joseph would more than suffice to overcome Esau. Not only so, but Joseph survived because of the merit of his ancestors:

A. "She caught him by his garment. . . . but he left his garment in her hand and fled and got out of the house. [And when she saw that he had left his garment in her hand and had fled out of the house, she called to the men of her household and said to them, 'See he has brought among us a Hebrew to insult us; he came in to me to lie with me, and I cried out with a loud voice, and when he heard that I lifted up my voice and cried, he left his garment with me and fled and got out of the house']" (Gen. 39:13–15):

B. He escaped through the merit of the fathers, in line with this verse: "And he brought him forth outside" (Gen. 15:5).

C. Simeon of Qitron said, "It was on account of bringing up the bones of Joseph that the sea was split: 'The sea saw it and fled' (Ps. 114:3), on the merit of this: '. . . and fled and got out.'"

Gen. R. LXXXVII:VIII.1

How then do people acquire merit? Through acts of supererogatory grace they gain God's special love, for both themselves and their descendants. Here is a concrete example of how acts of worth or merit accrue to the benefit of the heirs of those that do them:

A. "When they came to the threshing floor of Atad, which is beyond the Jordan, they lamented there with a very great and sorrowful lamentation, and he made a mourning for his father seven days" (Gen. 50:10):

B. Said R. Samuel bar Nahman, "We have reviewed the entire Scripture and found no other place called Atad. And can there be a threshing floor for thorns [the Hebrew word for thorn being *atad*]?

C. "But this refers to the Canaanites. It teaches that they were worthy of being threshed like thorns. And on account of what merit were they saved? It was on account of the acts of kindness that they performed for our father, Jacob [on the occasion of the mourning for his death]."

D. And what were the acts of kindness that they performed for our father, Jacob?

E. R. Eleazar said, "[When the bier was brought up there,] they unloosened the girdle of their loins."

F. R. Simeon b. Laqish said, "They untied the shoulder-knots."

G. R. Judah b. R. Shalom said, "They pointed with their fingers and said, 'This is a grievous mourning to the Egyptians' (Gen. 50:11)."

H. Rabbis said, "They stood upright."

I. Now is it not an argument a fortiori: now if these, who did not do a thing with their hands or feet, but only because they pointed their fingers, were saved from punishment, Israel, which performs an act of kindness [for the dead] with their adults and with their children, with their hands and with their feet, how much the more so [will they enjoy the merit of being saved from punishment]!

J. Said R. Abbahu, "Those seventy days that lapsed between the first letter and the second match the seventy days that the Egyptians paid respect to Jacob. [Seventy days elapsed from Haman's letter of destruction until Mordecai's letter announcing the repeal of the decree (cf. Est. 3:12, 8:9). The latter letter, which permitted the Jews to take vengeance on their would-be destroyers, should have come earlier, but it was delayed seventy days as a reward for the honor shown by the Egyptians to Jacob]" (Freedman, p. 992, n. 6).

Gen. R. C:VI.1

The Egyptians gained merit by honoring Jacob in his death, so Abbahu. This same point then registers for the Canaanites. The connection is somewhat farfetched, through the reference to the threshing floor, but the point is a strong one. Yet merit derives not only from exceptional deeds of a religious or moral character. People attain merit simply through hard work, through living up to their calling.

A. "If the God of my father, the God of Abraham and the Fear of Isaac, had not been on my side, surely now you would have sent me away empty-handed. God saw my affliction and the labor of my hand and rebuked you last night" (Gen. 31:41–2):

B. Zebedee b. Levi and R. Joshua b. Levi:

C. Zebedee said, "Every passage in which reference is made to 'if' tells of an appeal to the merit accrued by the patriarchs. [Freedman, p. 684, n. 2: It introduces a plea for or affirmation of protection received for the sake of the patriarchs.]"

D. Said to him R. Joshua, "But it is written, 'Except we had lingered' (Gen. 43:10) [a passage not related to the merit of the patriarchs]."

E. He said to him, "They themselves would not have come up except for the merit of the patriarchs, for if it were not for the merit of the patriarchs, they never would have been able to go up from there in peace."

F. Said R. Tanhuma, "There are those who produce the matter in a different version." [It is given as follows:]

G. R. Joshua and Zebedee b. Levi:

H. R. Joshua said, "Every passage in which reference is made to 'if' tells of an appeal to the merit accrued by the patriarchs except for the present case."

I. He said to him, "This case too falls under the category of an appeal to the merit of the patriarchs."

J. R. Yohanan said, "It was on account of the merit achieved through sanctification of the divine name."

K. R. Levi said, "It was on account of the merit achieved through faith and the merit achieved through Torah.

L. "The merit achieved through faith: 'If I had not believed . . .' (Ps. 27:13).

M. "The merit achieved through Torah: 'Unless your Torah had been my delight' (Ps. 119:92)."

Gen. R. LXXIV:XII.1

A. "God saw my affliction and the labor of my hand and rebuked you last night" (Gen. 31:41–2):

B. Said R. Jeremiah b. Eleazar, "More beloved is hard labor than the merit achieved by the patriarchs, for the merit achieved by the patriarchs served to afford protection for property only, while the merit achieved by hard labor served to afford protection for lives.

C. "The merit achieved by the patriarchs served to afford protection for property only: 'If the God of my father, the God of Abraham and the Fear of Isaac, had not been on my side, surely now you would have sent me away empty-handed.'

D. "The merit achieved by hard labor served to afford protection for lives: 'God saw my affliction and the labor of my hand and rebuked you last night.'"

Gen. R. LXXIV:XII.2

The main interest at the end is in the theology of merit. No. 1 investigates the meaning of an expression used in the base verse, among other passages. The exegesis is not particular to our base verse. No. 2 serves to prove a syllogism on the basis of the verses

before us, standing closer to the formulation of the verses themselves. The issue of the merit of the patriarchs comes up in the reference to the God of the fathers. The conception of the merit of the
patriarchs is explicit, not general. It specifies what later benefit to the
heir, Israel the family, derived from which particular action of a
patriarch or matriarch.

A.   "And Abram gave him a tenth of everything" (Gen. 14:20):
B.   R. Judah in the name of R. Nehorai: "On the strength of that blessing
     the three great pegs on which the world depends, Abraham, Isaac,
     and Jacob, derived sustenance.
C.   "Abraham: 'And the Lord blessed Abraham in *all* things' (Gen. 24:1)
     on account of the merit that 'he gave him a tenth of *all* things' (Gen.
     14:20).
D.   "Isaac: 'And I have eaten of *all*' (Gen. 27:33), on account of the merit
     that 'he gave him a tenth of *all* things' (Gen. 14:20).
E.   "Jacob: 'Because God has dealt graciously with me and because I have
     all' (Gen. 33:11) on account of the merit that 'he gave him a tenth of *all*
     things' (Gen. 14:20).

Gen. R. XLIII:VIII.2

A.   Whence did Israel gain the merit of receiving the blessing of the
     priests?
B.   R. Judah said, "It was from Abraham: '*So* shall your seed be' (Gen.
     15:5), while it is written in connection with the priestly blessing: '*So*
     shall you bless the children of Israel' (Num. 6:23)."
C.   R. Nehemiah said, "It was from Isaac: 'And I and the lad will go *so* far'
     (Gen. 22:5), therefore said the Holy One, blessed be he, '*So* shall you
     bless the children of Israel' (Num. 6:23)."
D.   And rabbis say, "It was from Jacob: 'So shall you say to the house of
     Jacob' (Ex. 19:3) (in line with the statement, '*So* shall you bless the
     children of Israel' (Num. 6:23)."

Gen. R. XLIII:VIII.3

No. 2 links the blessing at hand with the history of Israel. Now the
reference is to the word "all," which joins the tithe of Abram to the
blessing of his descendants. Because the blessing of the priest is at
hand, No. 3 treats the origins of the blessing. The picture is clear.
"Israel" constitutes a family as a genealogical and juridical fact. It inherits the estate of the ancestors. It hands on that estate. It lives by
the example of the matriarchs and patriarchs, and its history exem-
plifies events in their lives.

To conclude, let us survey a systematic statement of the power of
merit to redeem Israel. This statement appeals to the binding of Isaac
as the source of the merit, deriving from the patriarchs and matriarchs, which will in the end lead to the salvation of Israel.

A. ". . . and we will worship [through an act of prostration] and come again to you" (Gen. 22:5):

B. He thereby told him that he would come back from Mount Moriah whole and in peace [for he said that *we* shall come back].

Gen. R. LVI:II.4

A. Said R. Isaac, "And all was on account of the merit attained by the act of prostration.

B. "Abraham returned in peace from Mount Moriah only on account of the merit owing to the act of prostration: '. . . and we will worship [through an act of prostration] and come [then, on that account] again to you' (Gen. 22:5).

C. "The Israelites were redeemed only on account of the merit owing to the act of prostration: And the people believed . . . then they bowed their heads and prostrated themselves' (Ex. 4:31).

D. "The Torah was given only on account of the merit owing to the act of prostration: 'And worship [prostrate themselves] you afar off' (Ex. 24:1).

E. "Hannah was remembered only on account of the merit owing to the act of prostration: 'And they worshiped before the Lord' (1 Sam. 1:19).

F. "The exiles will be brought back only on account of the merit owing to the act of prostration: 'And it shall come to pass in that day that a great horn shall be blown and they shall come that were lost . . . and that were dispersed . . . and they shall worship the Lord in the holy mountain at Jerusalem' (Is. 27:13).

G. "The Temple was built only on account of the merit owing to the act of prostration: 'Exalt you the Lord our God and worship at his holy hill' (Ps. 99:9).

H. "The dead will live only on account of the merit owing to the act of prostration: 'Come let us worship and bend the knee, let us kneel before the Lord our maker' (Ps. 95:6)."

Gen. R. LVI:II.5

The entire history of Israel flows from its acts of worship ("prostration") and is unified by a single law. Every sort of advantage Israel has ever gained came about through that act of worship. Hence what is besought, in the elegant survey, is the law of history. The Scripture then supplies those facts from which the governing law is derived. The governing law is that Israel constitutes a family and inherits the merit laid up as a treasure for the descendants by the ancestors.

v.   The Nations as Families in Genesis Rabbah

As I pointed out in an earlier context, once sages had defined the social entity of Israel by analogy with a family, they naturally imposed upon social entities round about the same metaphor, which in its nature is inclusive and not exclusive. That instrument of thought therefore allowed sages to explain within a single, unitary theory what happened to both Israel and everyone else that mattered. A brief account of the outcome of extending the same metaphor suffices. If Abraham, Isaac, and Jacob stand for Israel later on, then Ishmael, Edom, and Esau represent Rome. Hence whatever sages find out about those figures tells them something about Rome and its character, history, and destiny. God has unconditionally promised to redeem Israel, but if Israel repents, then the redemption will come with greater glory. Here, in context of that conviction, is Ishmael's lesson:

A. ["He shall be a wild ass of a man, [his hand against every man and every man's hand against him, and he shall dwell over against all his kinsmen] . . . his hand against every man and every man's hand against him" (Gen. 16:12)]: Said R. Eleazar, "When is it the case that 'his hand is against every man and every man's hand against him'?

B. "When he comes concerning whom it is written: 'And wheresoever the children of men, the beasts of the field and the fowl of the heaven dwell, has he given them into your hand' (Dan. 2:38). [Freedman, p. 386, n. 2: In the days of Nebuchadnezzar, whose ruthless policy of conquest aroused the whole world against him.]

C. "That is in line with the following verse of Scripture: 'Of Kedar and of the kingdoms of Hazor, which Nebuchadrezzar smote' (Jer. 49:28). His name is spelled, 'Nebuchadrezzar' because he shut them up in the wilderness and killed them. [Freedman, p. 386, n. 4: A play on the name, which, with the present spelling, ends in *asar*, spelled with an *alef*, as though it were *asar*, spelled with an *ayin* and yielding the meaning, shut up.]"

Gen. R. XLV:IX.3

A. ["... and he shall dwell over against all his kinsmen"] (Gen. 16:12):

B. Here the word choice is "dwell" while later on it is "he fell" (Gen. 25:18).

C. So long as Abraham was alive, "he [Ishmael] shall dwell." Once he died, "he fell." [His father's merit no longer protected him.]

D. Before he laid hands on the Temple, "he shall dwell." After he laid hands on the Temple, "he fell."

E. In this world "he shall dwell." In the world to come, "he fell."

Gen. R. XLV:IX.4

Nos. 3 and 4 move from the figure of Ishmael to those like him, Nebuchadnezzar, then Rome. The temple was destroyed by each of these persons, in the tradition of Ishmael. The conclusion then provides the hope to Israel that the enemy will perish, at least in the world to come. So the passage is read as both a literal statement and also as an effort to prefigure the history of Israel's suffering and redemption. Ishmael, standing now for Christian Rome, claims God's blessing, but Isaac gets it, as Jacob will take it from Esau. The following works the contrast of Ishmael as against Isaac, yielding the same polemic against Rome:

A. "[God said, 'No, but Sarah your wife [shall bear you a son, and you shall call his name Isaac. I will establish my covenant with him as an everlasting covenant for his descendants after him.] As for Ishmael, I have heard you. Behold, I will bless him and make him fruitful and multiply him exceedingly. He shall be the father of twelve princes, and I will make him a great nation]'" (Gen. 17:19–20).

B. R. Yohanan in the name of R. Joshua b. Hananiah, "In this case the son of the servant woman might learn from what was said concerning the son of the mistress of the household:

C. "'Behold, I will bless him' refers to Isaac.

D. "'. . . and make him fruitful' refers to Isaac.

E. "'. . . and multiply him exceedingly' refers to Isaac.

F. "'. . . As for Ishmael, I have informed you' through the angel. [The point is, Freedman, p. 401, n. 4, explains, Ishmael could be sure that his blessing too would be fulfilled.]"

G. R. Abba bar Kahana in the name of R. Birai: "Here the son of the mistress of the household might learn from the son of the handmaiden:

H. "'Behold, I will bless him' refers to Ishmael.

I. "'. . . and make him fruitful' refers to Ishmael.

J. "'. . . and multiply him exceedingly' refers to Ishmael.

K. "And by an argument a fortiori: 'But I will establish my covenant with Isaac' (Gen. 17:21)."

Gen. R. XLVII:V.1

A. Said R. Isaac, "It is written, 'All these are the twelve tribes of Israel' (Gen. 49:28). These were the descendants of the mistress [Sarah].

B. "But did Ishmael not establish twelve?

C. "The reference to those twelve is to princes, in line with the following verse: 'As princes and wind' (Prov. 25:14). [But the word for *prince* also stands for the word *vapor*, and hence the glory of the sons of Ishmael would be transient (Freedman, p. 402, n. 2).]

D. "But as to these tribes [descended from Isaac], they are in line with this verse: 'Sworn are the tribes of the word, selah' (Hab. 3:9). [Freedman, p. 402, n. 3: The word for *tribe* and for *staff* or *rod*, in the cited verse, are synonyms, both meaning tribes, both meaning rods, and so these tribes would endure like rods that are planted.]"

Gen. R. XLVII:V.2

Nos. 1 and 2 take up the problem of the rather fulsome blessing assigned to Ishmael. One authority reads the blessing to refer to Isaac, the other maintains that the blessing refers indeed to Ishmael, and Isaac will gain that much more. No. 2 goes over the same issue, now with the insistence that the glory of Ishmael will pass like vapor, while the tribes of Isaac will endure as well-planted rods. The polemic against Edom–Rome, with its transient glory, is familiar. These brief passages suffice to illustrate the main point, which concerns the metaphor of the group as family and the working of that metaphor to encompass other families, the important ones placed into relationship with Israel and so explained with reference to Israel.

The challenge of Christianity from the beginning had come from its spiritualization of "Israel." Here that challenge finds its answer in the opposite and counterpart: the utter and complete "genealogization" of Israel. To state matters negatively, the people could no more conceive that they were not the daughters and sons of their fathers and mothers than that they were not one large family, that is, the family of Abraham, Isaac, and Jacob: Israel after the flesh. That is what "after the flesh" meant. The powerful stress on the enduring merit of the patriarchs and matriarchs, the social theory that treated Israel as one large, extended family, the actual children of Abraham, Isaac, and Jacob – these now-familiar metaphors for the fleshly continuity met head on the contrary position framed by Paul and restated by Christian theologians from his time onward.

The metaphor of "Israel" as family therefore served a powerful polemical purpose in engaging with the new political facts of the age. But the metaphor did not originate in the fourth century. It originated in Scripture itself. Adopting the metaphor simply formed a stage in the metaphorization of "Israel" in the here and now by appeal to the "Israel" of Scripture. The potential of "Israel" as family existed as soon as thinkers about the social entity, "Israel," realized that they and their contemporaries in the here and now constituted that same "Israel" that Scripture had portrayed. But the metaphor of family proved remarkably apt for the requirements of the new era, and that is why the potential metaphor came to realization in just this age. In the uses to which sages in Genesis Rabbah put the metaphor, we see the impact of those requirements upon their authorship. For we look in vain in the pages of the Mishnah, tractate Abot, Tosefta, and related writings for appeal to "Israel" as family or, even in Sifra and the two Sifrés, for systematic exploitation of that metaphor for polemical purposes.

Metaphor serves not within the aesthetic requirements of literature, but in the social logic of political struggle. Present at the start, our metaphor surfaces not in accident or even in idle, speculative exploration of inner meanings. It emerged out of the cunning of intellect in mortal confrontation. We may find evidence for that proposition in the contrast between neglect of an available metaphor and profound exploration of the implications of that same metaphor. That is how we find powerful testimony to the way in which a given system, in this case, the Judaism of the dual Torah, makes its own choices and then imposes them upon a reading of Scripture.

Were we to conclude, however, that the motive of the system and therefore its metaphorical imagination derived wholly from without, a mere chapter in the longer history of a social group's responding to its circumstance, I believe we should miss an important part of the metaphor's power. For, as I stressed at the outset, the metaphor of the family served to bring within the shelter of a single encompassing theory all of the components of that society, "Israel," covered by the abstraction at hand. "Family" explained the composition of the household, an economic unit of production. "Family" accounted for the interrelationships of households of a certain sort – the Jewish sort – in a mixed village or in a village made up of only Jewish households. As I said earlier, "family" allowed Jews to relate their own social entity to those other entities the political presence of which they chose to take account. In all, the power of the metaphor lay in its possibility of joining all social entities, whether groups, whether classes, whether of another order altogether, into a single and uniform entity: "the families of humanity," whether of Israel or of Esau. But the power of the metaphor also contained its pathos. "Family" – whether Israel, whether Esau – left "Israel" different but not at all singular. That is why the metaphor of family by itself could not, and did not, suffice. For sages found self-evident the fact that they, "Israel," formed a group not at all like other groups. They were not merely the better wing of a common family. They formed a different type of group altogether from other groups, if a nation, then a singular nation – a proposition that now captures our attention.

NOTES

1 Whether such a theory of society as a whole and in its constituents can be identified in other Judaisms seems to me an interesting question. For a systemic statement on the social entity, the "Israel," may exhibit diverse qualities and serve a range of theoretical purposes. Such a statement need not address the issues worked out in an encompassing theory of society. My sense is that the Priestly Code accounted for the whole, all together and all at once. Whether other of the pentateuchal statements did, whether we may locate in the prophetic ideology a theory of society at large and in detail

– these are questions I do not know how to answer. The comparison of Judaisms (as of other systems) will find in this consideration a taxonomic trait, I should imagine.

2 M. Freedman, trans., *Genesis Rabbah* (London: Soncino Press, 1948). Hereafter cited as Freedman.

CHAPTER 8

"Israel" as Family and Also Singular Nation

i. Mixing Metaphors

The metaphor of the family hardly exhausted the choices facing the fourth-century sages in the Land of Israel. "Israel" stood for not only family among families, but also people or nation among entities of the same genus. Long before the advent of Christianity, Jews, quite naturally thinking of themselves within the biblical record as embodying, now, the people Scripture had called "Israel," of course had attained consciousness of their singularity among the peoples or nations of the world. In the debate with Christianity sages evoked not only "family" but also "nation," or "people," an altogether political entity. In framing the metaphor of a social entity like, yet not alike, all other social entities – hence a nation, but a singular nation – sages prepared for their adversaries yet a second point-by-point reply to a critical challenge, one closely related to but distinct from the metaphor deriving from the family. The reason sages required this second metaphor – nation unlike other nations – is that, for their part, the Christians spoke in political, as well as genealogical, terms. They too invoked in explaining the social entity constituted by them the metaphor of people or nation, one of a peculiar order to be sure. Consequently, the polemical task directed attention to the metaphor built not upon genealogy but upon a different sort of polity.

ii. The Family-Nation and the Confrontation with Christianity

The Christians from the beginning saw themselves as a people without a past, a no-people, a people gathered from the peoples. Then who they can claim to be hardly derives from who they have been.

145

Identifying with ancient Israel was a perfectly natural and correct initiative, well founded on the basis of the Christian canon, encompassing the Hebrew Scriptures as "the old testament." It admirably accounted for the Christian presence in humanity, provided a past, explained to diverse people what they had in common. One problem from Christian theologians' perspective demanded solution: the existing Israel, the Jewish people, which revered the same Scriptures and claimed descent, after the flesh, from ancient Israel. The Jews traced their connection to ancient Israel, seeing it as natural, and also supernatural. The family tie, through Abraham, Isaac, and Jacob, formed a powerful apologetic indeed. The Jews furthermore pointed to their family record, the Scriptures, to explain whence they come and who they are. So long as the two parties to the debate shared the same subordinated political circumstance, Jewry could quite nicely hold its own in the debate. But with the shift in the politics of the Empire, the terms of debate changed. The parvenu became paramount, as the Christian party to the debate invoked its familiar position now with the power of the state in support.

The confrontation with Christianity, we already realize, in sages' thought took the form of a family dispute about who is the legitimate heir to the same ancestor. Judaic sages and Christian theologians addressed the same issue in pretty much the same terms, with a single mode of argument – appealing to a shared body of facts, the Scriptures – joining the two into a common debate. Before we address the sages' position, let us rapidly survey the opposition's framing of the issue. To show us how a fourth-century Christian theologian addressed the question at hand – namely, who is Israel in the light of the salvation of Jesus Christ – we turn to Aphrahat, a Christian monk in Mesopotamia, ca. 300–50 C.E., who wrote in Syriac a sustained treatise on the relationship of Christianity and Judaism. His demonstrations, written in 337–44 C.E., take up issues facing the Syriac-speaking Church in the Iranian Empire. Like sages in their appeal to Scripture, Aphrahat presents his case on the base of historical facts shared in common by both parties to the debate. He rarely cites the New Testament in his demonstrations on Judaism. Moreover, when he cites the Hebrew Scriptures, he ordinarily refrains from a fanciful or allegoristic reading of them, but, like the rabbis whose comments we have surveyed, he stressed that his interpretation rested solely on the plain and obvious factual meaning at hand. His arguments thus invoked rational considerations and historical facts: This is what happened, this is what it means. Scriptures therefore present facts on which all parties concur, the basis for a family argument. We take up Aphrahat's explanation of that polity, or political entity, of people or nation: "The people which is of the peoples," the people "which is no people," and then proceed to his address to Israel after the flesh. In this way we place into context sages' representation of "Israel" as a people unlike other peoples and set the stage for our reading of sages' representation of "Israel" as utterly sui generis.

The two issues as framed by the Christian theologians complement one another. Once the new people formed out of the peoples enters the status of Israel, then the old Israel loses that status. And how to express that judgment? By denying the premise of the life of Israel after the flesh, that salvation for the people of God would come in future time. If enduring Israel would never enjoy salvation, then Israel had no reason to exist: that is the premise of the argument framed in behalf of the people that had found its reason to exist (from its perspective) solely in its salvation by Jesus Christ. So what explained to the Christian community how that community had come into being also accounted, for that same community, for the (anticipated) disappearance of the nation that had rejected that very same nation-creating event.

Let me point to Aphrahat's *Demonstration Sixteen, "On the Peoples which are in the Place of the People."* Aphrahat's message is this:

> The people Israel was rejected, and the peoples took their place. Israel repeatedly was warned by the prophets, but to no avail, so God abandoned them and replaced them with the gentiles. Scripture frequently referred to the gentiles as "Israel." The vocation of the peoples was prior to that of the people of Israel, and from of old, whoever from among the people was pleasing to God was more justified than Israel: Jethro, the Gibeonites, Rahab, Ebedmelech the Ethiopian, Uriah the Hittite. By means of the gentiles God provoked Israel.

First, Aphrahat maintains,

> The peoples which were of all languages were called first, before Israel, to the inheritance of the Most High, as God said to Abraham, "I have made you the father of a multitude of peoples" (Gen. 17:5). Moses proclaimed, saying, "The peoples will call to the mountain, and there will they offer sacrifices of righteousness." (Deut. 33:19)

Not only so, but God further rejected Israel. That is why God turned to the peoples:

> When he saw that they would not listen to him, he turned to the peoples, saying to them, "Hear O peoples, and know, O church

> which is among them, and hearken, O land, in its fullness." (Jer.
> 6:18–19)

So who is now Israel? It is the peoples, no longer the old Israel: "By
the name of Jacob [now] are called the people which is of the
peoples."

That is the key to Aphrahat's case. The people that was a no-
people, that people that had assembled out of the people, has now
replaced Israel. Like Eusebius, Aphrahat maintained that the peoples
had been called to God before the people of Israel. The people that
was a no-people should not regard itself as alien to God:

> If they should say, "Us has he called alien children," they have
> not been called alien children, but sons and heirs . . . But the
> peoples are those who hearken to God and were lamed and
> kept back from the ways of their sins.

Indeed, the peoples produced believers who were superior in every
respect to Israel. Aphrahat here refers to the Gibeonites, Rahab, and
various other gentiles mentioned in the scriptural narrative. So he
concludes,

> This brief memorial I have written to you concerning the
> peoples, because the Jews take pride and say, "We are the peo-
> ple of God and the children of Abraham." But we shall listen to
> John [the Baptist] who, when they took pride [saying], "We are
> the children of Abraham," then said to them, "You should not
> boast and say, Abraham is father unto us, for from these very
> rocks can God raise up children for Abraham." (Matthew 3:9)

In *Demonstration Nineteen, "Against the Jews, on account of their
saying that they are destined to be gathered together,"* Aphrahat
proceeds to the corollary argument, that the Israel after the flesh has
lost its reason to endure as a nation. Why? Because no salvation awaits
them in the future. The prophetic promises of salvation have all
come to fulfillment in the past, and the climactic salvation for Israel,
through the act of Jesus Christ, brought the salvific drama to its conclusion. Hence the Jews' not having a hope of "joining together" at
the end of their exile forms a critical part of the entire picture. Here
is my summary of the argument:

The Jews expect to be gathered together by the Messiah, but this
expectation is in vain. God was never reconciled to them but has rejected them. The prophetic promises of restoration were all fulfilled
in the return from Babylonia. Daniel's prayer was answered, and his
vision was realized in the time of Jesus and in the destruction of
Jerusalem. It will never be rebuilt. When, in 362–3 C.E., the emperor

Julian, intending to embarrass Christianity, allowed Jews to undertake the rebuilding of the temple in Jerusalem, the project failed. The issue therefore proved live, the possibility vivid, and, later on, the outcome struck Christian theologians as decisive evidence of who now is Israel, God's people, and who is not.

We see that, to Aphrahat's indictment of unbelieving "Israel," the metaphor of family proves inconsequential. The political metaphor involving "people" or "nation" takes over. For the challenge of those who held such views as Aphrahat expresses, the case is complete: the people that is no-people, the people that is of the peoples, have taken the place of the people that claims to carry forward the salvific history of ancient Israel. The reason is in two complementary parts. First, "Israel" (not called "after the flesh") has rejected salvation and so lost its reason to exist, and, second, the no-people have accepted salvation and so gained its reason to exist.

iii. "Israel" as People or Nation in Leviticus Rabbah

The several threads of the dispute draw together into a tight fabric: The shift in the character of politics, marked by the epochal triumph of Christianity in the state, bears profound meaning for the messianic mission of the Church and, further, imparts a final judgment on the salvific claim of the competing nations of God: the Church and Israel. What possible answer can sages have proposed to this indictment? Because at the heart of the matter lies the Christians' claim that scriptural "Israel" persists in the salvific heritage that has passed to the Christians, sages reaffirm that scriptural "Israel" persists – just as Paul had framed matters, to which we return in the concluding part of this study – after the flesh, an unconditional and permanent status. But that consideration formed only part of the matter. Another part concerned the political entity, "Israel," not merely the genealogical entity "children of Abraham and Sarah." The issue addressed the holiness of "Israel" as political entity, people or nation. That accounts for the joining of two metaphors, the one drawn from genealogy, the other from politics.

A cogent and propositional commentary to the book of Leviticus, Leviticus Rabbah, ca. 400–50 C.E., reads the laws of the ongoing sanctification in nature of the life of Israel as an account of the rules of the one-time salvation in history of the polity of "Israel." To the framers of Leviticus Rabbah, one point of emphasis proved critical: "Israel" remains "Israel," the Jewish people, after the flesh, not only because Israel today continues the family begun by Abraham, Isaac, Jacob, Joseph, and the other tribal founders and bears the heritage bequeathed by them. "Israel" is what it is also because of its character as holy nation, not merely family. For salvific issues addressed not solely to individuals but to concerns of history and eschatology frame themselves as political, dealing corporate social entities. Maintaining, as the Christian theologians did, that Israel would see no future salvation amounted to declaring that Israel, the Jewish people (no longer merely family), pursued no worthwhile purpose in continuing to endure. Indeed, in light of Paul's use of the metaphor of genealogy, the metaphor of the family could not serve to convey the proposition that "Israel" (after the flesh) had had its salvation in the return to Zion and would have no future salvation at all. Accordingly, from the perspective of the Christian theologian represented by Aphrahat, the shift from genealogical to political metaphors was necessary. When the argument joined the question, Who is Israel? to the question, Who enjoys salvation? the metaphor therefore shifted from family to political entity.

We find in Leviticus Rabbah clear address to the political metaphor, that is, the position that "Israel" constitutes a polity, not therefore conforming to a genealogical metaphor at all. I can find no more suitable way of recapitulating their reply to the linked questions, Who is Israel? and Is Israel saved? than by a brief survey of one of the sustained essays they present on the subject in Leviticus Rabbah. For that purpose we proceed briefly to survey the unfolding, in Leviticus Rabbah Parashah Two, of the theme: Israel is precious. We find an invocation of the genealogical justification for the election of Israel:

> B. He said to him, "Ephraim, head of the tribe, head of the session, one who is beautiful and exalted above all of my sons will be called by your name: [Samuel, the son of Elkanah, the son of Jeroham,] the son of Tohu, the son of Zuph, an Ephraimite" [1 Sam. 1:1]; "Jeroboam son of Nabat, an Ephraimite" [1 Kings 11:26]. "And David was an Ephraimite, of Bethlehem in Judah" (1 Sam. 17:12).
>
> Lev. R. II:III.2

Because Ephraim, that is, Israel, had been exiled, the deeper message cannot escape our attention. Whatever happens, God loves Ephraim. However Israel suffers, God's love endures, and God cares. In context, this is framed as a genealogy. But in fact, the matter in the syllogistic presentation of the *parashah* at hand extends not to family but to a social entity defined in other terms entirely. That message brings powerful reassurance. Facing a Rome gone Christian, sages first had to state the obvious, which no longer seemed self-evident at all. God is especially concerned with Israel – again, viewed not as a family but as a social group of unrelated persons, who share a common viewpoint and pattern of life (within the definitions offered in Chapter 1).

A. . . . "Speak to the children of Israel" (Lev. 1:2).
B. R. Yudan in the name of R. Samuel b. R. Nehemiah: "The matter may be compared to the case of a king who had an undergarment, concerning which he instructed his servant, saying to him, 'Fold it, shake it out, and be careful about it!'
C. "He said to him, 'My lord, O king, among all the undergarments that you have, [why] do you give me such instructions only about this one?'
D. "He said to him, 'It is because this is the one that I keep closest to my body.'
E. "So too did Moses say before the Holy One, blessed be he, Lord of the Universe: 'Among the seventy distinct nations that you have in your world, [why] do you give me instructions only concerning Israel? [For instance,] "Command the children of Israel" [Num. 28:2], "Say to the children of Israel" [Ex. 33:5], "Speak to the children of Israel'" [Lev. 1:2].
F. "He said to him, 'The reason is that they stick close to me, in line with the following verse of Scripture: "For as the undergarment cleaves to the loins of a man, so have I caused to cleave unto me the whole house of Israel"'" (Jer. 13:11).

Lev. R. II:IV.1

Here the metaphor of family plays no role, while the metaphor of "Israel" as corporate polity predominates. That fact emerges from the point of stress before us. We do well to dwell on the reason: "They stick close to me." That is an appeal not to genealogy but to a different type of trait entirely. "Israel" is a social entity by reason of its relationship to God. Cleaving to God involves the way of life and worldview of the people that is distinctive and singular, and these are what mark "Israel" as singular. On that basis I point to the notion at hand as an application of a metaphor not of family but of "people" or "nation," that is, a polity defined by external traits of belief and behavior, rather than inherent ones of genealogy. This quite distinct approach to the metaphor appropriate to "Israel" therefore is different from, though it complements, the one that speaks of "Israel after the flesh."

G. Said R. Abin, "[The matter may be compared] to a king who had a purple cloak, concerning which he instructed his servant, saying, 'Fold it, shake it out, and be careful about it!'
H. "He said to him, 'My Lord, O king, among all the purple cloaks that you have, [why] do you give me such instructions only about this one?'
I. "He said to him, 'That is the one that I wore on my coronation day.'

J.   "So too did Moses say before the Holy One, blessed be he, Lord of the Universe: 'Among the seventy distinct nations that you have in your world, [why] do you give instructions to me only concerning Israel? [For instance,] "Say to the children of Israel," "Command the children of Israel," "Speak to the children of Israel."'

K.   "He said to him, 'They are the ones who at the [Red] Sea declared me to be king, saying, "The Lord will be king"' (Ex. 15:18)."

Lev. R. II:IV.1

The point of the passage has to do with Israel's particular relationship to God: Israel cleaves to God, declares God to be king, and accepts God's dominion. Further evidence of God's love for Israel derives from the commandments themselves. God watches over every little thing that Jews do, even caring what they eat for breakfast. That is what marks "Israel" off from other peoples, who form a common genus but diverse species. The familiar stress on the keeping of the laws of the Torah as a mark of hope finds fulfillment here: the laws testify to God's deep concern for Israel. So there is sound reason for high hope, expressed in particular in keeping the laws of the Torah. Making the matter explicit, Simeon b. Yohai translates this fact into a sign of divine favor:

A.   Said R. Simeon b. Yohai, "[The matter may be compared] to a king who had an only son. Every day he would give instructions to his steward, saying to him, 'Make sure my son eats, make sure my son drinks, make sure my son goes to school, make sure my son comes home from school.'

B.   "So every day the Holy One, blessed be he, gave instructions to Moses, saying, 'Command the children of Israel,' 'Say to the children of Israel,' 'Speak to the children of Israel.'"

Lev. R. II:V.1

We now come to the statement of how Israel wins and retains God's favor. The issue at hand concerns Israel's relationship to the nations before God, which is corollary to what has gone before. It is in two parts. First of all, Israel knows how to serve God in the right way. Second, the nations, though they do what Israel does, do things wrong. First, Israel does things right. Why then is Israel beloved? The following answers that question.

A.   R. Simeon b. Yohai taught, "How masterful are the Israelites, for they know how to find favor with their creator."

...

E.   Said R. Hunia [in Aramaic:], "There is a tenant farmer who knows how to borrow things, and there is a tenant farmer who does not know how to borrow. The one who knows how to borrow combs his hair, brushes off his clothes, puts on a good face, and then goes over to the overseer of his work to borrow from him. [The overseer] says to him, 'How's the land doing?' He says to him, 'May you have the merit of being fully satisfied with its [wonderful] produce.' 'How are the oxen doing?' He says to him, 'May you have the merit of being fully satisfied with their fat.' 'How are the goats doing?' 'May you have the merit of being fully satisfied with their young.' 'And what would you like?' Then he says, 'Now if you might have an extra ten denars, would you give them to me?' The overseer replies, 'If you want, take twenty.'

F. "But the one who does not know how to borrow leaves his hair a mess, his clothes filthy, his face gloomy. He too goes over to the overseer to borrow from him. The overseer says to him, 'How's the land doing?' He replies, 'I hope it will produce at least what [in seed] we put into it.' 'How are the oxen doing?' 'They're scrawny.' 'How are the goats doing?' 'They're scrawny too.' 'And what do you want?' 'Now if you might have an extra ten denars, would you give them to me?' The overseer replies, 'Go, pay me back what you already owe me!'"

Lev. R. V:VIII.1

If Aphrahat had demanded a direct answer, he could not have provoked a more explicit one. He claims Israel does nothing right. Sages counter, speaking in their own setting of course, that they do everything right. And here too, at issue is public conduct of a polity, not the extended life of a household, a family. Sages then turn the tables on the position of Aphrahat, again addressing it head on. While the nations may do everything Israel does, they do it wrong. As is clear, the traits that matter do not derive from ancestors but from contemporary conduct of like-minded persons: a social group, not a family, and, among social groups, a polity, or, in metaphorical language, a "people" or "nation."

iv. "Israel" as Both Family and Polity in Genesis Rabbah and Leviticus Rabbah: The Special Problem of the Confrontation with Rome

It was one thing to read "Israel" as a singular nation. It was another to interpret "Rome" in the same way, and, so far as I can see, the writings before us do not present such an interpretation. "Rome" is not represented as counterbalance and opposite of "Israel" as nation, in the way in which "Rome" forms the anti-Israel of "Israel" as family. The reason is that, once we treat "Israel" within the metaphor of nation or people, we have no occasion to differentiate other nations or peoples from one another. That sort of differentiation would form exactly the opposite of what is pertinent. "Israel" as singular nation is differentiated from all nations equally, in identical measure and for the same reasons, and "Rome" is not going to be represented as also singular. We understand, therefore, why within the present frame-work, the argument concerning "Israel" as singular, we have to revert to the familiar notion of "Israel" and "Esau." That remained, for sages, the preferred mode of metaphorization, when "Rome" in particular came under discussion. We therefore return to the familiar ground covered in Chapter 7. But in a moment, we shall see why we have to consider "Rome" as not only sibling and enemy, but also as nation and counterpart nation.

We begin with the familiar, "Rome" as "family." What is important in the metaphor of Israel as family is how that metaphor governs the conceptualization of the other political components of the sages' world. We recognize the result for the treatment of Rome: Rome is Edom, Ishmael, Esau. In my view, that reading of Rome within the family metaphor accords with the sages' larger apologetic and po-lemic task of explaining who Israel is in a world gone Christian. For were the sages' picture merely of Rome as tyrant and destroyer of the temple, we should have no reason to link the text to the problems of the age of redaction and closure. But now, as we have already seen, it is Rome as Israel's brother, counterpart, and nemesis. Rome is now what stands in the way of Israel's, and the world's, ultimate salvation, not a political Rome but a messianic Rome, participating in the sacred (i.e., the familial) history of Israel. That is at issue: Rome as surrogate for Israel, Rome as obstacle to Israel. The sages' message to the claim of now-Christian Rome to constitute Israel and to succeed Israel is this: "Indeed, it is as you say, a kind of Israel, an heir of Abraham as your texts explicitly claim. But we remain the sole legitimate Israel, the bearer of the birthright – we and not you. So you are our brother: Esau, Ishmael, Edom." And the rest follows.

Sages in Genesis Rabbah and in Leviticus Rabbah developed an important theory on who is Rome. The characterization of Rome in Leviticus Rabbah bears the burden of their judgment on the defini-tion of the Christian people, as much as the sages' characterization of Rome in Leviticus Rabbah expressed their judgment of the place of Rome in the history of the family, "Israel." To understand that posi-tion on the character of Rome, we have to note that it constitutes a radical shift in the characterization of Rome in the unfolding canon of the sages' Judaism. Rome in the prior writings, the Mishnah (ca. 200 C.E.) and the Tosefta (ca. 300–400 C.E.), stood for a particular place. We begin, once more, with the view of the Mishnah. For matters show a substantial shift in the characterization of Rome from the earlier to the later writings. Had matters remained pretty much the same from the earlier (late second-century) to later (fourth- and early fifth-century) writings, we could not maintain that what is said in the fourth-century documents testifies in particular to intellectual events of the fourth century. We should have to hold that, overall, the doctrine was set and endured in its original version. What happened later on would then have no bearing upon the doctrine at hand, and my claim of a confrontation on a vivid issue would not find validation. But the doctrine of Rome does shift from the Mishnah to the fourth-century sages' writings – Leviticus Rabbah, Genesis Rabbah, and the Talmud of the Land of Israel. That fact proves the consequence, in the interpretation of ideas held in the fourth century, of the venue of documents in that time.

This brings us to "Rome" as not only or mainly family but now "Rome" as a state – nation, people – within the genus of "Israel" as nation or people. The reason is simple. In what is to follow, we see how "Rome" as family shades over into "Rome" as empire and state, comparable with "Israel" as a nation or state – and as the coming empire too. That shading explains why I have called the treatment of Rome a special problem. For while "Rome" stands for "Esau," the metaphorization of Rome moves into fresh ground, comparing Rome to animals as well as to the near-family. We have already seen the adumbration of the position that, in Leviticus Rabbah, would come to remarkably rich expression. For Rome now stood for much more than merely a place among other places, or even a people or nation among peoples or nations. Rome took up a place in the unfolding of the empires – Babylonia, Media, Greece, then Rome. "Israel" takes its place in that unfolding pattern, and hence is consubstantial with Babylonia, Media, Greece, and Rome. In that context, "Rome" and "Israel" do form counterparts and opposites. Still more important Rome is the penultimate empire on earth. Israel will constitute the ultimate one. That message, seeing the shifts in world history in a pattern and placing at the apex of the shift Israel itself, directly and precisely takes up the issue made urgent just now: the advent of the Christian emperors. Why do I maintain, as I do, that in the characterization of Rome as the fourth and penultimate empire– animal, sages address issues of their own day? Because Rome, among the successive empires, bears special traits, most of which derive from the distinctively Christian character of Rome. We realize that we have moved very far from the genealogical metaphor.

Yet the comparison of "Israel" and "Rome" with states, nations, peoples, and empires rests on and is generated by the genealogical metaphor. For now "Rome" is like "Israel" in a way in which no other state or nation is like "Israel," and, consequently, in the odd metaphors of Rome as an animal unlike other animals or Rome as an empire unlike other empires we have to appeal to a special relationship between "Rome" and "Israel." And that special relationship, already prepared, can only be genealogical. How so? Rome emerges as both like and also not-like "Israel," in ways in which no other nation is ever represented as "like-Israel"; and, it follows, "Israel" is like "Rome" in ways in which "Israel" is not like any other people or nation.

The most suggestive disposition of Rome as a matter of fact moved beyond the metaphor of the family. Esau is compared to a pig. The reason for the aptness of the analogy is simple. The pig exhibits public traits expected of a suitable beast, in that it shows a cloven hoof, such as the laws of acceptable beasts require. But the pig does not exhibit the inner traits of a suitable beast, in that it does not chew the cud. Accordingly, the pig confuses and deceives. The polemic against Esau = Rome is simple. Rome claims to be Israel in that it adheres to the Old Testament, that is, the written Torah of Sinai. Specifically, Rome is represented as only Christian Rome can have been represented: it superficially *looks* kosher but it is unkosher. Pagan Rome cannot ever have looked kosher, but Christian Rome, with its appeal to continuity with ancient Israel, could and did and moreover claimed to. It bore some traits that validate, but lacked others that validate – just as Jerome said of Israel. It would be difficult to find a more direct confrontation between two parties to an argument. Now the issue is the same: Who is the true Israel? and the proof texts are the same, and, moreover, the proof texts are read in precisely the same way. Only the conclusions differ!

The polemic represented in Genesis Rabbah and Leviticus Rabbah by the symbolization of Christian Rome makes the simple point, first, that Christians are no different from, and no better than, pagans; they are essentially the same. Christians' claim to form part of Israel then requires no serious attention. Because Christians came to Jews with precisely that claim, the sages' response – they are another Babylonia – bears a powerful polemic charge. But that is not the whole story, as we see. Second, just as Israel had survived Babylonia, Media, Greece, so would they endure to see the end of Rome (whether pagan, whether Christian). But there is a third point. Rome really does differ from the earlier, pagan empires, and that polemic shifts the entire discourse, once we hear its symbolic vocabulary properly. For the new Rome really did differ from the old. Christianity was not merely part of a succession of undifferentiated modes of paganism. The symbols assigned to Rome attributed worse, more dangerous traits than those assigned to the earlier empires. The pig pretends to be clean, just as the Christians give the signs of adherence to the God of Abraham, Isaac, and Jacob. That much the passage concedes. For the pig is not clean, exhibiting some, but not all, of the

required indications, and Rome is not Israel, even though it shares
Israel's Scripture.

And that brings us to that mixture of metaphors in which genealogy explains relationships between polities. Let us begin with a
simple example of how ubiquitous is the shadow of Ishmael/Esau/
Edom/Rome. Wherever in Genesis Rabbah sages reflect on future
history, their minds turn to their own day. They found the hour
difficult, because Rome, now Christian, claimed that very birthright
and blessing that they understood to be theirs alone. Christian Rome
posed a threat without precedent. Now another dominion, besides
Israel's, claimed the rights and blessings that sustained Israel. Wherever in Scripture they turned, sages found comfort in the iteration
that the birthright, the blessing, the Torah, and the hope all belonged
to them and to none other. Here is a striking statement of that constant proposition.

A. "[So she said to Abraham, 'Cast out this slave woman with her son,
for the son of this slave woman shall not be heir with my son Isaac.']
And the thing was very displeasing to Abraham on account of his son.
But God said to Abraham, 'Be not displeased because of the lad and
because of your slave woman; whatever Sarah says to you, do as she
tells you, for through Isaac shall your descendants be named'" (Gen.
21:12):

B. Said R. Yudan bar Shillum, "What is written is not 'Isaac' but 'through
Isaac.' [The matter is limited, not through all of Isaac's descendants but
only through some of them, thus excluding Esau.]"

Gen. R. LIII:XII.2

A. R. Azariah in the name of Bar Hutah, "The use of the B, which stands
for two, indicates that he who affirms that there are two worlds will
inherit both worlds [this age and the age to come]."

B. Said R. Yudan bar Shillum, "It is written, 'Remember his marvelous
works that he has done, his signs and the judgments of his mouth' (Ps.
105:5). I have given a sign, namely, it is one who gives the appropriate
evidence through what he says. Specifically, he who affirms that there
are two worlds will be called 'your seed.'

C. "And he who does not affirm that there are two worlds will not be
called 'your seed.'"

Gen. R. LIII:XII.3

Nos. 2 and 3 interpret the limiting particle, "in," that is, *among* the
descendants of Isaac will be found Abraham's heirs, but not all the
descendants of Isaac will be heirs of Abraham. No. 2 explicitly
excludes Esau, that is Rome, and No. 3 makes the matter doctrinal in
the context of Israel's inner life. As the several antagonists of Israel
stand for Rome in particular, so the traits of Rome, as sages perceived

them, characterized the biblical heroes. Esau provided a favorite target. From the womb Israel and Rome contended.

A.   "And the children struggled together [within her, and she said, 'If it is thus, why do I live?' So she went to inquire of the Lord. And the Lord said to her, 'Two nations are in your womb, and two peoples, born of you, shall be divided; the one shall be stronger than the other, and the elder shall serve the younger'] " (Gen. 25:22–3):

B.   R. Yohanan and R. Simeon b. Laqish:

C.   R. Yohanan said, "[Because the word, 'struggle,' contains the letters for the word, 'run,'] this one was running to kill that one and that one was running to kill this one."

D.   R. Simeon b. Laqish: "This one releases the laws given by that one, and that one releases the laws given by this one."

Gen. R. LXIII:VI.1

A.   R. Berekhiah in the name of R. Levi said, "It is so that you should not say that it was only after he left his mother's womb that [Esau] contended against [Jacob].

B.   "But even while he was yet in his mother's womb, his fist was stretched forth against him: 'The wicked stretch out their fists [so Freedman[1]] from the womb' (Ps. 58:4)."

Gen. R. LXIII:VI.2

A.   "And the children struggled together within her":

B.   [Once more referring to the letters of the word "struggled," with special attention to the ones that mean, "run,"] they wanted to run within her.

C.   When she went by houses of idolatry, Esau would kick, trying to get out: "The wicked are estranged from the womb" (Ps. 58:4).

D.   When she went by synagogues and study houses, Jacob would kick, trying to get out: "Before I formed you in the womb, I knew you (Jer. 1:5)."

Gen. R. LXIII:VI.3

A.   "Two nations are in your womb, [and two peoples, born of you, shall be divided; the one shall be stronger than the other, and the elder shall serve the younger]" (Gen. 25:23):

B.   There are two proud nations in your womb, this one takes pride in his world, and that one takes pride in his world.

C.   This one takes pride in his monarchy, and that one takes pride in his monarchy.

D.   There are two proud nations in your womb.

E.   Hadrian represents the nations, Solomon, Israel.

F.   There are two who are hated by the nations in your womb. All the nations hate Esau, and all the nations hate Israel.

G.   [Following Freedman's reading:] The one whom your creator hates is in your womb: "And Esau I hated" (Mal. 1:3).

Gen. R. LXIII:VII.2

A. "and two peoples, born of you, shall be divided":
B. Said R. Berekhiah, "On the basis of this statement we have evidence that [Jacob] was born circumcised."

Gen. R. LXIII:VII.3

A. ". . . the one shall be stronger than the other, [and the elder shall serve the younger]" (Gen. 25:23):
B. R. Helbo in the name of the house of R. Shila: "Up to this point there were Sabteca and Raamah, but from you will come Jews and Romans." [Freedman, p. 561, n. 8: "Hitherto even the small nations such as Sabteca and Raamah counted; but henceforth all these will pale into insignificance before the two who will rise from you."]

Gen. R. LXIII:VII.4

A. ". . . and the elder shall serve the younger" (Gen. 25:23):
B. Said R. Huna, "If he has merit, he will be served, and if not, he will serve."

Gen. R. LXIII:VII.5

The passage LXIII:VI.1–3 takes for granted that Esau represents Rome, and Jacob, Israel. Consequently the verse underlines the point that there is natural enmity between Israel and Rome. Esau hated Israel even while he was still in the womb. Jacob, for his part, revealed from the womb those virtues that would characterize him later on, eager to serve God as Esau was eager to worship idols. The text invites just this sort of reading, and LXIII:VII proceeds along the same lines. Rome is not really valid, any more than a pig, despite its public traits, is valid. Here we see a statement of that view, in the ample and handsomely articulated version of Leviticus Rabbah:

A. Moses foresaw what the evil kingdoms would do [to Israel].
B. "The camel, rock badger, and hare" (Deut. 14:7). [Compare: "Nevertheless, among those that chew the cud or part the hoof, you shall not eat these: the camel, because it chews the cud but does not part the hoof, is unclean to you. The rock badger, because it chews the cud but does not part the hoof, is unclean to you. And the hare, because it chews the cud but does not part the hoof, is unclean to you, and the pig, because it parts the hoof and is cloven-footed, but does not chew the cud, is unclean to you" (Lev. 11:4–8).]
C. The camel refers to Babylonia [in line with the following verse of Scripture: "O daughter of Babylonia, you who are to be devastated!], Happy will be he who requites you, with what you have done to us" (Ps. 147:8).
D. "The rock badger" (Deut. 14:7) – this refers to Media.
E. Rabbis and R. Judah b. R. Simon.
F. Rabbis say, "Just as the rock badger exhibits traits of uncleanness and traits of cleanness, so the kingdom of Media produced both a righteous man and a wicked one."

G.   Said R. Judah b. R. Simon, "The last Darius was Esther's son. He was clean on his mother's side and unclean on his father's side."

H.   "The hare" (Deut 14:7) – this refers to Greece. The mother of King Ptolemy was named "Hare" [in Greek: lagos].

I.   "The pig" (Deut. 14:7) – this refers to Edom [Rome].

J.   Moses made mention of the first three in a single verse and the final one in a verse by itself [(Deut. 14:7, 8)]. Why so?

K.   R. Yohanan and R. Simeon b. Laqish.

L.   R. Yohanan said, "It is because [the pig] is equivalent to the other three."

M.   And R. Simeon b. Laqish said, "It is because it outweighs them."

N.   R. Yohanan objected to R. Simeon b. Laqish, "'Prophesy, therefore, son of man, clap your hands [and let the sword come down twice, yea thrice]' (Ez. 21:14)."

O.   And how does R. Simeon b. Laqish interpret the same passage? He notes that [the threefold sword] is doubled (Ez. 21:14).

Gen. R. XIII:V.9

In the apocalypticizing of the animals of Lev. 11:4–8/Deut. 14:7 (the camel, rock badger, hare, and pig), the pig, standing for Rome, again emerges as different from the others and more threatening than the rest. Just as the pig pretends to be a clean beast by showing the cloven hoof but in fact is an unclean one, so Rome pretends to be just but in fact governs by thuggery. Edom does not pretend to praise God but only blasphemes. It does not exalt the righteous but kills them. These symbols concede nothing to Christian monotheism and veneration of the Torah of Moses (in its written medium). Of greatest importance, whereas all the other beasts bring further ones in their wake, the pig does not: "It does not bring another kingdom after it." It will restore the crown to the one who will truly deserve it, Israel. Esau will be judged by Zion (so Ob. 1:21). Now how has the symbolization delivered an implicit message? It is in the treatment of Rome as distinct, but essentially equivalent to the former kingdoms. This seems to me a stunning way of saying that the now-Christian empire in no way requires differentiation from its pagan predecessors. Nothing has changed, except matters have gotten worse. Beyond Rome, standing in a straight line with the others, lies the true shift in history, the rule of Israel and the cessation of the dominion of the (pagan) nations. Rome in the fourth century became Christian. Sages responded by facing that fact quite squarely and saying, "Indeed, it is as you say, a kind of Israel, an heir of Abraham as your texts explicitly claim. But we remain the sole legitimate Israel, the bearer of the birthright – we and not you. So you are our brother: Esau, Ishmael, Edom." And the rest follows.

The contrast between Israel and Esau produced the following

anguished observation. But here the Rome is not yet Christian, so far as the clear reference is concerned. A further important point was that Esau–Rome ruled now, but Jacob–Israel will follow in due course. This claim is made explicit:

A. "And Jacob sent messengers before him":
B. To this one [Esau] whose time to take hold of sovereignty would come before him [namely, before Jacob, since Esau would rule, then Jacob would govern].
C. R. Joshua b. Levi said, "Jacob took off the purple robe and threw it before Esau, as if to say to him, 'Two flocks of starlings are not going to sleep on a single branch' [so we cannot rule at the same time].'"

Lev. R. LXXV:IV.2

A. ". . . to Esau his brother":
B. Even though he was Esau, he was still his brother.

Lev. R. LXXV:IV.3

Nos. 2 and 3 make a stunning point. It is that Esau remains Jacob's brother, and that Esau rules before Jacob will. The application to contemporary affairs cannot be missed, both in the recognition of the true character of Esau – a brother! – and in the interpretation of the future of history. This same point is made in another way in the following:

A. "These are the kings who reigned in the land of Edom before any king reigned over the Israelites: Bela the son of Beor reigned in Edom, the name of his city being Dinhabah" (Gen. 36:31–2):
B. R. Isaac commenced discourse by citing this verse: "Of the oaks of Bashan they have made your oars" (Ez. 27:6).
C. Said R. Isaac, "The nations of the world are to be compared to a ship. Just as a ship has its mast made in one place and its anchor somewhere else, so their kings: 'Samlah of Masrekah' (Gen. 36:36), 'Shaul of Rehobot by the river' (Gen. 36:27), and: 'These are the kings who reigned in the land of Edom before any king reigned over the Israelites.'"

Lev. R. LXXXIII:I.1

A. ["An estate may be gotten hastily at the beginning, but the end thereof shall not be blessed" (Prov. 20:21)]: "An estate may be gotten hastily at the beginning": "These are the kings who reigned in the land of Edom before any king reigned over the Israelites."
B. ". . . but the end thereof shall not be blessed:" "And saviors shall come up on mount Zion to judge the mount of Esau" (Ob. 1:21).

Lev. R. LXXXIII:I.2

No. 1 contrasts the diverse origin of Roman rulers with the uniform origin of Israel's king in the house of David. No. 2 makes the same point still more forcefully. How so? Freedman makes sense of No. 2 as follows: Though Esau was the first to have kings, his land will even-

tually be overthrown (Freedman, p. 766, n. 3). So the point is that Israel will have kings after Esau no longer does, and the verse at hand is
made to point to the end of Rome, a striking revision to express the
importance in Israel's history to events in the lives of the patriarchs.

A. "These are the kings who reigned in the land of Edom before any king
    reigned over the Israelites: Bela the son of Beor reigned in Edom, the
    name of his city being Dinhabah" (Gen. 36:31–2):

B. Said R. Aibu, "Before a king arose in Israel, kings existed in Edom:
    'These are the kings who reigned in the land of Edom before any king
    reigned over the Israelites.'" [Freedman, p. 766, n. 4: "1 Kgs. 22:48
    states, 'There was no king in Edom, a deputy was king.' This refers to
    the reign of Jehoshaphat. Subsequently in Jehoram's reign, Edom
    revolted and 'made a king over themselves' (2 Kgs. 8:20). Thus from
    Saul to Jehoshaphat, in which Israel had eight kings, Edom had no king
    but was ruled by a governor of Judah. Aibu observes that this was to
    balance the present period, during which Edom had eight kings while
    Israel had none. For that reason, Aibu employs the word for deputy
    when he wishes to say 'existed' thus indicating a reference to the verse
    in the book of Kings quoted above."]

C. R. Yose bar Haninah said, "[Alluding to a mnemonic, with the first
    Hebrew letter for the word for kings, judges, chiefs, and princes:]
    When the one party [Edom] was ruled by kings, the other party [Israel]
    was ruled by judges, when one side was ruled by chiefs, the other side
    was ruled by princes."

D. Said R. Joshua b. Levi, "This one set up eight kings and that one set up
    eight kings. This one set up Bela, Jobab, Husham, Samlah, Shaul,
    Hadad, Baalhanan, and Hadar. The other side set up Saul, Ishbosheth,
    David, Solomon, Rehoboam, Abijah, Asa, and Jehoshaphat.

E. "Then Nebuchadnezzar came and overturned both: 'That made the
    world as a wilderness and destroyed the cities thereof' (Is. 14:17).

F. "Evil-merodach came and exalted Jehoiakin, Ahasuerus came and ex-
    alted Haman."

Lev. R. LXXXIII:II.1

The passage once more stresses the correspondence between
Israel's and Edom's governments, respectively. The reciprocal character of their histories is then stated in a powerful way, with the
further implication that, when the one rules, the other waits. So now
Israel waits, but it will rule. The same point is made in what follows,
but the expectation proves acute and immediate.

A. "Magdiel and Iram: these are the chiefs of Edom, that is Esau, the
    father of Edom, according to their dwelling places in the land of their
    possession" (Gen. 36:42):

B. On the day on which Litrinus came to the throne, there appeared to R.
    Ammi in a dream this message: "Today Magdiel has come to the
    throne."

C.   He said, "One more king is required for Edom [and then Israel's turn will come]."

Lev. R. LXXXIII:II.3

A.   Said R. Hanina of Sepphoris, "Why was he called Iram? For he is destined to amass [a word using the same letters] riches for the king-messiah."
B.   Said R. Levi, "There was the case of a ruler in Rome who wasted the treasuries of his father. Elijah of blessed memory appeared to him in a dream. He said to him, 'Your fathers collected treasures and you waste them.'
C.   "He did not budge until he filled the treasuries again."

Lev. R. LXXXIII:II.4

No. 3 presents once more the theme that Rome's rule will extend only for a foreordained and limited time, at which point the Messiah will come. No. 4 explains the meaning of the name Iram. The concluding statement also alleges that Israel's saints even now make possible whatever wise decisions Rome's rulers make. That forms an appropriate conclusion to the matter. Ending in the everyday world of the here and the now, we note that sages attribute to Israel's influence anything good that happens to Israel's brother, counterpart, opposite, whether family, whether polity, Rome.

iv.   Mixed Metaphor, Uniform Outcome

In the end, we are struck by the mixture of the two metaphors, the one appealing to genealogy, the other to polity. Representing "Israel" as singular invokes a narrowly political metaphor: nation or people, in the same genus as others, but, among them, singular and special by reason of service to God. But as soon as "Rome" enters discourse, that original metaphor fails, for reasons I regard as intrinsic to the conflicting claims. "Rome" too claims to serve God, the same God in the same way. The political metaphor fails, even while the political issues prevail. Accordingly, we find a reversion, when it comes to Rome in particular, to the genealogical metaphor, now framed in terms that, at their foundations, can be only political. So the "family" at one and the same time constitutes the "people" or "nation." The upshot is the same.

NOTES

---

1 M. Freedman, trans., *Genesis Rabbah* (London: Soncino Press, 1948). Hereafter cited as Freedman.

CHAPTER 9

"Israel" as Sui Generis

i. From Sentence to Statement: "Israel" in the Here and Now

Representing themselves as critical to the everyday governance of the Jews, sages in the documents of the second phase in the formation of the Judaism of the dual Torah took the view that the "Israel" that they saw every day formed a unique social entity. They concentrated their thought on the particularities of this "Israel," yielding a conception of "Israel" as sui generis, and in seeing "Israel" as unique they left off the matter of comparison, contrast, and classification. That too is, of course, a kind of metaphorization, because seeing the social group as unlike all other social groups represents an act of comparison and contrast too. This view of "Israel" as sui generis, sustained in the documents at hand as it was rare in the first set, we see in two blatant traits. First, we find a sustained interest in the natural laws governing "Israel" in particular, statements of the rules of the group's history viewed as a unique entity within time. Sentences out of the factual record of the past formed into a cogent statement of the laws of "Israel"'s destiny, laws unique to the social entity at hand. Second, the teleology of those laws for an Israel that was sui generis focused upon salvation at the end of history, that is, an eschatological teleology formed for a social entity embarked on its own lonely journey through time.

"Israel" beyond all metaphor, unavailable for comparison and contrast, that people "dwelling alone," thus was now the object of intense study on the part of the thoughtful sages, governing from day to day but also gazing beyond the far horizon. Indeed, I am inclined to think that seeing "Israel" as sui generis and not merely an abstraction and instrumentality for classification of entities may well represent a perspective natural to a group within the political class of the population. For, one may suppose, concrete issues in the here and now tended to highlight differences between group and group and to obliterate those points in common that permitted comparison and contrast in the philosophical mode. Portraying themselves as engaged with a real social group on a day-to-day basis, sages searched within the life of that group for the rules and orderly regulations that governed. Seeking commonalities of pattern, they centered their interest on what they deemed particular.

ii. The Rules of Nature, the Rules of History, and the Supernatural Governance of "Israel" in Leviticus Rabbah

The definition of "Israel" comes to us not only in what people expressly mean by the word, but also in the implicit terms yielded by how they discuss the social entity. In Leviticus Rabbah the conception of "Israel" as sui generis reaches expression in an implicit statement that Israel is subject to its own laws, which are distinct from the laws governing all other social entities. These laws may be discerned in the factual, scriptural record of "Israel"'s past, and that past, by definition, belonged to "Israel" alone. It followed, therefore, that by discerning the regularities in "Israel"'s history, implicitly understood as unique to "Israel," sages recorded the view that "Israel" like God was not subject to analogy or comparison. Accordingly, though not labeled a genus unto itself, Israel is treated in that way.

To understand how this view of "Israel" comes to expression, we have to trace the principal mode of thought characteristic of the authorship of Leviticus Rabbah.[1] It is an exercise in the proving of hypotheses by tests of concrete facts. The hypotheses derive from theology of Israel. The tests are worked out by reference to those given facts of social history that Scripture, for its part, contributes. As with the whole range of ancient exegetes of Scripture, typified in this context by Aphrahat and the rabbinic exegetes of Genesis Rabbah that were cited in the preceding chapter, so the authorship at hand treated Scripture as a set of facts. These facts concerned history, not nature, but they served, much as did the facts of nature availed the Greek natural philosophers, to prove or disprove hypotheses. The hypotheses concerned the social rules to which Israel was subjected. The upshot was that Israel was subject to its own rules, revealed by the historical facts of Scripture.

If I had to point to the single most common way in which sages made the implicit statement that "Israel" is sui generis, I would point to their "as if" mode of seeing "Israel"'s reality. Sages read "Israel"'s history not as it seems – that is, not as it would appear when treated in accord with the same norms as the histories of other social entities – but as a series of mysteries. The facts are not what appearances suggest. The deeper truth is not revealed in those events that happen, in common, to "Israel" and to (other) nations over the face of the earth. What is really happening to "Israel" is wholly other, different from what seems to be happening and what is happening to ordinary groups. The fundamental proposition pertinent to "Israel" in Leviticus Rabbah is that things are not what they seem. "Israel"'s reality does not correspond to the perceived facts of this world.

The source of this particular mode of thinking about "Israel" is easily identified. The beginning of seeing "Israel" as if it were other than the social group people saw lay in the original metaphorization of the social group. When people looked at themselves, their households and villages, their regions and language group, and thought to themselves, "What more are we? What else are we?" they began that process of abstraction that took the form of an intellectual labor of comparison, contrast, and analogy that led to metaphorization. The group is compared with something else (or to nothing else) and hence is treated as not fully represented by the here and the now but as representative, itself, of something else beyond. And that very mode of seeing things, lying in the foundations of the Mishnah's authorship's thought, implicit in the identification of the survivors as the present avatar of Scripture's "Israel," yielded an ongoing process of metaphorization. The original use of the metaphor "Israel," to serve as the explanation of who the surviving groups were, made it natural from that time forward to see "Israel" under the aspect of the "as if." How this mode of thought worked itself out in the documents at hand is clear. The exegetes at hand maintained that a given statement of Scripture, in the case of Leviticus, stood for and signified something other than that to which the verse openly referred. If – as was a given for these exegetes – water stands for Torah, the skin disease mentioned in Lev. 13 (in Hebrew called *saraat* and translated as leprosy) stands for and is caused by evil speech – the reference to some thing to mean some other thing entirely – then the mode of thought at hand is simple.

What is decisive for our inquiry is that *that mode of thought pertained to "Israel" alone*. Solely in the case of "Israel" did one thing symbolize another, speak not of itself but of some other thing entirely. When other social entities (e.g., Babylonia, Persia, or Rome) stood for something else, it was in relationship to "Israel" and in the context of the metaphorization of Israel. When treated in a natural context, by contrast, we find no metaphors – for example, Alexander of Macedonia in the story considered earlier is a person, and no symbol stands for that person. When Greece appears in the sequence of empires leading finally to the rule of "Israel," then Greece may be symbolized by the hare. From the opposite perspective, other symbols such as the bear and the eagle could stand for the empires, but – in that metaphorical context – then "Israel" stands only for itself. Whichever way we have it, therefore, implicit in that view and mode of thought is the notion of "Israel" as sui generis, lacking all counterpart or parallel entity for purposes of comparison and contrast. The importance of the mode of reading Scripture "as if" it meant something else than what it said, in the case of the exegesis of Leviticus Rabbah, should not be missed. What lies beneath or beyond the surface – there is the true reality, the world of truth and meaning.

This mode of thinking about "Israel" applies a prevailing hermeneutic. Specifically, in the authorship at hand – encompassing not only Leviticus Rabbah but a far broader sector of the sages' writings in this period – a common object or symbol really represented an uncommon one. Nothing says what it means. Everything important speaks metonymically, elliptically, parabolically, symbolically. All statements carry deeper meaning, which inheres in other statements altogether. Accordingly, if we ask the single prevalent literary construction to testify to the prevailing frame of mind, its message is that things are never what they seem. All things demand interpretation. Interpretation begins in the search for analogy, for that to which the thing is likened, hence the deep sense in which all exegesis at hand is parabolic. It is a quest for that for which the thing in its deepest structure stands. When sages represented "Israel" as sui generis in the manner just now spelled out, they therefore brought to bear upon that social entity, the social group, a mode of thought deriving initially from their manner of reading Scripture. When we consider their ordering of matters, we have further to observe that they read Scripture the way Scripture taught them, to begin with, to encounter God: "in our image, after our likeness," that is, metaphorically and parabolically. Once more we find ourselves following theological sociology into the realm of theological anthropology.

Because the exegetes by definition applied the mode of thought at hand solely to Israel and not to the nations, it follows, in my view, that Israel constituted an entity that was sui generis. For its affairs alone generated that search for a deeper, other meaning than the one that floated at the surface. The Jews of this period (and not then alone), so long used to calling themselves God's first love, now saw others with greater worldly reason claiming that same advantaged relationship.

Not in mind only, but still more in the politics of the world, the people that remembered its origins along with the very creation of the world and founding of humanity, that recalled how it alone served and serves the one and only God, for more than three hundred years had confronted a quite different existence. The radical disjuncture between the way things were and the way Scripture said things were supposed to be – and in actuality would some day become – surely imposed an unbearable tension. It was one thing for the slave born to slavery to endure. It was another for the free man sold into slavery to accept that same condition. The vanquished people, the nation that had lost its city and its temple, that had, moreover, produced another nation from its midst to take over its Scripture and much else, could not bear too much reality. That defeated people will then have found refuge in a mode of thought that trained vision to see things otherwise than as the eyes perceived them. Among the diverse ways by which the weak and subordinated accommodate to their circumstance, the one of iron-willed pretense in life is most likely to yield the mode of thought at hand: things never are, because they cannot be, what they seem.

What happens in Leviticus Rabbah is that, reading one thing in terms of something else, the builders of the document systematically adopted for Israel today the reality of the Scripture, its history and doctrines – again with the consequence that "Israel" constituted a social entity that was sui generis, now once more by definition. They transformed that unique history from a sequence of one-time events, leading from one place to some other, into an ever-present mythic world. No longer was there one Moses, one David, one set of happenings of a distinctive and never-to-be-repeated character. Now whatever happens, of which the thinkers propose to take account, must enter and be absorbed into that established and ubiquitous pattern and structure founded in the patterns of Scripture's truth. It is not that biblical history repeats itself. Rather, biblical history no longer constitutes history as a story of things that happened once long ago and pointed to some one moment in the future, but it becomes an account of things that happen every day – hence, an ever-present mythic world. "Israel" now lived on a mythic plane of being, an eternity that happened to be caught up in time, so to speak, but truly, a social entity different in genus, not only in species.

What the sages of Leviticus Rabbah now proposed was a reconstruction of Israel's social existence along the lines of the ancient design of Scripture as they read it. What that meant was that everything that happened was turned from a sequence of one-time and linear events into a repetition of known and already experienced paradigms – hence, once more, a mythic being of a unique social entity. The source and core of the myth, of course, derive from Scripture, which was reread, renewed, and reconstructed along with the society that revered Scripture. So, to summarize, the mode of thought that dictated the issues and the logic of the document, telling the thinkers to see one thing in terms of something else, addressed Scripture in particular and collectively. Thinking as they did, the framers of the document saw Scripture in a new way, just as they saw their own circumstance afresh, rejecting their world in favor of Scripture's, reliving Scripture's world in their own terms.

The doctrinal substance of the theory of Israel as sui generis may be stated in a single paragraph.

God loves Israel (now without its quotation marks), so gave them the Torah, which defines their life and governs their welfare (the position noted previously, when God explains God's particular concern for "Israel" by reason of "Israel"'s cleaving to God). Israel is alone in its category (sui generis), proved by the fact that what is a virtue to Israel is a vice to the nation, life giving to Israel, poison to the gentiles. True, Israel sins, but God forgives that sin, having punished the nation on account of it. Such a process has yet to come to an end, but it will culminate in Israel's complete regeneration. Meanwhile, Israel's assurance of God's love lies in the many expressions of special concern, for even the humblest and most ordinary aspects of the national life: the food the nation eats, the sexual practices by which it procreates. These life-sustaining, life-transmitting activities draw God's special interest, as a mark of his general love for Israel. Israel then is supposed to achieve its life in conformity with the marks of God's love. These indications moreover signify also the character of Israel's difficulty, namely, subordination to the nations in general but to the fourth kingdom, Rome, in particular. Both food laws and skin diseases stand for the nations. There is yet another category of sin, also collective and generative of collective punishment, and that is social. The moral character of Israel's life, the treatment of people by one another, the practice of gossip and small-scale thuggery – these too draw down divine penalty. The nation's fate therefore corresponds to its moral condition. The moral condition, however, emerges not only from the current generation. Israel's richest hope lies in the merit of the ancestors, thus in the Scriptural record of the merits attained by the founders of the nation, those who originally brought it into being and gave it life.

If we now ask about further recurring themes or topics, there is one that is utterly commonplace. It is expressed by recurrent lists of events in Israel's (unique) history, meaning, in this context, Israel's history solely in scriptural times, down through the return to Zion. The lists again and again ring the changes on the one-time events of the generation of the flood; Sodom and Gomorrah; the patriarchs and the sojourn in Egypt; the exodus; the revelation of the Torah at Sinai; the golden calf; the Davidic monarchy and the building of the Temple; Sennacherib, Hezekiah, and the destruction of northern Israel; Nebuchadnezzar and the destruction of the temple in 586 B.C.E.; the life of Israel in Babylonian captivity; Daniel and his associates, Mordecai and Haman. These events occur over and over again. They turn out to serve as paradigms of the everyday social reality of the community of Israel, perceived in the here and now: an "as if" way of speaking about the social facts of sin and atonement, steadfastness and divine intervention, and equivalent lessons. We find, in fact, a fairly standard repertoire of scriptural heroes or villains, on the one side, and conventional lists of Israel's enemies and their actions and downfall, on the other. The boastful, for instance, include the generation of the flood, Sodom and Gomorrah, Pharaoh, Sisera, Sennacherib, Nebuchadnezzar, the wicked empire (Rome) – all in contrast to Israel, "despised and humble in this world." The four kingdoms recur again and again, always ending, of course, with Rome, with the repeated message that after Rome will come Israel. But Israel has to make this happen through its faith and submission to God's will. Lists of enemies ring the changes on Cain, the Sodomites, Pharaoh, Sennacherib, Nebuchadnezzar, Haman.

Accordingly, the mode of thought brought to bear upon the theme of "Israel," now with reference to Israel's (unique) history, remains exactly the same as in the Mishnaic stratum: classification, accomplished through list making, with data exhibiting similar taxonomic traits drawn together into lists based on common monothetic traits or definitions. But the outcome of the inquiry into the social rules of "Israel" viewed as a problem in natural philosophy is not the same as in the Mishnaic system. Where the making of rules yielded an "Israel" in genus like, in species unlike, other social entities, now the discovery of rules produced an "Israel" that was sui generis. For the lists through the power of repetition make a single enormous point and prove a social law of history. The catalogs of exemplary heroes and historical events provide a model of how contemporary events are to be absorbed into the biblical paradigm unique to "Israel." Because biblical events exemplify recurrent happenings, sin and redemption, forgiveness and atonement, they lose their one-time character. At the same time and in the same way, current events find a place within the ancient, but eternally present, paradigmatic scheme. So no new historical events, other than exemplary episodes in lives of heroes, demand narration because, through what is said about the past, what was happening in the times of the framers of Leviticus Rabbah would also come under consideration. This mode of dealing with biblical history and contemporary events produces two reciprocal effects. The first is the mythicization of biblical stories, their removal from the framework of ongoing, unique patterns of history and sequences of events and their transformation into accounts of things that happen all the time. The second is that contemporary events too lose all of their specificity and enter the paradigmatic framework of established mythic existence. So the Scripture's myth happens every day, and every day produces reenactment of the Scripture's myth. That is, in concrete terms, what it means to state what of a unique entity cannot be said. If we speak of an entity unlike all others, then, by rights, we should not be able to make intelligible statements. But, as we see, sages can and do.

The outcome of the "as if" mode of thought is to restate everything in an unexpected way. That is why the message of Leviticus Rabbah attaches itself to the book of Leviticus, as if that book had come from prophecy and addressed the issue of history and salvation. But Leviticus came from the priesthood and spoke of sanctification. The paradoxical syllogism – the as if reading, the opposite of how things seem – of the composers of Leviticus Rabbah therefore reaches simple formulation. In the very setting of sanctification we find the promise of salvation. In the topics of the cult and the priesthood we uncover the national and social issues of the moral life and redemptive hope of Israel. The repeated comparison and contrast of priesthood and prophecy, sanctification and salvation, turn out to produce a complement, which comes to most perfect union in the text at hand. The basic mode of thought – denial of what is at hand in favor of a deeper reality – proves remarkably apt. The substance of thought concerning the unique social entity, beyond all metaphor, confronts the acute crisis of the present circumstance:

Are we lost for good to the fourth empire, now-Christian Rome? No, we may yet be saved.

Has God rejected us forever? No, aided by the merit of the patriarchs and matriarchs and of the Torah and religious duties, we gain God's love.

What must we do to be saved? We must *do* nothing, we must *be* something: sanctified.

That status we gain through keeping the rules that make Israel holy. So salvation is through sanctification, all embodied in Leviticus read as rules for the holy people.

The Messiah will come not because of what a pagan emperor does or, indeed, because of Jewish action either, but because of Israel's own moral condition. When Israel enters the right relationship with God, then God will respond to Israel's condition by restoring things to their proper balance. Israel cannot, but need not, so act as to force the coming of the Messiah. Israel can attain the condition of sanctification, by forming a moral and holy community, so that God's response will follow the established prophecy of Moses and the prophets. So the basic doctrine of Leviticus Rabbah is the metamorphosis of Leviticus. Instead of holy caste, we deal with holy people. Instead of holy place, we deal with holy community, in its holy land. The deepest exchange between reality and inner vision, therefore, comes at the very surface: the rereading of Leviticus in terms of a different set of realities from those to which the book, on the surface, relates. No other biblical book would have served so well; it had to be Leviticus. Only through what the framers did on that particular book could they deliver their astonishing message and vision.

In their reflection on "Israel" as a unique entity, the authorship of Leviticus Rabbah pursued knowledge much as did philosophers, indeed, natural philosophers. Greek science focused upon physics. Then the laws of Israel's salvation serve as the physics of the sages. But Greek science derived facts and built theorems on the basis of other sources besides physics; the philosophers also studied ethnography, ethics, politics, and history. What made Greek science science was its power of generalization, of following curiosity beyond the case at hand. Similarly, for the sages, parables, exemplary tales, and completed paragraphs of thought deriving from other sources (not to exclude the Mishnah, Tosefta, Sifra, Genesis Rabbah, and such literary compositions that had been made ready for the Talmud of the Land of Israel) make their contribution of data subject to analysis. All of these sources of truth, all together, were directed toward the discovery of philosophical laws of history. But these laws were for the understanding of Israel's life, now and in the age to come, and concerned that generality, all of humanity, only through the anthropology beginning with "Israel" as the counterpart and opposite of the fallen Adam. In so stating, we have moved far beyond our original inquiry, because we have discovered, not for the first time, how theological sociology leads us backward toward that theological anthropology that, in the Judaism of the dual Torah, weighed in the balance the first Adam against Israel (again, no quotation marks) and found in Israel not the social entity but the model and likeness, "in our image, after our likeness," of what it meant to be human, like

God. These observations carry us far beyond the limits of this book, namely, to a later inquiry, into the personality of God and the theological metaphors of Judaism.

Israel thus emerges as a unique social entity. What we have in Leviticus Rabbah, therefore, is the result of the mode of thought not of prophets or historians but of philosophers and scientists. The framers propose not to lay down but to discover rules governing Israel's life. I state with necessary emphasis: As we find the rules of nature by identifying and classifying facts of natural life, so we find rules of society by identifying and classifying the facts of Israel's social life. In both modes of inquiry we make sense of things by bringing together like specimens and finding out whether they form a species, then bringing together like species and finding out whether they form a genus – in all, classifying data and identifying the rules that make possible the classification. That sort of thinking lies at the deepest level of list making, which is, as I said, work of offering a proposition and facts (for social rules) as much as a genus and its species (for rules of nature). Once discovered, the social rules of Israel's national life of course yield explicit statements, such as that God hates the arrogant and loves the humble. The readily assembled syllogism follows: If one is arrogant, God will hate him, and if he is humble, God will love him.

The logical status of these syllogistic statements, based on facts and yielding propositions of their own to which reasonable persons must accede, in context is as secure and unassailable as the logical status of statements about physics, ethics, or politics, as these emerge in philosophical thought. What differentiates the statements is not their logical status – as sound, scientific philosophy – but only their subject matter, on the one side, and distinctive rhetoric, on the other. The heart of the matter lies in laying forth the rules of life – of Israel's life and salvation. These rules – particular to their subject, which is therefore sui generis – derive from the facts of history, as much as the rules of the Mishnah derive from the facts of society (and, in context, the rules of philosophy derive from the facts of nature). In their search for the rules of Israel's life and salvation, sages in Leviticus Rabbah found their answer not in the one-time events of history but in paradigmatic facts, social laws of salvation of the unique social entity. The perspective of "Israel" in the here and now has produced an astonishing vision indeed, one that translates the everyday into eternal verities concerning a unique society-people-nation. And we have therefore to ask why. The answer derives in my view from the standpoint, in that society and nation, of the sages represented by our documents' authorships.

iii. The Sage and "Israel"'s Governance, and "Israel"'s Salvation in the Yerushalmi

The Judaism of the dual Torah represents the social entity "Israel" not only as subject to laws pertaining only to that entity. That same system, in its second formative period, also defines in unique terms the teleology of that same social entity. These terms once more express the conception of Israel as sui generis, because, as a matter of definition and doctrine, the salvific, eschatological teleology can apply solely to Israel, severally and jointly. The goal of the Judaic system at hand centers upon the social group, not the individual or any class of individuals within the group, and marks for salvation – as the Mishnah's statement of the matter in its taxonomic terms has already suggested – the group as a whole. But the second phase of the system as represented by the Yerushalmi portrays that systemic teleology, with its social focus, in a very special way. And that portrait leads us deep into the formative processes of that same metaphorical thinking, the results of which lie spread out before us.

To state my thesis simply: We have in the writings of the sages the statement of how a social group, thinking about a social group, writes large its conception of itself. The thesis is in two parts. First, what we have in the authoritative literature at hand is the consensus of a small group of sages, hence the thought of a social group. And the consensus addresses the encompassing social group, all the Jews, or "Israel." Accordingly, we deal with a social group thinking about a social group. The substance of that doctrine of the group, the shape of that social metaphor, second, tells us how that group sees the social entity in its own image. For that small group, the sages, testifies concerning its shared vision, and, we shall see with great clarity, when that small group expresses its vision for the sheltering society imagined to encompass the world beyond, that vision of the whole highlights traits remarkably congruent to the characteristics, in the ideal form at least, of the small social group responsible for the larger vision.

The portrait of the sages' role in society, as they lay matters out, alerts us to what is at stake for them in their theory of "Israel" as sui generis. For the teleological doctrine of the sages, as it encompasses all Israel, endows with the traits of those sages' social group in particular the larger nation or people in general. The pertinence to the proposition of Israel as sui generis then is straightforward. Israel is sui generis in that it exhibits the traits of the sages, and the sages' group's traits, for their part, have no counterpart, in sages' view, in this world but only in heaven. In God's image, after God's likeness, Moses "our rabbi" forms the model for sages, and sages, for "Israel."[2] When, therefore, we grasp the salvific doctrine that expresses the sages' teleology for the system as a whole, we shall see the result of how a group of clerk-lawyer-philosopher-wonderworkers projected outward, onto "Israel," those traits of supernatural standing that to begin with it fantasized for itself.

Sages' shared consensus did not provide for the individual, except as part of the group, Israel. This we saw in the first, and rather sparse, statement of Israel as sui generis: The group as a whole was destined for a single fate, from which, for unfortunate convictions, individuals might exempt themselves. For both the nation and the individual, the systemic teleology had to be the same – to attain salvation. For the individual that meant the life of the world to come, and for the nation, the return to, and restoration of, Jerusalem and its holy temple. The system's teleology is not stated with great frequency in discourse even on theological issues: It is never expressed in a clear way in discussion of legal ones. Yet, once emerging with force and authority, the purpose of the system as a whole is amply clear. The profundity of the message, its decisive place at the center and heart of matters, and its power to impart to the Judaism to which the Judaism of the dual Torah attests life force and meaning – all become self-evident, once a statement of the ultimate and critical points of insistence comes forth. The premise of that statement proves pertinent to our inquiry. It is that Israel is absolutely sui generis, having no counterpart in any other social entity on the face of the earth.

We recall that in Leviticus Rabbah the first premise of the social entity as sui generis was its yielding social laws particular to itself. The teleological shape of these laws forms the second premise. It is to secure the salvation of the social entity. The keeping of the law as the sages defined and kept it defined the condition of salvation, with the consequence that what marked the individual Jew as different, his or her adherence to certain customs or ceremonies, was raised to the level of social definition through the systemic teleology. The Yerushalmi expressly links salvation to keeping the law. This means that the issues of the law were drawn upward into the highest realm of Israelite consciousness. Keeping the law in the right way is represented as not merely right or expedient. It is the way to bring the Messiah, the son of David. This is stated by Levi, as follows:

X.   Said R. Levi, "If Israel would keep a single Sabbath in the proper way, forthwith the son of David would come.

Y.   "What is the Scriptural basis for this view? 'Moses said, Eat it today, for today is a sabbath to the Lord; today you will not find it in the field' (Ex. 16:25)."

Z. And it says, "For thus said the Lord God, the Holy One of Israel, 'In returning and rest you shall be saved; in quietness and in trust shall be your strength. And you would not' (Is. 30:15)."

Y. Ta. 1:1.IX

The coming of the Messiah, moreover, was explicitly linked to the destruction of the temple. How so? The Messiah was born on the day the temple was destroyed. Accordingly, as the following story makes explicit, the consolation for the destruction of the temple lay in the coming of the son of David.

A. The rabbis said, "This messiah king if he comes from among the living, David will be his name; if he comes from among the dead, it will be David himself."

B. Said R. Tanhuma, "I say that the Scriptural basis for this teaching is, 'And he shows steadfast love to his messiah, to David and his descendants forever' (Ps. 18:50)."

C. R. Joshua b. Levi said, "'Sprout' (semah) is his name."

D. R. Yudan, son of R. Aibo, said, "Menahem is his name."

E. Said Hananiah son of R. Abahu, "They do not disagree. The numerical value of the letters of one name equals the numerical value of the other – semah (= 138) is equal to menahem (= 138)."

F. And this story supports the view of R. Yudan son of R. Aibo. "Once a Jew was plowing and his ox snorted once before him. An Arab who was passing and heard the sound said to him, 'Jew, loosen your ox and loosen the plow and stop plowing. For today your Temple was destroyed.'

G. "The ox snorted again. He [the Arab] said to him, 'Jew, bind your ox and bind your plow. For today the messiah king was born.' He said to him, 'What is his name?' 'Menahem.' He said to him, 'What is his father's name?' He said to him, 'Hezekiah.' He said to him, 'Where is he from?' He said to him, 'From the royal capital of Bethlehem in Judea.'

H. "He went and sold his ox and sold his plow. And he became a peddler of infants' felt clothes. And he went from place to place until he came to that very city. All of the women bought from him. But Menahem's mother did not buy from him. He heard the women saying, 'Menahem's mother, Menahem's mother, come buy for your child.' She said, 'I want to bring him up to hate Israel. For on the day he was born the Temple was destroyed.' They said to her, 'We are sure that on this day it was destroyed and on this day it will be rebuilt.'

I. "She said to him [the peddler], 'I have no money.' He said to her, 'It is no matter to me. Come and buy for him and pay me when I return.' A while later he returned to that city. He said to her, 'How is the infant doing?' She said to him, 'Since the time you saw him a wind came and carried him off away from me.'"

Y. Ber. 2:3 [Zahavy[3]]

These two stories provide a glimpse into a far larger corpus of theories about the coming of the Messiah. The former, as we have noted, explicitly links the coming of the Messiah to the proper observance of the law as sages propound and exemplify it. The story bears ample proof of how the sages' thought about their own group extends to the definitive traits of the sheltering society of Israel beyond. When I represent the sages' doctrine of "Israel" as the outcome of a small social group's thought about a larger social group, the story at hand provides a fine instance of the matter.

The latter story presents a series of rather generalized messianic sayings and in no way addresses the distinctive concerns of rabbis and clerks. What is the given of the story makes the deepest impression on us. It is the representation of the Messiah as – of course – a sage or rabbi, hence the "rabbinization" of the messianic hope. Here we find the key to the larger theory of "Israel" as sui generis. It is "Israel"'s Messiah in the model of the sage, who for his part is sui generis among "Israel," in the model of Moses, our rabbi, "in our image, after our likeness."

We should not ignore, of course, the political utility of the doctrine. The "rabbinization" of the messianic hope required its neutralization, so that people's hopes would not be raised prematurely, with consequent, incalculable damage to the defeated nation. This meant, first of all, that rabbis insisted the Messiah would come in a process extending over a long period of time, thus not imposing a caesura upon the existence of the nation and disrupting its ordinary life. Accordingly, the Yerushalmi treats the messianic hope as something gradual, to be worked toward, not a sudden cataclysmic event. That conception was fully in accord with the notion that the everyday deeds of people formed a pattern continuous with the salvific history of Israel.

A. One time R. Hiyya the Elder and R. Simeon b. Halapta were walking in the valley of Arabel at daybreak. They saw that the light of the morning star was breaking forth. Said R. Hiyya the Elder to R. Simeon b. Halapta, "Son of my master, this is what the redemption of Israel is like – at first, little by little, but in the end it will go along and burst into light.

B. "What is the Scriptural basis for this view? 'Rejoice not over me, O my enemy; when I fall, I shall rise; when I sit in darkness, the Lord will be a light to me' (Mic. 7:8).

C. "So, in the beginning, 'When the virgins were gathered together the second time, Mordecai was sitting at the king's gate' (Est. 2:19).

D. "But afterward: 'So Haman took the robes and the horse, and he arrayed Mordecai and made him ride through the open square of the city, proclaiming, Thus shall it be done to the man whom the king delights to honor' (Est. 6:11).

E.   "And in the end: 'Then Mordecai went out from the presence of the king in royal robes of blue and white, with a great golden crown and a mantle of fine linen and purple, while the city of Susa shouted and rejoiced' [Est. 8:15].

F.   "And finally: 'The Jews had light and gladness and joy and honor' (Est. 8:16)."

Y. Yoma 3:2.III

We may regard the emphasis upon the slow but steady advent of the Messiah's day as entirely consonant with the notion that the Messiah will come when Israel's condition warrants it. The improvement in standards of observing the Torah, therefore, to be effected by the nation's obedience to the clerks will serve as a guidepost on the road to redemption. The moral condition of the nation ultimately guarantees salvation. God will respond to Israel's regeneration, planning all the while to save the saved, that is, those who save themselves. The implicit conviction of "Israel" as sui generis hardly requires repetition at this point. The doctrine of salvation as it applies to the social entity, living in accord with laws that apply only to that entity, provides ample evidence for what it means to regard a social entity, a group, as unlike all (other) groups.

What is most interesting in Yerushalmi's picture is that the hope for the Messiah's coming is further joined to the moral condition of each individual Israelite. Hence the messianic fulfillment was made to depend on the repentance of Israel, which stands for the universal conformity to the sages' model. The entire drama, envisioned by others in earlier types of Judaism as a world-historical event, was reworked in context into a moment in the life of the individual and the people of Israel collectively. The coming of the Messiah depended not on historical action but on moral regeneration. So from a force that moved Israelites to take up weapons on the battlefield, the messianic hope and yearning were transformed into motives for spiritual regeneration and ethical behavior. The energies released in the messianic fervor were then linked to rabbinic government, through which Israel would form the godly society.

J.   "'The oracle concerning Dumah. One is calling to me from Seir, "Watchman, what of the night? Watchman, what of the night?" (Is. 21:11).'"

K.   The Israelites said to Isaiah, "O our Rabbi, Isaiah, What will come for us out of this night?"

L.   He said to them, "Wait for me, until I can present the question."

M.   Once he had asked the question, he came back to them.

N. They said to him, "Watchman, what of the night? What did the Guardian of the ages tell you?"

O. He said to them, "The watchman says: 'Morning comes; and also the night. If you will inquire, inquire; come back again' (Is. 21:12)."

P. They said to him, "Also the night?"

Q. He said to them, "It is not what you are thinking. But there will be morning for the righteous, and night for the wicked, morning for Israel, and night for idolaters."

R. They said to him, "When?"

S. He said to them, "Whenever you want, He too wants [it to be] – if you want it, He wants it."

T. They said to him, "What is standing in the way?"

U. He said to them, "Repentance: 'Come back again' (Is. 21:12)."

V. R. Aha in the name of R. Tanhum b. R. Hiyya, "If Israel repents for one day, forthwith the son of David will come.

W. "What is the Scriptural basis? 'If today you would hearken to his voice'" (Ps. 95:7).

Y. Ta. 1:1:IX

What serves the present argument concerning the available social metaphors – in this case, the unique and incomparable character of "Israel" – is the statement clearly presented in the story that Israel's social definition and character are what govern Israel's salvation.

The case I proposed at the outset to make, that Israel is conceived to be sui generis, and that the systemic teleology amply expressed that conception, can enjoy no more complete demonstration than in the stories we have reviewed, representative as they are of the sages' consensus as portrayed by the Yerushalmi. The rule of Heaven and the learning and authority of the rabbi on earth were identified with one another. Salvation for Israel depended upon adherence to the sage and acceptance of his discipline. Both God's will in Heaven and the sage's words on earth constituted Torah. And Israel would be saved through Torah, so the sage was the savior. All of these doctrines, critical to the teleology of the Yerushalmi's version of the Judaism of the dual Torah, expressed at their foundations a single conviction – that Israel, God's nation, conformed to a different law from the nations, worked out a history that was subject to its own rules, and constituted a social entity with no counterpart, not merely as to species but especially as to genus.

What made Israel a unique society was its possession of the Torah – a perspective surely distinctive to sages, masters as they were of the Torah in the way in which they thought the Torah should be read. From the sages' perspective, Israel in the model of the Torah from Heaven constituted Heaven's projection onto earth. Analysis of traditions on earth corresponded to the discovery of the principles of creation; the full realization of the teachings of Torah on earth, in the life of Israel, would transform Israel into a replica of heaven on earth. It was an axiom of all forms of Judaism that, because Israel had sinned, it was punished by being given over into the hands of earthly empires; when it atoned, it was, and again would be, removed from their power. The means of atonement, reconciliation with God, were specified by the sages' system as study of Torah, practice of commandments, and doing good deeds. Why so? The answer is distinctive to the matrix of the sages' system. And the proposition at hand completes the argument for the view that, in the sages' statement of "Israel" as sui generis, they expressed, concerning the larger group, the consensus of that smaller group they themselves composed. To state matters with emphasis:

When Jews in general had mastered Torah, they would become rabbis, just as some now had become rabbis, saints, or holy men. When *all* Jews had become rabbis, they would no longer lie within the power of the nations, that is, of history. *Then* the Messiah would come. Redemption then depended upon all Israel's accepting the yoke of the Torah. At that point all Israel would attain a full and complete embodiment of Torah, revelation, as the sages taught it. Then all Israel would fulfill its unique character and destiny.

Thus conforming to God's will and replicating Heaven, Israel on earth, as a righteous, holy community would exercise the supernatural power of Torah. They would be able as a whole to do what some few saintly rabbis now could do. With access to supernatural power, redemption would naturally follow. When we contemplate the case of a small group's expressing a consensus on the character and destiny of the larger social entity, we now see in a clear way the meaning of that mode of social reflection. The sage exercised supernatural power as a kind of living Torah, his very deeds served to reveal law, as much as his word expressed revelation. The sage stood for the larger society, the social entity, Israel. That this fundamental fact reached expression in the reading of Scripture itself, as we shall now see, constitutes the proof for the proposed interpretation of the social metaphor before us.

The clearest picture of the Yerushalmi's theory of Israel's salvation – therefore of Israel's status as a social entity that is sui generis – is to be found in the sages' reading of Scripture. Specifically, the worldview projected by them upon the heroes of ancient Israel most clearly reveals the Yerushalmi's sages' view of themselves and their world. Sages naturally took for granted that the world they knew in the fourth century had flourished a thousand and more years earlier. The values they embodied and the supernatural powers they fantasized for themselves were projected backward onto biblical figures. Seeing Scripture in their own model, sages took the position that the Torah of old, its supernatural power and salvific promise, in their own day continued to endure – among themselves. In consequence, the promise of salvation contained in every line of Scripture was to be kept in every deed of learning and obedience to the law effected under their auspices. So while they projected backward the things they cherished in an act of (to us) extraordinary anachronism, in their eyes they carried forward, to their own time, the promise of salvation for Israel contained within the written Torah of old.

If David, King of Israel, was like a rabbi today, then a rabbi today would be the figure of the son of David who was to come as King of Israel. It is not surprising, therefore, that among the many biblical heroes whom the talmudic rabbis treated as sages, principal and foremost was David himself, now made into a messianic rabbi or a rabbinic Messiah. He was the sage of the Torah, the avatar and model for the sages of their own time. That view was made explicit, both specifically and in general terms. I give one striking expression of the proposition at hand. If a rabbi was jealous to have his traditions cited in his own name, it was because that was David's explicit view as well. In more general terms, both David and Moses are represented as students of Torah, just like the disciples and sages of the current time.

A. It is written, "And David said longingly, 'O that someone would give me water to drink from the well of Bethlehem [which is by the gate]'" (1 Chron. 11:17).
B. R. Hiyya bar Ba said, "He required a teaching of law."
C. "Then the three mighty men broke through [the camp of the Philistines]" (1 Chron. 11:18).
D. Why three? Because the law is not decisively laid down by fewer than three.
E. "But David would not drink of it; [he poured it out to the Lord, and said, 'Far be it from me before my God that I should do this. Shall I drink the lifeblood of these men? For at the risk of their lives they brought it']" (1 Chron. 11:18–19).
F. David did not want the law to be laid down in his own name.
G. "He poured it out to the Lord" – establishing [the decision] as [an unattributed] teaching for the generations, [so that the law should be authoritative and so be cited anonymously].

Y. San. 2:6.IV

O. David himself prayed for mercy for himself, as it is said, "Let me dwell in thy tent for ever! Oh to be safe under the shelter of thy wings, selah" (Ps. 61:4).
P. And did it enter David's mind that he would live for ever?

Q. But this is what David said before the Holy One, blessed be he, "Lord of the world, may I have the merit that my words will be stated in synagogues and schoolhouses."

R. Simeon b. Nazira in the name of R. Isaac said, "Every disciple in whose name people cite a teaching of law in this world – his lips murmur with him in the grave, as it is said, 'Your kisses are like the best wine that goes down smoothly, gliding over lips of those that sleep' (Song 7:9).

S. "Just as in the case of a mass of grapes, once a person puts his finger in it, forthwith even his lips begin to smack, so the lips of the righteous, when someone cites a teaching of law in their names – their lips murmur with them in the grave."

Y. Sheq. 2:4.V

O. "I will awake the dawn" (Ps. 5:7, 8) – I will awaken the dawn; the dawn will not awaken me.

P. David's [evil] impulse tried to seduce him [to sin]. And it would say to him, "David. It is the custom of kings that awakens them. And you say, I will awake the dawn. It is the custom of kings that they sleep until the third hour [of the day]. And you say, At midnight I rise." And [David] used to say [in reply], "[I rise early] because of thy righteous ordinances (Ps. 119:62)."

Q. And what would David do? R. Phineas in the name of R. Eleazar b. R. Menahem [said], "[He used to take a harp and lyre and set them at his bedside. And he would rise at midnight and play them so that the associates of Torah should hear. And what would the associates of Torah say? 'If David involves himself with Torah, how much more so should we.' We find that all of Israel was involved in Torah [study] on account of David."

Y. Berakhot 1:1.XII [Zahavy]

E. R. Yohanan, "All these forty days that Moses served on the mountain, he studied the Torah but forgot it. In the end it was given to him as a gift. All this why? So as to bring the stupid students back to their studies [when they become discouraged]."

Y. Horayot 3:5.I

This long extract has shown us how the Talmud's authorities readily saw their concerns in biblical statements attributed to David. "Water" meant "a teaching of Torah." "Three mighty men" were of course judges. At issue was whether the decision was to be stated in David's own name – and so removed from the authoritative consensus of sages. David exhibits precisely those concerns for the preservation of his views in his name that, in earlier sections, we saw attributed to rabbis.

All of this scarcely conceals the sages' deeper convictions, for, we remember, David the rabbi also was in everyone's mind David the

Messiah. The principal development attested by the Yerushalmi is the figure of the sage, honored with the title of rabbi, his centrality in the social and salvific world of the Jewish nation. Sages so defined the national historical life of Israel that it was matched by and joined to the local and private life of the village. The whole social entity "Israel" thereby served as a paradigm of ultimate perfection, sanctification and hence salvation. I can imagine no more decisive proof for the conviction that "Israel" constituted a social entity that was in genus, not solely in species, absolutely unique on the face of the earth. The closer the sages came to the everyday realities of "Israel"'s life, the more concrete the abstraction "Israel" became, and the more the sages represented the abstraction – beginning with themselves and their most concrete social group (not merely "entity") – as an "Israel" that was not merely particular but unique.

NOTES

1 I must confess that of all rabbinic documents I have studied beginning to end and attempted to describe in a systematic and thorough way, Leviticus Rabbah turned out to be the single most subtle and attractive one. Since I found myself profoundly moved by all of the writings of late antiquity I have translated and analyzed, that is a considerable judgment.
2 And "Israel," in proper context, for Adam. But that comes in a later study, as I have said.
3 Tzvee Zahavy, *The Talmud of the Land of Israel: I. Berakhot* (Chicago: University of Chicago Press, in press). Hereafter cited as Zahavy.

CHAPTER 10

The Second Phase of the Judaism of the Dual Torah and Its Social Metaphors

i.   Intransitive "Israel"

The single remarkable fact before us has proved so obvious as not to require much comment. It is the concrete and this-worldly way in which sages in the surveyed writings thought about "Israel." The social component of their Judaism, "Israel" now circulated in discourse not as an abstraction but as a concrete and palpable social fact: a real group of people thoughtfully imagined, profoundly loved, intimately known – a social group in the concrete sense defined in Chapter 1. Thus "Israel" found definition in its own terms, meaning what "we" are absolutely, and not principally in terms of who, or what, an "Israel" – an "it" – was not. The reason that that concrete trait of mind is remarkable obviously derives from the comparison with the manner of thought about "Israel" and its definition that we found characteristic of the writings of the earlier phase in the formation of Judaism, the Mishnah and associated documents: "Israel" as against "non-Israel," "Israel" as against Levite or priest. The categories that portray "Israel" not in relationship to "non-Israel" – for example, a family formed by a common genealogy and sustained by the shared inheritance of the merit of the ancestors, or Israel as sui generis and therefore a supernatural entity – served discourse only at severely limited points.

And what a difference a metaphor makes! For now we have the definition of "Israel" in its own terms, the representation of "Israel" as a concrete and material society or nation or family, the protracted account of "Israel" in the social world of nations and not solely in the theoretical and abstract world of classifying things (including, incidentally, nations), and the attention to the history and eschatological salvation of this "Israel." These marks of a different mode of thought have characterized the results of each of our surveys. But until now we have not taken sufficient notice of the fundamentally different way of perceiving the social world that has come to expression in the fresh results at hand. Our task is now to account for the contrast between "Israel" in one corpus of writing and "Israel" in the continuator writings of that same corpus, to explain not merely the different points of emphasis but rather the striking shift – from abstract and speculative to concrete and fleshly – in the character of thought concerning the social component of the Judaism of the dual Torah.

Let me frame the question very simply. What explains in the fourth- and fifth-century documents the appearance of new metaphors, or the neglect of the received ones? Two metaphors, scarcely explored in the writings of the first stage in the formation of the Judaism of the dual Torah, in the second stage came to prominence: first, the view of "Israel" as a family, the children and heirs of the man, Israel; second, the conception of Israel as sui generis. Whereas "Israel" in the first phase of the formation of Judaism perpetually finds definition in relationship to its opposite, "Israel" in the second phase constituted an intransitive entity, defined in its own terms and not solely or mainly in relationship to other comparable entities. The enormous investment in the conception of "Israel" as sui generis makes that point blatantly. But "Israel" as family bears that same trait of autonomy and self-evident definition. In the first phase, just as "gentile" was an abstract category, so was "Israel." *Kohen* was a category, and so too "Israel." When we see "Israel" as classifier and taxonomic category, we confront an abstraction in a system of philosophy. The "Israel" we have seen in the second stratum of the literature of the dual Torah by contrast bears a socially vivid sense. The contrast is clear. "Israel" when viewed in the this-worldly framework of most of the Mishnah's discussions emerges through a series of contrasts and comparisons, not as intrinsically important, systemically determinative facts. We know in that literature what "Israel" or "an Israel" is mainly when we can specify the antonym.

I cannot think of a more opposite result than the one we have now attained in our survey of the three most important documents of the fourth and fifth centuries. Now, I need hardly underscore, "Israel" stands for a real social group, not merely an entity in theory. "Israel" forms a family, and an encompassing theory of society, built upon that conception of "Israel," permits us to describe the proportions and balances of the social entity at hand, showing how each component both is an "Israel" and contributes to the larger composite as well. "Israel" as sui generis carried in its wake a substantial doctrine of definition, a weighty collection of general laws of social history governing the particular traits and events of the social group. In comparing transitive with intransitive "Israel," we move from "Israel" as not-gentile and "Israel" as not-priest to powerful statements of what "Israel" *is*. To account for the metaphorical revolution at hand, I see two important changes: one out at the borders of, the other within, the Jews' group.

ii.   Social Metaphors of Judaism despite Christianity

In both metaphorical definitions of "Israel," sages worked out in a specific way a larger and encompassing problem presented not to their "Israel" but the other "Israel." Let me first specify in detail how I think that the two notions of "Israel" responded to the crisis of the political triumph of Christianity. From the viewpoint of the Christians, the shift signified by the conversion of Constantine marked a caesura in history. The meaning of history commencing at Creation pointed for Christians toward Christ's triumph in the person of the Emperor and the institution of the Christian state. To Israel, the Jewish people, what can these same events have meant? The received Scriptures of ancient and recent Israel, both Judaic and Christian, now awaited that same sort of sifting and selection that had followed earlier turnings of a notable order, in 586 B.C.E., and after 70 C.E., for example: Which writing had now been proved right, which irrelevant? So Christians asked themselves, as they framed the canon of the Bible, both Old and New Testaments. Then to Israel, the Jewish people, what role and what place for the received Torah of Sinai, in its diversity of scrolls? The dogged faith that Jesus really was Christ, Messiah and King of the world, now found vindication in the events of the hour. What hope endured for the salvation of Israel in the future? In the hour of vindication the new Israel confronted the old, the one after the spirit calling into question the legitimacy of the one after the flesh: What now do you say of Christ? For Israel, the Jewish people, what was there to say in reply, not to Christ but to Christians? These three issues frame our principal concerns: the meaning of history, the realization of salvation, and the definition of one's own group in the encounter with the other.

To state matters simply, by claiming that "Israel" constituted "Israel after the flesh," the actual, living, present family of Abraham and Sarah, Isaac and Rebecca, Jacob and Leah and Rachel, sages met head on the Christian claim that there was – or could ever be – some other "Israel," of a lineage not defined by the family connection at all, and that the existing Jews no longer constituted "Israel." By representing "Israel" as sui generis, sages moreover focused upon the systemic teleology, with its definition of salvation, in response to the Christian claim that salvation is not of Israel but of the Church, now enthroned in this world as in heaven. The sage, model for Israel, in the model of Moses, our rabbi, on earth represented the Torah that had come from heaven. Like Christ, in earth as in heaven, like the Church, the body of Christ, ruler of earth (through the emperor) as of heaven, the sage embodied what Israel was and was to be. So Israel as family in the model of the sage, like Moses our rabbi, corresponded in its social definition to the Church of Jesus Christ, the New Israel, the source of salvation of the savior of humanity. The metaphors given prominence in the sages' writings of the late fourth and fifth centuries formed a remarkable counterpoint to the social metaphors important in the mind of significant Christian theologians, as both parties reflected on the political revolution that had taken place.

The social entity formed by "the Church," or "Israel after the spirit," like "Israel" or the Jews as they defined themselves, required a metaphor by which to account for itself. And revering the Scriptures, Christians too had long found in "Israel" the metaphor to account for its existence as a distinct social entity. The debate between Christians and Jews on "Israel" and the broader problem of the social entity constituted by each gained intensity because of a further peculiarity of the discourse between these two groups but no others of the day. Both concurred that the group chosen by God will bear the name, Israel. God's choice among human societies would settle the question: Which nation does God love and favor? Jews, we know full well, saw themselves as the Israel of today joined in the flesh to the Israel of the scriptural record. Christians explained themselves as the Israel formed just now, in recent memory, even in the personal experience of the living, among those saved by faith in God's salvation afforded by the resurrection of Jesus Christ. In these statements on who is Israel, the parties to the debate chose to affirm, each for its own part, its own unique legitimacy and to deny the other's right to endure at all as a social and national entity.

But both parties shared common premises as to definitions of issues and facts to settle the question.[1] They could mount a sustained argument between themselves because they talked about the same thing, invoked principles of logic in common, and shared the definition of the pertinent facts. They differed only as to the outcome. The issue of who is Israel articulated in theological, not political, terms covers several topics: Are the Jews today "Israel" of ancient times? Was, and is, Jesus Christ? If so, who are the Christians, both on their own and also in relationship to ancient Israel? These questions scarcely can be kept distinct from one another. And all of them cover the familiar ground we have already traversed concerning the social entity, its teleology, and (in concrete terms) salvation, and that accounts for my insistence that we consider, in the context of defining "Israel," a picture of salvation as sages portrayed the matter.

The Christian agenda may be stated simply enough. First, was, and is, Jesus the Christ? If so, then the Jews who rejected him enjoyed no share in the salvation at hand. If not, then they do. The Christian challenge comes first. If Jesus was and is Christ, then Israel "after the flesh" because of its unbelief no longer enjoys the status of the people who bear salvation. Salvation has come, and Israel "after the flesh" has denied it. If he is Christ, then what is the status of those – whether Jews or gentiles – who did accept him? They have received the promises of salvation and their fulfillment. The promises to Israel have been kept for them. Then there is a new Israel, one that is formed of the saved, as the prophets had said in ancient times that Israel would be saved.

A further issue that flowed from the first – the rejection of Jesus as Christ – concerns the status of Israel, the Jewish people, now and in time to come. Israel after the flesh, represented from the Gospels forward as the people who rejected Jesus as Christ and participated in his crucifixion, claims to be the family of Abraham, Isaac, and Jacob. Then further questions arise. First, does Israel today continue the Israel of ancient times? Israel maintains that Israel now continues in a physical and spiritual way the life of Israel then. Second, will the promises of the prophets to Israel afford salvation for Israel in time to come? Israel "after the flesh" awaits the fulfillment of the prophetic promise of salvation. Clearly, a broad range of questions demanded sorting out. But the questions flow together into a single issue, faced in common. The Christian position on all these questions came to expression in a single negative: No, Israel today does not continue the Israel of old, no, the ancient promises will not again bear salvation, because they have already been kept, so, no, the Israel that declines to accept Jesus' claim to be the Christ is a no-people.

Contained in the emphases of the documents we have surveyed, the response of Israel's sages to these same questions proves equally unequivocal. Yes, the Messiah will come in time, and yes, he will come to Israel of today, which indeed continues the Israel of old. And yes, the Messiah will be a sage, for "Israel" is the model of sages. To state matters more abstractly, the Torah defined matters for the "Israel" of the sages of the Judaism of the dual Torah, as much as Christ defined matters for the "Israel" that had joined at the cross. So the issue is squarely and fairly joined. Who is Israel raises a question that stands second in line to that of the Messiah, with which we have already dealt. And, it must follow, the further question of who are the Christians requires close attention to that same messianic question.

Before Christianity had addressed the issue of who the Christians were, Paul had already asked what the Jews were not. Christians formed the true people of God.[2] So the old and lasting Israel, the Jewish people, did not. Paul had called into question "Israel's status as God's chosen people," because (in Rosemary Ruether's words) "Israel had failed in its pursuit of righteousness based on the Torah . . . had been disobedient . . . [so that] the privileged relation to God provided by the Mosaic covenant has been permanently revoked." So from its origins, Christianity had called into question Israel's former status, and, as John Gager says, held that "Israel's disobedience is not only not accidental to God's plan of salvation, it has become an essential part of its fulfillment." The Christian position on one side of the matter of who is Israel, namely, who is not Israel, had reached a conclusion before the other aspect of the matter – the Christians' status as a New Israel – came to full expression.[3] Reflections on the classification of the new group – superior to the old, sui generis, and whatever the occasion of polemic requires the group to be – fill the early Christian writings. In general there were three: Greeks or gentiles, Jews, and the Christians as the new People.

When Christians asked themselves what sort of group they formed, they answered that they constituted a new group, and a group of a new type altogether. They identified with the succession to Israel after the flesh, with Israel after the spirit, with a group lacking all parallel or precedent, with God fearers and lawkeepers before Judaism was given at Sinai. The dilemma comes to expression in the statement of Eusebius, biographer of Constantine and founder of the Christian tradition of historiography in the fourth century:

> In the oracles directed to Abraham, Moses himself writes prophetically how in the times to come the descendants of Abraham, not only his Jewish seed but all the tribes and all the nations of the earth, will be deemed worthy of divine praise because of a common manner of worship like that of Abraham. . . . How could all the nations and tribes of the earth be blessed in Abraham if no relationship of either a spiritual or a physical nature existed between them? . . . How therefore could men reared amid an animal existence . . . be able to share in the blessings of the godly, unless they abandoned their savage ways and sought to participate in a life of piety like that of Abraham? . . . Now Moses lived after Abraham, and he gave the Jewish race a certain corporate status which was based upon the laws provided by him. If the laws he established were the same as those

by which godly men were guided before his time, if they were capable of being adopted by all peoples so that all the tribes and nations of the earth could worship God in accordance with the Mosaic enactments, one could say that the oracles had foretold that because of Mosaic laws men of every nation would worship God and live according to Judaism. . . . However since the Mosaic enactments did not apply to other peoples but to the Jews alone . . . , a different way, a way distinct from the law of Moses, needed to be established, one by which the nations of all the earth might live as Abraham had so that they could receive an equal share of blessing with him.[4]

Because, with the advent of Constantine, a political dimension served to take the measure of the Christian polity, we have to ask about the political consciousness of the Church in its original formulation. In this matter Harnack points out that the political consciousness of the Church rests on three premises, first, the political element in the Jewish apocalyptic, second, the movement of the gospel to the Greeks, and third, the ruin of Jerusalem and the end of the Jewish state. He says, "The first of these elements stood in antithesis to the others, so that in this way the political consciousness of the church came to be defined in opposite directions and had to work itself out of initial contradictions."[5] From early times, Harnack says, the Christians saw Christianity as "the central point of humanity as the field of political history as well as its determining factor." That had been the Jews' view of themselves. With Constantine the corresponding Christian conception matched reality.

Now the Christians formed a new People, a third race. When the change came, with the Christianization of the Empire at the highest levels of government, the new people, the third race, had to frame a position and policy about the old people, enduring Israel "after the flesh." For its part, the Jewish people, faced with the Christian *défi*, found the necessity to reaffirm its enduring view of itself, now, however, in response to a pressure without precedent in its long past. The claim of the no-people that the now and enduring Israel is the no-people knew no prior equivalent. The age of Constantine marked the turning of the world: All things were upside down. How could Israel, the Jewish people, deal with a world that from its perspective had gone mad? Israel's answer, which we shall reach in due course, proves stunningly apropos: right to the issue, in precisely the terms of the issue.

That is one reason, in my view, that we find in the Judaism of the sages who redacted the principal documents of Judaism that reached closure in the century beyond the conversion of Constantine both a doctrine of who is "Israel," the family of the original Jacob = Israel, and an apologetic for the "Israel" at hand, a social entity that was sui generis and destined for salvation. Both proved remarkably relevant to the issues presented to Christianity and Judaism by the crisis of Christianity's worldly triumph. A shared program brought the two religions into protracted confrontation on an intersecting set of questions, a struggle that has continued until our own time – originated in the fact that, to begin with, both religions agreed on almost everything that mattered. They differed on little, so made much of that little. Scripture taught them both that vast changes in the affairs of empires came about because of God's will. History proved principles of theology. In that same Torah prophets promised the coming of the Messiah, who would bring salvation. Who was, and is, that Messiah, and how shall we know? And that same Torah addressed a particular people, Israel, promising that people the expression of God's favor and love. But who is Israel, and who is not Israel? In this way Scripture defined the categories shared in common, enabling Judaism and Christianity to engage, if not in dialogue, then in two monologues on the same topics. The terms of this confrontation continued for centuries because the conditions that precipitated it, the rise to political dominance of Christianity and the subordination of Judaism, remained constant for fifteen hundred years.

The reply to Christianity in terms of the metaphors of Israel, of course, carries us far from the framing of issues of social definition familiar in the writings of the first stage in the literature of formative Judaism. There, thinking about the social entity "Israel" formed a chapter in the larger discourse of thought about other topics; "Israel" as we have noticed had formed a taxonomic category and indicator. Now, in response to the challenge of Christianity, thought about "Israel" centered on the issues of history and salvation, issues made not merely chronic but acute by the political triumph. That accounts for what I believe is an unprecedented reading of the outsider, contained in the two propositions of Rome, first, as Esau or Edom or Ishmael, that is, as part of the family; and second, of Rome as the pig. Differentiating Rome from other gentiles represented a striking concession indeed. Rome is represented as only Christian Rome can have been represented: It looks kosher but it is unkosher. Pagan Rome cannot ever have looked kosher, but Christian Rome, with its appeal to ancient Israel, could and did and moreover claimed to. It bore some traits that validate, but lacked others that validate.

The other metaphor, that of the family, proved equally pointed. Sages framed their political ideas within the metaphor of genealogy, because to begin with they appealed to the fleshly connection, the family, as the rationale for Israel's social existence. A family beginning with Abraham, Isaac, and Jacob, Israel today could best sort out its relationships by drawing into the family other social entities with which it found it had to relate. So Rome became the brother. That affinity came to light only when Rome had turned Christian, and that point marked the need for the extension of the genealogical net. But the conversion to Christianity also justified the sages' extending membership in the family to Rome, for Christian Rome shared with Israel the common patrimony of Scripture, and said so. The character of the sages' thought on Israel therefore proved remarkably congruent to the conditions of public discourse that confronted them. But the substance of their doctrine – the rejection of metaphor in favor of the claim that Israel formed an entity that was sui generis – derived from within, as we shall now observe.

iii.   Social Metaphors of an Authorship with Authority

When we grasp how the authorship understood itself, we may compare that representation of matters with its thinking about the larger social group subject to re-visioning in the systematic statement at hand. "Israel" writ large, I have already suggested, represented the sages' conception of themselves. A small social group reflecting on a larger social group, sages projected outward their sense of their own group. Their social metaphors germinated, to begin with, out of the seed of that singular authorship's own social imagination of itself. This thesis then is to be tested against the authorship's representation of its own social entity. Because we have, in the Yerushalmi and its related writings, the results of a social group reflecting upon a social group, we turn to the representation of their own standing in heaven and earth as imagined by the authorship of the Yerushalmi. All things, in that portrait, stood in hierarchical connection and relationship, with sages at the end of the chain begun at Sinai (a conception that would not have surprised the authorship of tractate Abot). Consequently if we wish to understand metaphors for "all Israel," we begin with the "us" constituted by the sages. And what we find is that conception of Israel as sui generis, standing in unique relationship to God in heaven, that has impressed us as a principal way of imagining "Israel" in the documents of the late fourth and fifth centuries.

A.   "And it came to pass in the days of Ahaz" (Is. 7:1):

B.   "The Aramaeans on the east and the Philistines on the west devour Israel with open mouth" (Is. 9:12):

C.   The matter [of Israel's position] may be compared to the case of a king who handed over his son to a tutor, who hated the son. The tutor thought, "If I kill him now, I shall turn out to be liable to the death penalty before the king. So what I'll do is take away his wet-nurse, and he will die on his own."

D. So thought Ahaz, "If there are no kids, there will be no he-goats. If there are no he-goats, there will be no flock. If there is no flock, there will be no Shepherd, if there is no Shepherd, there will be no world."

E. So did Ahaz plan, "If there are no children, there will be no adults. If there are no adults, there will be no disciples. If there are no disciples, there will be no sages. If there are no sages, there will be no prophets. If there are no prophets, the Holy One, blessed be he, will not allow his presence to come to rest in the world." [Lev. R.: . . . Torah. If there is no Torah, there will be no synagogues and schools. If there are no synagogues and schools, then the Holy One, blessed be he, will not allow his presence to come to rest in the world.]

F. That is in line with the following verse of Scripture: "Bind up the testimony, seal the Torah among my disciples" (Is. 8:16).

G. R. Huna in the name of R. Eleazar: "Why was he called Ahaz? Because he seized (ahaz) synagogues and schools."

Gen. R. XLII:III.2

Israel formed that locus in the world in which God's presence came to rest. Sages stand within a chain of not tradition but encounter with God. In Torah study they prepare the way for prophecy. Israel, all together, forms God's domain on earth, and sages in the nature of things constitute the medium that links prophecy to people. The version of Leviticus Rabbah is still more tightly linked to the reality of our authorship, which locates in its principal institutions, synagogues and schools, that place at which God comes to rest on earth. The vision of an "Israel" that takes shape around synagogues and schools carries us deep into our authorship's understanding of Israel as God's (unique) people. That definition then forms part of a larger public conception of "Israel" within the metaphor of a God who takes up residence within a social group.

That rather general observation sets the stage for our consideration of the representation of Israel's social reality, and of the sages' place within it, in the pages of the Yerushalmi in particular. That document, hanging like a necklace around the Mishnah, formed their most sustained and substantial statement to, and therefore also about, the social world of "Israel." What we observed in the theological statement in hand, an "Israel" formed around the centerpiece made up of sages, we shall now see portrayed in a series of case reports. The authorship of the Yerushalmi[6] presents a world in which sages made concrete decisions in the governance of a palpable and material society, made up of real people doing real things, and the "Israel" before us – in my view, reflecting the social experience of our authorship – therefore takes on the flesh and bones of an ongoing society, a social entity in fields and streets, not a mere abstraction for philosophical speculation, a principal component of the hierarchization of the world out there and in here alike. For sages – our authorship – are portrayed as exercising authority not only over their own circles (i.e., people who agreed with them) but over the Jewish community at large.

This authority was practical and involved very specific powers. The first and most important sort of power a rabbi under some circumstances and in some cases maintained he could exercise was to sort out and adjudicate rights to property and personal status affecting property. The rabbi is described as able to take chattels or real estate from one party and to give them into the rightful ownership of some other. The second sort of power rabbis are supposed to have wielded was to tell people what to do, or not to do, in matters not involving property rights. The Yerushalmi's authorship repeatedly and consistently alleges that rabbis could tell people outside the circles of their own disciples and estate how to conduct themselves. A rabbi is presented as able to coerce someone to do what that ordinary Jew might otherwise not wish to do, or to prevent him from doing what he wanted. The first kind of authority may be called judicial, the second, moral. But the distinction is ours, not theirs. The Yerushalmi's authorship does not distinguish among the various kinds of authority and power of coercion exercised by rabbis. Let us now spell out the character of rabbinic authority.

The Yerushalmi's authorship takes for granted that rabbis could define the status of persons in such ways as to affect property and marital rights and standing. It is difficult to imagine a more effective form of social authority. As we shall see, our authorship treats as settled fact a range of precedents, out of which the character of the law is defined. In those precedents, rabbis declare a woman married or free to marry; permitted as wife of a priest to eat food in the status of heave offering or prohibited from doing so; enjoying the support of a husband's estate or left without that support; having the right to collect a previously contracted marriage settlement or lacking that right. In all of these ways, as much as in their control of real estate, commercial, and other material and property transactions among Jews, the rabbis held they governed the Jewish community as effective political authorities. Whatever beliefs or values they proposed to instill in the people, or realize in the collective life of the community, they effected not through moral suasion or pretense of magical power. It was not hocus-pocus but political power resting on the force of government authority. They could tell people what to do and force them to do it. That is the type of social authority implicit in the Talmud; that is the system of politics attested and assumed in our documents.

The Yerushalmi's authorship is remarkably reticent about the basis for rabbis' power over the Jews' political institutions: Who bestowed this-worldly legitimacy and supplied the force? To be sure, the systematic provision of biblical proof texts for Mishnaic laws presents an ample myth for the law. Given by God to Moses at Mount Sinai, the law, including the Mishnah's laws, represents the will of Heaven. But with all the faith in the world, on the basis of such an assertion about God's will, the losing party to a litigation over a piece of real estate will surely have surrendered his property to the other side only with the gravest reservations, if at all. He more likely will have complained to some other authority, if he could. Short of direct divine coercion, upon which a legal system cannot be expected to rely, there had to be more reliable means of making the system work. What these were, however, the Yerushalmi's authorship hardly tells us. So, for the present purpose, we cannot pretend to know. We only know rabbis held that they could run courts and make decisions for Jews who were not rabbis or disciples.

One thing is clear. Jews did not live in territorial units, ethnically uniform and distinct from areas inhabited by other, equally distinct groups. Every page of the Yerushalmi bespeaks a polyglot and multiform society, with diverse political entities at hand. Even towns such as Sepphoris and Tiberias, with mainly Jewish populations, are described as sheltering non-Jewish populations, each one with its particular status and rights. What must follow is that imagining "Israel" as a cogent social entity appealed to an ethnic, not a territorial, domain. The Yerushalmi's authorship's perspective is that of a very low level of bureaucracy. In the larger political system, the rabbis' courts constituted a trivial detail. The courts in their hands, powerful though they were in affecting the lives of ordinary Israelites, took up minor matters, with which the great powers of government and state – out there, way up and beyond – did not care to deal. So before us is the world of power portrayed by ethnarchic clerks, nobodies in the larger scheme of things.

The single most striking trait of reports about what rabbis said and did as judges in courts is the practical character of the authority imputed to rabbis. Our authorship portrays sages as judges able to take property from one party and assign it to some other. Decisions are carried out not by persuasion or threats of supernatural retaliation but through coercion (though the political basis is not specified). Rabbinic judges exercised unchallenged de jure power in their courts.

The power to transfer ownership from one party to some other, or to govern transactions with that same effect, represents the single most important testimony to the character of the authority of the sage or rabbi as judge. Courts exercising authority over an ethnic group spread out among other ethnic groups need not have enjoyed jurisdiction over real estate transactions. The Yerushalmi's authorities believed their courts could settle litigation over the title to land and the sale of land by minors. These reports, the first on a defense against a claim of title by usucapion, the second on the sale of real property by a minor, leave no doubt as to this Talmud's view of the state of affairs. Sages furthermore claimed jurisdiction over lesser chattels and transactions in movables. Such issues involving conflicting claims on the terms of a property lease, and appropriate utilization of property subject to neighbors' rights, are portrayed.

While authority over real transactions in real estate, gifts, and testaments is most striking, ordinary folk would more regularly have encountered rabbinic authority in litigating conflicts of movables, especially arising in trade and commerce, as well as in collection of debts and bailments. These kinds of cases, being trivial in value as compared with those entailing transfer of real property, are apt to have been more common. Breach of contract, for example in commercial transactions, came under rabbinical supervision. Rabbinic courts were called upon to settle cases involving collection of debts. As in the case of breach of contract, their power involved imposition of frightening oaths, which people tried to avoid. The rabbinic judges claimed the power to force the collection of outstanding debts, not only from the debtor himself but also from the guarantor of the debt. They also imposed their own reading on bonds of indebtedness in a case in which the writing was unclear. Finally, they assumed full authority to determine the facts of the matter. The sages' courts dealt not only with property, but also with threats to sound social policy. For instance, the sale of animals to gentiles was discouraged, whether on grounds that the beasts might serve some idolatrous purpose, that the beasts would be so worked as to violate the Sabbath law, or that the raising of small cattle posed a severe threat to the ecology of the Land.

The power of the court to summon a litigant or a witness rested upon the capacity to declare a recalcitrant party to be ostracized or excommunicated. This had the effect of removing him from the Jewish community. Because the penalty is taken for granted as effective, we learn that the rabbis behind the following tale assumed general support from the Jewish community for their judicial activities.

A. R. Joshua b. Levi summoned a man to his court three times, and the man did not come. He sent him the message, "If it were not the case that in my entire life I have never declared a man to be subject to a herem [ostracism], I should have declared you to be in herem."

B. For twenty-four reasons they excommunicated a person, and this is one of them.

C. "And that if any one did not come within three days, by order of the officials and the elders all his property should be forfeited, and he himself banned from the congregation of the exiles" (Ezra 10:8).

D. Said R. Isaac b. R. Eleazar, "There are many more than those twenty-four cases scattered throughout the Mishnah."

Y. M.Q. 3:1:VII

For the penalty of ostracism to work, there had to be general compliance with rabbis' authority. Yet the sanction was invoked, in particular, to force compliance with the court's procedures, not obedience to its decisions in a case of conflicting property claims. There a more formidable sanction had to come into play, for the courts could hardly depend for effective authority only upon a common consensus about what, to begin with, was subject to conflict.

If the Jewish nation at large is represented as accepting the sovereignty of rabbinic courts in property disputes, the reason may have been the power of the courts not only to persuade or elicit general support, but also to call upon the power of the state to transfer ownership of real and movable property from one party to another. But there was a kind of jurisdiction that, in the end, had to enjoy not merely passive acquiescence through fear of ostracism but active support of the people at large, namely, determinations of personal status. Although the courts might call upon the state to back up their rulings about property, they are not likely to have enjoyed equivalent support in matters to which the government was probably indifferent, such as whether a given woman was betrothed and so not free to marry anyone but the fiancé, or whether she was not betrothed and so free to marry anyone of her choice. Persistent meddling in such affairs can have generated only widespread protest, unless the community at large acquiesced and indeed actively supported the right of the courts to make such decisions.

Nonetheless, even behind these evidences of rabbinic authority, based as they are on sanctions of moral authority, as distinct from the imperial government's ultimate threat of force, there still were elements of exchange of property or things of value. Consequently, when we deal with personal status, we take up yet another aspect of the rabbis' power to judge property cases. For rulings in cases involving personal status – whether a woman was betrothed or married, a slave was freed, a man was a valid priest – always carried in their wake material considerations. Indeed, even if the courts were set up only to settle questions of personal status in accordance with the law of the Jewish nation, something of slight concern to the government, the courts would have had to enjoy the power to transfer real property and movables from one party to another. We may hardly be surprised, therefore, to find a substantial repertoire about how rabbis decided questions of the status of women, slaves, and similar sorts of persons in a subordinate or otherwise special status.

Consequently, the authorship that stood behind the Yerushalmi preserved a vast number and wide variety of cases in which, so far as they were concerned, rabbinic courts exercised a kind of authority we may regard only as political and bureaucratic. Persons and property of Israel came under their authority. So the Yerushalmi's authorship represents itself as a set of authorities possessed of considerable concrete power of a political and not merely charismatic character, judges of litigation and administrators of questions of personal status. Decisions are represented, moreover, as precedents, accepted in theorizing about law and uniformly authoritative for courts spread over a considerable territory. Accordingly, rabbinic judges saw themselves as part of a system and a structure, not merely local strong men or popular sages. A fully articulated system of politics and government, staffed by people who knew the Mishnah and how to apply its law to concrete cases and who had the full power to do so, is represented here. Rabbinic judges knew what to do and had full confidence in their authority to do it.

This Talmud represents the rabbi not only as a part of a national government and bureaucracy but also, and more important to our problem, as prefect in his own community. The basis of his authority in this second role was partly the same as with his court role. He could effect judgments bearing significant consequences for the disposition of property, for example, in trade and commerce. But other sorts of decisions shade off into less tangible issues, leading us to a view of the rabbi as something other than a solely political figure. The same local authority who could settle litigations and direct the course of commerce also could tell the people the rules of public fasting. He further could give directions for the disposition of synagogue property and the conduct of worship, though his presence is scarcely represented as important in the liturgy of the synagogue.

The principal evidence of the character of the sage or rabbi as a public figure exercising at one and the same time political and religious authority (again, a distinction important now, not then) derives from stories about the rabbi as the figure mediating between Jews and the outside world. In this context the rabbi comes forth as head of the Jewish nation in his locale. This is because of his power to represent the nation in its dealings with other groups, or to direct Jews on how to conduct those transactions. Whatever the condition of the Jews' government in the country at large (whether, as seems likely, there was a central institution with power over local prefects, for instance), it is in this context that we see the rabbi as the Big Man (in the anthropological sense) of the Jews. But that portrait emerges from the rabbis' own writings. We do not know how others saw them. What is important is the implication that the rabbi of a locale served as authority not only in municipal court but also in governing relationships with the state. Yet his authority continued to rest solely on his mastery of the law. That is, he could permit actions normally prohibited in the law. He is represented not as negotiating, only as accommodating. Accordingly, so far as the Jewish nation of the Land of Israel was represented in ongoing relationships with the government, some other sort of figure than the rabbi presumably took charge. Furthermore, the unstated supposition is that Israel stands in a subordinated relationship, able to resist only with difficulty, and then at a very high cost. The alternative to submission is assumed to be death. So the domain over which the rabbi presided flourished on the edge of an active volcano.

The rabbi's authority as representative of the Jewish nation and mediator between that nation and the gentile world in general, and the government in particular, bore heavy symbolic weight. But in shaping the Jewish community to accord with "the Torah," the rabbi's local authority outside the court produced far more significant, concrete results. It is at this point that we see the shading off of the character of the rabbi's decisions, as they dealt less with disposition of persons and property and more with intangible matters of proper conduct and observance of religious taboos. These matters still presented public and social issues in which the rabbi not merely exemplified but also enforced law. Rabbinic authority is represented as extending not only to public observances. Rabbis also instructed individuals on the way to carry out personal rites of a nonprivate character, such as burials. At issue here are decisions on reburial of the deceased; when the rites of mourning, following burial, actually come into effect; and the applicability of rites of mourning to a priest in doubt as to his relationship to the deceased. Private conduct was deemed subject to public authority, and the rabbi is represented as the source of rulings on them.

The rabbi stood on the intersecting borders of several domains: political and private, communal and individual. He served as both legal and moral authority, decider and exemplar, judge and clerk, administrator and governor, but also holy man and supernatural figure. The rabbi as a public official was expected to, and did, perform certain supernatural or magical deeds. He stood at the border between heaven and earth, as much as he stood at the frontier between Israel and the nations: wholly liminal, entirely exemplary, at one and the same time. What is important here is the representation of the rabbi as public authority deemed to exercise supernatural power. His task was to use his supernatural power in pretty much the same context and for the same purpose as he used his political-judicial and legal power and learning, on the one side, and his local influence and moral authority, on the other. What is striking is that sages exercised their responsibility equally through this-worldly and other-worldly means.

One striking type of story makes the point. Rabbis made rules on public fasting. For their part, they possessed sufficient merit so that, if they personally fasted, they were supposed to be able to bring rain. Yet another area in which supernatural, as distinct from this-worldly, authority came to the fore was in preventing epidemics. The first story provides a routine instance of rainmaking; the second, of bringing rain and stopping a pestilence, by two themes being joined together.

A.   R. Aha carried out thirteen fasts, and it did not rain. When he went out, a Samaritan met him. [The Samaritan] said to him [to make fun of him], "Rabbi, take off our cloak, because it is going to rain."

B.   He said to him, "By the life of that man [you]! Heaven will do a miracle, and this year will prosper, but that man will not live to see it."

C.   Heaven did a miracle, and the year prospered, and that Samaritan died.

D.   And everybody said, "Come and see the fruit [the man's corpse] [lying in the] sun."

Y. Ta. 3:4.V

A.   There was a pestilence in Sepphoris, but it did not come into the neighborhood in which R. Haninah was living. And the Sepphoreans said, "How is it possible that that elder lives among you, he and his entire neighborhood, in peace, while the town goes to ruin?"

B.   [Haninah] went in and said before them, "There was only a single Zimri in his generation, but on his account, twenty-four thousand people died. And in our time, how many Zimris are there in our generation? And yet you are raising a clamor!"

C.   One time they had to call a fast, but it did not rain. R. Joshua carried out a fast in the South, and it rained. The Sepphoreans said, "R. Joshua

b. Levi brings down rain for the people in the South, but R. Haninah holds back rain for us in Sepphoris."

D. They found it necessary to declare a second time of fasting, and sent and summoned R. Joshua b. Levi. [Haninah] said to him, "Let my lord go forth with us to fast." The two of them went out to fast, but it did not rain.

E. He went in and preached to them as follows: "It was not R. Joshua b. Levi who brought down rain for the people of the South, nor was it R. Haninah who held back rain from the people of Sepphoris. But as to the Southerners, their hearts are open, and when they listen to a teaching of Light [Torah] they submit [to accept it], while as to the Sepphoreans, their hearts are hard, and when they hear a teaching of Light, they do not submit [or accept it]."

F. When he went in, he looked up and saw that the [cloudless] air was pure. He said, "Is this how it still is? [Is there no change in the weather?]" Forthwith, it rained. He took a vow for himself that he would never do the same thing again. He said, "How shall I say to the creditor [God] not to collect what is owing to him?"

Y. Ta. 3:4.I

The tale about Joshua and Haninah is most striking, because it presents a thoroughly rationalistic picture of the supernatural framework at hand. True, God could do miracles. But if the people caused their own disasters by not listening to rabbis' Torah teachings, they could hardly expect God always to forgo imposing the sanction for disobedience, which was holding back rain. Accordingly, there were reliable laws by which one could deal with the supernatural world that kept those laws too. The particular power of the rabbi was in knowing the law. The storyteller took for granted, to be sure, that in the end the clerk could bring rain in a pinch.

The Yerushalmi's authorship's account of rabbis' exercise of authority over the life of Israel leaves the impression that, in the main, rabbis formed an autonomous government, a collegium of sages. They not only learned the same law, namely, the Mishnah, with its associated traditions. They also saw themselves as subordinate to the same great authorities of the law, both of times past and of their own day. Accordingly, time and again the picture emerges of a well-organized Jewish government, working not only locally but throughout the Land of Israel, unified in perspective and policy throughout the Israelite sectors of the Land. In consequence we have a view of an effective national government, staffed by the rabbinic estate. The Yerushalmi posits the existence, in addition to the rabbinic bureaucrats, of a patriarch who hired them, used their services for the administration of the local affairs of the Jewish nation in the Land of Israel, and validated their decisions, even while maintaining his auton-

omy from, and superiority over, the clerks who made those decisions. Rabbis in their role as local authorities derived their authority
from the Jewish government of which they formed a mere part. The
rabbinic judges and clerks depended for political and legal legitima-
tion of their decisions and orders upon that government beyond
themselves, both close at hand, in the patriarchate, and far away, in
the Roman government itself. The Yerushalmi's authorship's picture
of the patriarchal government makes clear that the power of rabbis
to judge cases depended upon their status as legitimate clerks, con-
ferred by the patriarchate, probably more than on the brute force it
made available.

The Yerushalmi's authorship portrays the rabbi as an effective
authority over the everyday affairs and social life of the social group
("Israel"). True enough, details of the portrait time and again contradict its main lines. The rabbi was part of the administration of a man
who stood at the margins of the rabbinic estate, one foot in, the other out. The sage was further limited in his power by popular will and
consensus, by established custom. Furthermore, the rabbi as clerk
and bureaucrat dealt with matters of surpassing triviality, a fair
portion of them of no interest to anyone but a rabbi, I should
imagine. He might decide which dog a flea might bite. But would the
fleas listen to him? Accordingly, the Yerushalmi's voluminous evidence of the rabbis' quest for authority over the Jewish nation turns
out to present ambiguities about inconsequentialities. On the one
side, the rabbi could make some practical decisions. On the other, he
competed for authority over Israel with the patriarch and with local
village heads. In general, no Jew decided much. And, admittedly,
from the viewpoint of the Roman Empire, the rabbi was apt to have
been one among many sorts of invisible men, self-important non-
entities, treating as consequential things that concerned no one but
themselves, doing little, changing nothing. After all, in the very
period in which the tales before us were coming to closure and
beginning to constitute our Talmud as we know it, the power of the
Jewish nation to govern itself grew ever less, and came to an end, so
far as the patriarchal rule of the Land of Israel was concerned, in the
early decades of the fifth century. By harping on how they decided
things and inserting into the processes of legal theory precedents
established in their courts, and by representing the life of Israel in
such a way that the government of the nation was shown to be
entirely within the hands of the nation's learned, legitimate authorities, the Talmud's sages stated quite clearly what they thought was
going on. "Israel" remained Israel, wholly subject to its own law,

entirely in control of its own destiny, fully possessed of its own land –
measured by the model of the governing sage.

iv.   Theological Anthropology and Theological Sociology: The Society of the Sages and the Metaphor of "Israel"

Testimony to and vindication of the eternity of "Israel" lay in the
continuing authority of Israel's sages, fully in control of God's Torah
for "Israel" and modeling themselves and their nation "in our image,
after our likeness." In that context, we read "Israel" as the sages'
metaphorical vocabulary defined that social entity. That metaphorization has yielded the blatant conception of the social entity,
Jacob–Israel, as counterpart and opposite of Esau–Rome, that here-
commonplace notion of the social entity as sui generis, thus as God's
domain on earth. These metaphors derived from an authorship in full
charge (in its own mind at least) of the social entity to which, in its
imagination, it gave shape and imparted meaning – and, by the way,
definition. The "Israel" of the second phase in the formation of the
Judaism of the dual Torah formed a palpable and worldly reality
because the authorship of the principal documents of the Judaism of
the dual Torah imagined, for society at large, the world that that
authorship now composed. Authors with authority conceived of an
Israel that formed a political entity in a real world, from the village
and household in the immediacy of the here and now to the realm of
the ethnic state, and outward to the bounds of political reality: Israel
and Rome at the farthest limits of time now and ages to come.

NOTES

1 This is the argument of my *Judaism and Christianity in the Age of Constantine* (Chicago, 1987: University of Chicago Press).
2 Rosemary Radford Ruether, *Faith and Fratricide: The Theological Roots
of Anti-Semitism* (New York: Seabury Press, 1979), pp. 64ff.
3 Ibid.; and John G. Gager, *The Origins of Anti-Semitism: Attitudes Towards
Judaism in Pagan and Christian Antiquity* (New York: Oxford University
Press), pp. 256–8.
4 *The Proof of the Gospel* 12:, cited by Colm Luibheid, *The Essential
Eusebius* (New York: Mentor Omega, 1966), p. 41.
5 Adolf Harnack, *The Mission and Expansion of Christianity in the First
Three Centuries,* trans. and ed. James Moffatt (London; repr., Gloucester:
Pete Smith, 1908), p. 256–7.

6 In my *Judaism in Society: The Evidence of the Yerushalmi* (Chicago: University of Chicago Press, 1985), I worked from the literary forms outward to the attitudes of mind persistently contained at the deepest structural layers of the document, rhetorical and logical plan and topical program alike. It is on that basis that I represent matters as I do, maintaining that there is an authorship that, in the recurrent patterns of form and proposition, proposes to make a statement we can rehearse. In my *The Talmud of the Land of Israel. A Preliminary Translation and Explanation* (Chicago: University of Chicago Press, 1982) XXXV. *Introduction. Taxonomy,* I have pursued the same matter on a more narrowly formal and rhetorical front.

PART III

Same Metaphors, Other Systems

CHAPTER 11

Other Judaisms and Their Social Metaphors

i.   "Israel" and the Social Rules of Judaisms

In investigating the theories of "Israel" presented by the documentary evidence of that Judaism, I propose to outline the rules that
govern thinking about the social entity, or social thought, of one
important religious formation. I aim at establishing some rules, which
can be tested in the study of other Judaisms and other religious systems entirely. I have a very particular question in mind. What I really
want to know is where, when, and why a given systemic statement
will invoke one metaphor, and the conditions in which a different
metaphor proves compelling. Furthermore, I should like to find out
what images, issues, and points of self-evidence follow in the retinue
of a regnant metaphor. In asking, for the social thought of Judaic
systems, why this and not that, I therefore propose to enter into
processes of thought concerning the social consciousness of a given
group, as important statements of that consciousness come before
us. Rules of this kind are proposed in this chapter, and they generate
their own hypothesis.

What can we say about the modes of thought of that social group,
the sages who constituted the authorship of the canon of the Judaism
of the dual Torah? Not social facts, out there, but imagining society, in
here, yielded the sages' categories and definitions. Specifically, sages
began within, in imagination, and drew for detail upon their inner
vision. What they saw is what they expected and wanted to see. We
clearly see that fact when we take a look at the categories of king and
high priest that sages invoked in their picture of the governance of
Israel. At the time that sages produced the Mishnah, Israel had neither
king nor high priest. Long before the destruction of the temple in 70
C.E., Israel, the people-nation, hardly constituted a political entity

governed by the bicameral institution of "king" and "high priest."
"Israel" in its land was subject to diverse authorities, not all of them
Jewish, and none of them – so far as contemporary evidence suggests
– formed within the patterns presented by the Mishnah's authorities
as facts and norms of government. From that fact we gain a clear
notion of the power of imagination – hence of metaphor – in the
shaping of the doctrine of society, Israel, in the literature before us.
What we see is a group of people who make sense of the social world
not out of the facts of that world but out of the realities of the inner
mind and its perceptions. But another important point needs to be
emphasized. Because we deal with the result of a social process, a
consensus of individuals who speak as a society about a society, what
we shall analyze in this book is a set of social metaphors in a still
more subtle sense: metaphors – acts of imagination and of social art –
concerning a social entity, produced by a social entity.

Systems by definition attend to a social entity; otherwise all we have
is a book. And social groups – two or more persons sharing distinctive traits – commonly perceive what is not there to be seen, namely,
something other, and more, than what they are. Concrete traits stand
for an abstract social entity, present even when not perceived, indeed, imposing other traits besides those that are palpable. Accordingly, if our survey and analysis of how "Israel" serves as a metaphor
for the groups Jews form and how the metaphors imputed to an
"Israel" express shared concerns of such groups are to succeed, we
have now to generalize. Success in such an exercise will yield lessons
for the description, analysis, and interpretation of other systems and
their social entities, other groups and their shared metaphors for
themselves. But we require also an account of where and how Jews'
groups, with their intense awareness of forming a social entity subject
to stipulation and condition, may differ from others. Accordingly, I
propose hypotheses for general discourse deriving from the particular case at hand. And, to begin with, that requires comparison of
the Judaism we have treated with other Judaisms.

Generalizing on the detailed survey we have now completed, we
seek rules that will guide inquiry into three questions. First, we ask
how in other Judaisms, besides the Judaism of the dual Torah, "Israel"
will reach definition, hence metaphorical analogy and contrast. Second, we want to know whether we may predict the type of metaphor
a given system (even those outside Judaism) will prefer. Are there
circumstances that will provoke thought of one kind rather than
some other? Third, we should like to be able to predict when "Israel"
will form an indicative and central component of a system, active and
definitive of other traits of the system, and when the social entity

defined by system builders will prove inert and at best a dependent variable. These questions are meant to yield laws in Judaisms governing metaphors for the social entity. Such laws should help us to predict the shape and importance, if not the contents, of social metaphors in a Judaism and, further, should guide us in the analysis of how other religious formations work out the same issue as is met, in Judaisms, by imputing to "Israel" various traits of a social order.

We therefore move on to an exercise in generalization based on what we have now learned. I intend further, if tentatively, to compare and contrast those generalizations with the shape and structure of other Judaic systems, cursorily sketched to be sure.

ii. No Judaism without an "Israel"

Axiom: *An "Israel" serves as the social component of a Judaic system.*

The axiom of our analysis requires reiteration. It is that all Judaic systems appeal to a social entity and claim to address problems of not merely theology or intellect and philosophy but also of society. I state flatly there can be no Judaism without an "Israel." When, therefore, we speak of a Judaism, or a Judaic religious system, by definition we mean a cogent statement, covering both this world and the transcendent one, on the society and culture of a social group, covering three principal matters: the worldview, the way of life expressive of that worldview, and the social entity to which the worldview is addressed and that embodies the way of life. These three components form a system that in their union makes a cogent statement to a persistent social fact. What unites the three is an overriding and fundamental question addressed by the system as a whole, along with a self-evidently valid and compelling answer to that question, supplied implicitly by the entirety of the system, whole (in a well-formed system) also in every detail – an acute and critical question (however chronic in its persistence) commonly answered explicitly by the statement of the worldview of the system. The first social rule of course states what in fact has defined the premise of this inquiry, and hence constitutes not a rule or law but an axiom not subject to demonstration.

iii. The Social Rules of Judaisms: Three Propositions

Let us move directly to the principal result: What do we now know about "Israel" that we did not know at the outset, and could not necessarily have predicted? It is the now-proven fact that an "Israel" will find its definition within the Judaic system that it serves. An "Israel" will prove wholly congruent to the shape and structure of that system and will be formed of materials selected by the systemic authorship out of a miscellaneous, received or invented repertoire of possibilities.[1] The opposite proposition is that the social entity, "Israel," will appeal to facts dictated by the social world "out there," so that the system will struggle to absorb and assimilate the givens of a politics and imagination not formed by the system itself. That opposite but quite plausible proposition is false for the data we have examined. An "Israel" within a given system is the invention of the system builders, with those traits found relevant to the larger system – without appeal to facts or realities beyond the range of systemic control. Any notion that the character of the "Israel" will find defini-tion in a received corpus of facts not subject to the system's own processes of selection is false. Any conception that the system builders – sages, in the present instance, over a period of centuries – compose their "Israel" through collection of information and gener-alization of what they find is improbable. The system responds to its inner logic and makes things up from there. That is why neither the social data nor the repertoire of available "Israel"s makes a con-tribution on their own initiatives, respectively. I state the proposition in a simple way.

> Proposition 1: *The shape and meaning imputed to the social component, "Israel," will conform to the larger interests of the system and in detail express the system's main point.*

True enough, that is not the whole story, and a later rule will tell another chapter of the same story of systems. For, I think, crises of politics and social culture do precipitate system formation (or, as I have done, can be shown to correlate with one). But that is a separate consideration. It is one thing to interpret a system in its larger social context, as we do. It is quite another to relate directly and not through systemic mediation a component of a system that may refer to that larger context. That theory of an unmediated relationship between a theory of society and the actualities of a social group ignores the power of systematic thought to compose, whole and complete, a full account of all things, all together and all at once.

Within the systemic framework, therefore, an "Israel" will stand for the social entity, most commonly but not necessarily a social group (as defined in Chapter 1), and the mode of turning the abstraction into a concrete entity will express, in that detail, the larger proposition – that urgent question, that self-evidently valid answer – of the system viewed whole. Thought about "Israel" may draw upon the inherited writings, and attain concrete expression through appeal to metaphors of one sort or another. But that process of thought proves integral to the larger systemic program. That yields the question of what kind of "Israel" will emerge from a particular systemic process. But there are rules applicable to all systemic processes, which allow us to predict what sort of "Israel" will emerge within a determinate number of possibilities. We come to one recurrent proposition in the completed survey.

> Proposition 2: *What an "Israel" is depends on who wants to know. Philosophers imagine a philosophical "Israel," and politicians conceive a political "Israel."*

I appeal to the standing and circumstance of the system builders in explaining, quite tangentially and en passant, the character and use of the social metaphors selected within a given system. As we saw in Part I, philosophers interested in problems of classification utilize "Israel" as a systemic classifier, whether within the group, for hierarchization of castes, or at the boundaries of the group, for differentiation among nations (which, self-evidently, forms merely another exercise in hierarchization). For philosophers the sui generis presents an embarrassment, but "Israel" as superior species of a common genus fits well in an inquiry into theory. A program of encompassing classification will value "Israel" as essential to the work of setting all things in their proper place and order and giving them all their rightful names. But for the philosophers the social component formed part of the inert background of thought, not a principal component of the activity of system formation. What made their system work and imparted to it compelling urgency was not the matter of "Israel" at all, because that matter, when fully defined and displayed, answered no critical systemic questions. So much for "Israel" as "not-gentile," "not-priest."

Part II showed us as systemically prominent a different set of metaphors, deriving from genealogy and yielding the social group in the familial model. "Israel" as family permitted comparison with other lines of the same family, but not with other families. While joined to the antimetaphorical judgment of "Israel" as sui generis, the family metaphor permitted thought to encompass other political entities as well. These metaphors – for example, of family, of the "other" as part of the family, of the symbolization of the other (and hence, potentially, also of "Israel") by animals and foods – had been available but had played a slender part, if any, in the prior documents of the Judaism of the dual Torah. Both modes of thinking about the social entity – the one genealogical, the other categorically particularistic – found a place side by side within the same documentary statements, and that shows us how the authorships presented a single cogent version of the matter. Both representations of "Israel" treated the social entity as a this-worldly and concrete fact of society, appealing to traits of activity, interchange and action, not merely those of sheer being, of static classification. (An) "Israel" was not only to be but also to do, a category not only of ontology but also of sociology (and therefore history and politics).

And why not? For the sages who portrayed "Israel" in such fleshly terms as family and who also found in "Israel" a social entity without any categorical counterpart at all represented themselves as engaged, in the everyday and the here and now, with the life of that same "Israel." Their concrete experience, as they represented it, focused their attention on the near-at-hand particularities of their "Israel." Engaged in public life and administration, these sages conceived of "Israel" as a unique polity, one subject to its own rules, as much as they represented themselves as practitioners of the honorable professions of politician and bureaucrat. For the politician-clerks, the social consideration constituted a principal component of the system formation. Their urgent question had to do with the standing of "Israel" within the polity of heaven and earth: Who was "Israel" among several pretenders? Even within the modest sample of sources we have surveyed we may readily perceive the centrality of that question, which recurs and forms an urgent and acute matter. Framed in the setting of contemporary history, eschatology, theological disputation, the politics of the hour and the policy of the ages, the issue of "Israel" formed the overriding theme within argument beyond. What made the second phase of the system of the Judaism of the dual Torah work (for those for whom it did work) was the self-evidently valid response the system provided to the issue of "Israel" in particular. That matter contained within itself the critical systemic question. The contrast to the use and function of "Israel" in the Mishnaic phase of the Judaism of the dual Torah hardly needs to be drawn. Once we recognize that "Israel" will matter more to one system than to another, we come to another proposition of general interest, closely tied to the foregoing.

Proposition 3: *The systemic importance of the category "Israel" depends on the generative problematic – the urgent question – of the system builders, and not on their social circumstance. The place of "Israel" within the self-*

evidently true response offered by the system will prove
congruent to the logic of the system and that alone.

It is one thing to claim that philosophers give us a philosophical
"Israel," politicians a political one. It is another to explain merely by
reference to the social standing of the system builders that philosophical or political character imputed to the social entity. That
seems to me trivial, but also wrong. The larger character of the
system imparted to each detail the characteristic traits that defined it.
And that distinctive systemic character derived from the issue addressed by the system as a whole, not from the social standing of the
system builders.[2] Were we to have concluded the formation of our
laws of "Israel"s with the opening one, we should treat as a statement
of (mere) professional or class interest – whether of philosophers or
of politicians or of priests or intellectuals or householders for that
matter – what transcends class and transforms interest. It is the whole
that takes shape and defines the parts. In a well-crafted system – and
all of the systems we have before us are cogent – the details *express*
the whole, they do not merely add up to the whole. To make this
point stick, I have to explain how the "Israel" expressed in its detail
the systemic problematic that gave form and energy to the whole.

The authorships of the documents of the first phase of the Judaism
of the dual Torah worked out the generative problematic of "Israel"s
sanctification. To that matter "Israel" forms an obsessive concern but
supplies no probative data; it is part of the question, not the answer, a
premise and not a presence. The logic of the system of sanctification
would impute particular traits to "Israel" but no categorical imperative attached to "Israel." That same logic did not require "Israel" to
constitute a formative or definitive category. The first Judaism of the
dual Torah reflected on issues of *process*. The outcome of process is
what settled questions of classification. The system specifically derived its motive force from problems framed out of the conflict
between the workings of intentionality, and the matter of classification and categorization defined the arena of that conflict. Indeed,
by definition, issues of classification and finding the right category for
things constituted an inert component of thought: the question, not
the wherewithal for the framing of the answer. The motive for the
answer derived from issues of will and intentionality. The interplay
between human intentionality and the status of the world of things
and of nature, the power of the human being by intentionality to
shape and change the character of nature by reclassifying the givens
of this world from one category to some other – these form the
active force within the system. That is why the lively and vital source

of thought in the Mishnaic system is reflection not on *category* but on *process*. The curious paradox of the Mishnaic statement is that while the intent of the whole is to place all things into the proper category, to show them subject to their appropriate rule, it is the process of categorization, not the categories and their formation (for example), that fills up the entirety of the document. That accounts as well for the fundamental logic that assigns to "Israel" its modest speaking part, but also its towering place as the backdrop of thought.

The documents of the second phase of the Judaism of the dual Torah came to closure at the end of a century of political upheaval. When Christianity became the religion of the state, with the state extirpation of paganism as a matter of public policy and the reduction of Judaism to subordinated status, the Jews faced a critical question. Framing that question in terms of who is Israel encompassed all the important components of the crisis. That is why "Israel" became not a mere premise but an active and powerful presence in the narrative of the system as a whole – and why, also, the system resorted to narrative to make its statement. First, by the turn of the fifth century the Jews had to deal with the claim of Christianity that the political triumph confirmed the nearly four-hundred-year-old truth that Christ had been, and now was proved to be, the King of the world. Second, they had to contend with the Christian claim that the old Israel's salvation, promised by the prophets, had been realized in the original return to Zion, after 586 B.C.E. Third, they had to grapple with the Christians' allegation that the Hebrew Scriptures found their correct interpretation in the now-canonized New Testament, successor and completion of the Old. Fourth, they had to address the Christians' claim to constitute (the new) Israel, replacing the old in God's favor. One could list item after item on a long catalog of points of conflict, but all of them must (from Jews' viewpoint) come down to a single matter: Who now is "Israel"? And, it follows, the generative problematic, the urgent question facing the system builders at the end of the fourth century took the form of the issue of "Israel," and received the, to them self-evidently valid, answer that "we" are "Israel," and "the others" – the competition – are not.

To the acute issue of "Israel," the system's principal propositions – the metaphor of family joined to the principle of the sui generis character of "Israel" as a social entity (no longer a "group" in the category of other groups, however special a species of that genus) – formed a fitting response. The systemic character and also the importance of the category thus derived from the urgent question at hand. When the issues centered on politics, the response to the issues would appeal to the political definition of "Israel" as a concrete fact of palpable society, no longer a mere category in the hierarchical construction of theoretical social categories. Then, but only then, the system took over and worked out with reference to "Israel" its inner logic, order, proportion, and structural cogency.[3] To signal the final issue, I point to the hypothesis addressed in the concluding chapter: that the system builders' social (including political) circumstance defines the generative problematic that imparts self-evidence to the systemically definitive logic, encompassing its social component. We return to this issue presently.

iv. The Case of Paul and "Israel" after the Spirit

Proposition 1: *The shape and meaning imputed to the social component, "Israel," will conform to the larger interests of the system and in detail express the system's main point.*

For proof that the proposition is not particular to the case, we appeal to the "Israel" defined by Paul, who presents us with a metaphor for which, in the documents of the Judaism of the dual Torah, I can find no counterpart in this context.[4] "Israel" compared to an olive tree, standing for "Israel" encompassing gentiles who believe but also Jews by birth who do not believe, "Israel" standing for the elect and those saved by faith and therefore by grace – these complex and somewhat disjointed metaphors and definitions form a coherent and simple picture when we see them not in detail but as part of the larger whole of Paul's entire system. For the issue of "Israel" for Paul forms a detail of a system centered upon a case in favor of salvation through Christ and faith in him alone, even without keeping the rules of the Torah. So does the consensus of the familiar and rich corpus of scholarship on Paul present matters, and I take the results as definitive.[5]

Before we proceed to Paul in particular, let us consider the larger problem of social definition, therefore metaphorization, that confronted Christians in general. By way of exemplifying the range of choices available to a nascent group and underlining the critical importance of the issue of the social metaphor within a religious system, let us begin not at the center but at the fringe, with the problem of defining a social metaphor for the social group "Christians," as the earliest Christian thinkers contemplated the problem. Like Israel organizing its ancient Scriptures in the sixth century in the aftermath of the exile from the Land of Israel and return to the Land, Christian social thinkers in late antiquity understood themselves to be something essentially new, not merely a new group, but a new *kind* of group. A rapid survey of the repertoire of choices shows what is at stake. As soon as Christians coalesced into groups, they asked themselves what sort of groups they formed. They in fact maintained several positions. First, they held that they were a people, enjoying the status of the Jewish people, and that, as Harnack says, "furnished adherents of the new faith with a political and historical self-consciousness." So they were part of Israel, that is, a species of the genus Israel – a different part from the old, to be sure – and continued the Israel of ancient times; they were not a new group but a very old one. But, second, others further defined themselves as not only a new people, but as a new *type* of group, recognizing no taxonomic counterpart in the existing spectrum of human societies, peoples, or nations.

The claims of the Christians indeed varied according to circumstance, so Harnack summarizes matters in a passage of stunning acuity:

> Was the cry raised, "You are renegade Jews" – the answer came, "We are the community of the Messiah, and therefore the true Israelites." If people said, "You are simply Jews," the reply was, "We are a new creation and a new people." If again they were taxed with their recent origin and told that they were but of yesterday, they retorted, "We only seem to be the younger People; from the beginning we have been latent; we have always existed, previous to any other people; we are the original people of God." If they were told, "You do not deserve to live" the answer ran, "We would die to live, for we are citizens of the world to come, and sure that we shall rise again."[6]

The Christians found themselves, therefore, laying claim to a variety of identities as a social group, and not all of their identities proved mutually compatible. To be (part of) Israel after all is not the same thing as to be a wholly new people. To be citizens of Rome is not the same thing as to be denizens of the world to come. To be a third people, a no-people that has become a people, a people that has been called out of the people – all of these choices faced the new group. These reflections on the classification of the new group – superior to the old, sui generis, and whatever the occasion of polemic requires the group to be – fill the early Christian writings. In general there were three choices: Greeks or gentiles, Jews, and the Christians as the new People.

And this brings us to Paul. The generative problematic that tells Paul what he wishes to know about "Israel" derives from the larger concerns of the Christian system Paul proposes to work out. That problematic was framed in the need, in general, to explain the

difference, as to salvific condition, between those who believed in
Christ, and those who did not believe.[7] But it focused, specifically,
upon the matter of "Israel," and how those who believed in Christ
but did not derive from "Israel" related to both those who believed
and also derived from "Israel" and those who did not believe but
derived from "Israel." Do the first-named have to keep the Torah?
Are the nonbelieving Jews subject to justification? Because the issue
cannot have proved critical in the working out of an individual system
(but only in the address to the world at large), we may take for
granted that Paul's own Jewish origin made the question at hand
important, if not critical. What transformed the matter from a
chronic into an acute question – the matter of salvation through
keeping the Torah – encompassed also the matter of who is "Israel."

For his part, Paul appeals, for his taxic indicator of "Israel," to a
consideration we have not found commonplace at all, namely,
circumcision. It is certainly implicit in the Torah, but the Mishnah's
laws, we recall, accommodate as "Israel" persons who (for good and
sufficient reasons) are not circumcised, and treat as "non-Israel"
persons who are circumcised but otherwise do not qualify. So for the
Mishnah's system circumcision forms a premise, not a presence, a
datum but not a decisive taxic indicator. But Paul, by contrast, can
have called "Israel" all those who are circumcised, and "non-Israel" all
those who are not circumcised – pure and simple. That has been
shown, just now, by Jonathan Z. Smith,[8] who states:

> The strongest and most persistent use of circumcision as a taxic
> indicator is found in Paul and the deutero-Pauline literature.
> Paul's self-description is framed in terms of the two most
> fundamental halakic definitions of the Jewish male: circumcision
> and birth from a Jewish mother . . . . "Circumcised" is con-
> sistently used in the Pauline literature as a technical term for the
> Jew, "uncircumcised," for the gentile.

It must follow, as I said, that for Paul, "Israel" is "the circumcised
nation," and an "Israel" is a circumcised male. The reason for the
meaning attached to "Israel" is spelled out by Smith:

> What is at issue . . . is the attempt to establish a new taxon:
> "where there cannot be Greek and Jew, circumcised and un-
> circumcised, barbarian and Scythian" (Col. 3:11), "for neither
> circumcision counts for anything but uncircumcision but a new
> creation" (Gal. 6:15).

It follows that for Paul, the matter of "Israel" and its definition forms
part of a larger project of reclassifying Christians in terms not defined
by the received categories, now (as we recall from Chapter 1) a third

race, a new race, a new man, in a new story. Smith proceeds to make the matter entirely explicit to Paul's larger system:

> Paul's theological arguments with respect to circumcision have their own internal logic and situation: that in the case of Abraham, it was posterior to faith (Rom. 4:9–12); that spiritual things are superior to physical things (Col. 3:11–14); that the Christian is the "true circumcision" as opposed to the Jew (Phil. 3:3) . . . But these appear secondary to the fundamental taxonomic premise, the Christian is a member of a new taxon.

In this same context Paul's Letter to the Romans presents a consistent picture. In chapters 9–11 he presents his reflections on what and who is (an) "Israel." Having specified that the family of Abraham will inherit the world not through the law but through the righteousness of faith (Rom. 4:13), Paul confronts "Israel" as family and redefines the matter in a way coherent with his larger program. Then the children of Abraham will be those who "believe in him that raised from the dead Jesus our Lord, who was put to death for our trespasses and raised for our justification" (Rom. 4:24–5). For us the critical issue is whether Paul sees these children of Abraham as "Israel." The answer is in his address to "my kinsmen by race. They are Israelites, and to them belong the sonship, the glory, the covenants, the giving of the law, the worship, and the promises; to them belong the patriarchs, and of their race, according to the flesh, is the Christ. God who is over all be blessed for ever" (Rom. 9:3–4). "Israel" then is the holy people, the people of God. But Paul proceeds to invoke a fresh metaphor, "Israel" as olive tree, and so to reframe the doctrine of "Israel" in a radical way:

> Not all who are descended from Israel belong to Israel, and not all are children of Abraham because they are his descendants. . . . it is not the children of the flesh who are the children of God, but the children of the promise are reckoned as descendants. (Rom. 9:6–7)

Here we have an explicit definition of "Israel," now not after the flesh but after the promise. "Israel" then is no longer a family in the concrete sense in which we have seen the notion expressed in earlier materials. "Israel after the flesh" who pursued righteousness that is based on law did not succeed in fulfilling that law because they did not pursue it through faith (Rom. 9:31), "and gentiles who did not pursue righteousness have attained it, that is, righteousness through faith" (Rom. 9:30). Now there is an "Israel" after the flesh but *also* "a remnant chosen by grace . . . the elect obtained it" (Rom. 11:5–6); consequently the fleshly "Israel" remains, but gentiles ("a wild olive shoot") have been grafted "to share the richness of the olive tree" (Rom. 11:17). Do these constitute "Israel"? Yes and no. They share in the promise. They are "Israel" in the earlier definition of the children of Abraham. There remains an "Israel" after the flesh, which has its place as well. And that place remains with God: "As regards election they are beloved for the sake of their forefathers. For the gifts and the call of God are irrevocable" (Rom. 11:28–9).

This very rapid and schematic account makes the point at hand and illustrates the law with which we began: The shape and meaning imputed to the social component "Israel" here conform to the larger interests of the system constructed by Paul, both episodically and, in Romans, quite systematically. "Israel" as a detail expresses also the system's main point. For Paul's Judaic system, encompassing believing (former) "gentiles" but also retaining a systemic status for non-believing Jews, "Israel" forms an important component within a larger structure. More to the point, "Israel" finds definition on account of the logical requirements of that encompassing framework. Indeed, I cannot imagine making sense of Paul's remarkably complex metaphor of the olive tree without understanding the problem of thought that confronted him, and that he solved through, among other details, his thinking on "Israel." The notion of entering "Israel" through belief but not behavior ("works") in one detail expresses the main point of Paul's system, which concerns not who is "Israel" but what faith in Christ means.[9]

When I offered as a law applicable to many instances the proposition that the shape and meaning imputed to the social component "Israel" will conform to the larger interests of the system and in detail express the system's main point, I faced the task of giving another case in which the same proposition applies. Paul's case suffices. As we shall see presently, however, I could as well have appealed to Philo and to the Essenes of Qumran for further instances. Hence my proposition forms a law applicable to a variety of Judaisms, not merely a generalization deriving from only one particular case. Giving three cases does not demonstrate the validity of the law, but it does demonstrate that the law is a law and not merely a restatement of the traits pertinent to a single case. Now that we see how an "Israel" expresses the traits of the larger system that defines it, we want to know how to account for those definitive systemic traits. That carries us to the first of two propositions governing the formation of a system as a whole, for which I have invented the word, *systemopoiea*. The one concerns the character of the system builders, the other, the quality and shape of the critical question they proposed to answer. I have already appealed to that social law of Judaism(s) when I proposed to explain by reference to the social and political status of the respective authorships the systemic differences between the first and the second stages in the formation of the Judaism of the dual Torah. Now let us see whether I have given as a law what is in fact particular to its case.

v.   The Cases of Philo and of the Essenes of Qumran

> Proposition 2: *What an "Israel" is depends on who wants to know. Philosophers imagine a philosophical "Israel," and politicians conceive a political "Israel."*

By philosopher in the present context I mean an intellectual who attempts to state as a coherent whole, within a single system of thought and (implicit) explanation, diverse categories and classifications of data. By politician I mean a person of public parts, one who undertakes to shape a social polity, a person of standing in a social group such as a community, who proposes to explain in some theoretical framework the meaning and character of the life of that group or nation or society or community. I should classify the framers of the Mishnah as philosophers, those of the Yerushalmi and related writings (by their own word) as politicians. The related but distinct systems made by each group exhibit traits of philosophy and politics, respectively, for reasons I have now spelled out. The generalization is before us. Does it apply to more than our own case? For purposes of showing that the same phenomenon derives from other cases and therefore constitutes a law, I appeal to an individual, a philosopher, and an authorship, the formative intellects of the community at Qumran. Philo, the Jewish philosopher of Alexandria, serves as our example of the former, and the authorship of the more important writings of the Essene community of Qumran, the latter.

For Philo, Israel forms a paradigmatic metaphor, bearing three meanings. The first is ontological, which signifies the places of "Israel" in God's creation. The second is epistemological. This signifies the knowledge of God that Israel possesses. The third is political, referring to the polity that "Israel" possesses and projects in light of its ontological place and epistemological access to God.[10] Not wishing to pretend to know things that, firsthand, in fact I do not know, I turn to a quick survey of the role assigned to "Israel" in Philo's system, as that role is portrayed in the systematic pictures provided by the two modern masters of the subject, Harry A. Wolfson and Erwin R. Goodenough.[11] Our point of interest is achieved when we perceive even from a distance the basic contours of Philo's vision of "Israel."

What we shall see is that, for Philo, "Israel" formed a category within a larger theory of how humanity knows divinity, an aspect of ontology and epistemology. True, "Israel" emerges as, if not unique, then sui generis. But that is only in the framework of a system of classification, so "Israel" is not really sui generis in the way in which, in the second phase of the Judaism of the dual Torah, "Israel" has no counterpart in kind, not merely in species. What makes an "Israel" into "Israel" for Philo is a set of essentially philosophical considerations, concerning adherence to or perception of God. In the philosophical system of Philo, "Israel" constitutes a philosophical category, not a social entity in an everyday sense.[12]

Seeing "Israel" as "the people which is dedicated to his service," Philo holds that "Israel" is the best of races and is capable of seeing God, and this capability of seeing God is based upon the habit of his service to God.[13] The upshot is a capacity to receive a type of prophecy that comes directly from God, and one must be descended from "Israel" to receive that type of prophecy. An Egyptian, Hagar, cannot see the Supreme Cause.[14] The notion of inherited "merit" (in this context an inappropriate metaphor) bears more than a single burden; here "merit" or inherited capacity involves a clearer perception of God than is attained by those without the same inheritance – a far cry indeed from the "merit of the ancestors" as the fourth-century sages would interpret it.[15] Mere moral and intellectual qualifications, however, do not suffice. One has to enjoy divine grace, which Moses had, and which, on account of the merit of the patriarchs, the people have. Wolfson comments, "This view, that the revelation of the Law was a special gift to Israel, was by the time of Philo a common belief among the Jews, as is evidenced from Sirach."[16]

We see, therefore, that Philo defines "Israel" to mean "seeing God," and the people are "those who are members of that race endowed with vision," or "those to whose lot it has fallen to see the best, that is the truly existing."[17] The definitions at hand form part of a distinction, in Wolfson's words,

> . . . important to Philo, between the two methods of knowing God and with God also the Logos reflects the distinction made by Philo himself between the three kinds of knowledge of the mind, one that is indirectly derived from sense-perception, one that comes from a knowledge of the ideas, and a third, which is directly derived from God by revelation and prophecy. These three kinds of knowledge . . . correspond to [an epistemological scheme] which is found in Plato.

No wonder, then, that the name "Israel," applied to individual or nation alike, means "seeing God."[18]

Wolfson's account of Philo's political theory[19] covers a variety of subjects not germane to our interest. Wolfson points to Philo's definition of the Mosaic polity as "not common descent but the common heritage of the Law," and to his position on the "superiority of spiritual kindship to the kinship of blood," and the like. These issues are worked out in accord with a philosophical program; Wolfson compares Philo's position to Aristotle's, for example. The main point here is that "even the native-born Jew is a member of that polity [Israel], in the full sense of the term membership, not only because he is a descendant of the stock that founded that polity, but also, and primarily so, because he remained loyal to the Law which is the heritage of that stock."[20] Philo's main point in this context is that kinship based upon a common belief is superior to kinship based upon a common descent, a position he repeats in a number of passages.[21] The metaphor at hand, therefore, draws upon shared viewpoint or belief as the criterion for the definition of the entity. But whether the entity constitutes a social group is a subordinate question; the purpose for which definition is initially proposed is not an inquiry into the concrete meaning of an abstraction "Israel," or a search for the deeper, hence more abstract, meaning of a concrete group of people who exhibit shared traits, "Israel." From either perspective, Philo's "Israel" is scarcely visible.

In this respect, we find ourselves where we stood with Paul, who proposed to work out a definition of "Israel" within that larger system that encompassed "Israel" out of the past and also the "Israel" that would be grafted on. No wonder, then, that the "Israel" as the "one who sees God" – an "Israel" perhaps implicit throughout, but not brought to the surface in any of our sages' definitions – fits so well into Philo's larger quest but so poorly with the "Israel"s of the Judaism of the dual Torah. True, for both "Israel"s what is at stake is willingness to serve God, for example, by observing the Torah: "He commanded those who should live in this polity to follow God in this as in other matters." Wolfson repeats,

> The superiority of the kinship based upon the service of God to that based upon blood relationship is also asserted by him in his comment upon the verse, "The proselyte who is with you shall rise higher and higher, but you shall fall lower and lower." The proselyte, he says, will be exalted "because he has come over to God of his own accord . . . while the nobly born who had falsified the sterling of his high lineage will be dragged down to the lowest depths . . . in order that all men who behold this example may be corrected by it, learning that God received

gladly virtue which grows out of ignoble birth, utterly dis-
regarding its original roots."[22]

But Philo gives us an "Israel" not "after the flesh," or even, in Paul's
sense, "after the spirit" or "the promise," but rather, one that we
might characterize as an "Israel after a philosophical search": "those
to whose lot it has fallen to see the best, that is the truly existing."[23]
"Israel" then is made up of members of the Mosaic polity, those who
are sons of God in the sense that they are willing to serve God and
keep the Torah.

As to the Jews in his own day, Philo writes as though he speaks of a
different "Israel" from the one "whose lot it has fallen to see the best,
that is the truly existing." Now he addresses a concrete social entity,
and, not surprisingly, he invokes social traits to describe that political
entity:

> The Jews of Palestine and of all these colonies [in the diaspora]
> constitute to him one whole nation, of which the Jews in each
> locality are a part. That whole nation of the Jews forms a polity,
> which, in comparison with the local polities of each individual
> Jewish locality, is described by him as the more universal polity,
> which bears the general name of the nation, that is, the name of
> Israel, and which depends for its existence upon the existence of
> the Temple.[24]

Here we find different language used to describe a quite different
"Israel" indeed. Philo saw the Jews as a group formed by common
origin and common religion; he calls them a nation and a universal
polity of divine calling. According to Wolfson, Philo saw "Israel" as:

> . . . a number of individual communities, geographically and
> politically dispersed, but united by a common law, a common
> form of organized life, and a common way of living. . . . In this
> conception of Jews as constituting a nation which transcends
> race and local citizenship, Philo thus formulates a new concep-
> tion of nationality, one expressed not in terms of race or
> territory or political government, but rather in terms of religion
> or culture.[25]

It is not without solid reason that Wolfson finds in Paul a comparable
position, overall:

> Just as in Philo, the expression "divine ecclesia" is used as a
> description of the entire body of professing Jews, so also in
> Christianity the entire body of professing Christians is described
> as constituting an "ecclesia of God." Just as in Philo all those who
> profess Judaism, whether native-born Jews or converts, are

called "the sons of God," so also in Christianity all those who are "led by the spirit of God" are called "the sons of God." Just as in Philo all those who profess Judaism are called Israel, so also Christianity, considering itself the heir of Judaism, calls itself "the Israel of God" [Gal. 3:29]. Just as Philo describes the whole body of professing Jews as "the universal polity" by which he means "universal ecclesia" or "catholic church," so in Christianity the whole body of professing Christians came to be called "the universal ecclesia" or "catholic church."[26]

While interpreting Philo differently from Wolfson, Goodenough underlines the identical data in telling us Philo's definition and use of "Israel." For him, too, "Israel" constitutes a component in a philosophical system.[27] Philo identifies the patriarchs, Abraham, Isaac, and Jacob, with the Powers of God, and they are a medium for giving God's higher gifts to men:

> This august triad was made into "a royal priesthood and a holy race." This race has got the name of Israel, that is, "Seeing God," and is distinguished by the fact that it has the vision of God at the end of the mystic Road, the highest possible achievement, to which vision God draws the soul up the Road by the action of the divine powers. This is not a reference to the race of Israel, but first to the patriarchs, and then to those who got the vision, whether Jews or Gentiles, and only to those. For the true successors of the Patriarchs, who have themselves been thus elevated, are not those descended from them in the flesh but their spiritual successors.[28]

Goodenough's reading of Philo, like Wolfson's, gives us an "Israel" that is integral to a philosophical system, and that is the main point: The traits of this philosopher's "Israel" are profoundly philosophical and emphasize aspects of intellect.[29]

If Philo, serving as the counterpart to the authorship of the Mishnah, represents an intellectual's thinking about the entity "Israel," we do well to identify a political reading, placing into perspective, for comparison and contrast, the deeply political definitions of "Israel" formed by the authorships of the Yerushalmi, Genesis Rabbah, and Leviticus Rabbah. For they appeal to political metaphors – metaphors of the group as *polis*. They see "Israel" as a political entity matched against "Rome," or treated as sui generis, or compared to a family – anything but a mere category, by happenstance, a classification of persons, rather than of sexual abnormalities, to be set into a hierarchical system. For that purpose we turn to the library that was selected by, and therefore presumably speaks for, the builders of an "Israel" that is the best documented, in its original site and condition, of any in antiquity: the Essene community of Qumran.[30] Just as for Philo I appealed to the foremost authorities for guidance, so for the Essene community at Qumran I do the same.[31] Geza Vermes, translator of the more important documents and authority on the community, draws our attention to what is critical.[32]

The Essenes of Qumran serve as a test case for two distinct laws: First, what matters to begin with is dictated by the traits of the one to whom the subject is important, not by the objective and indicative characteristics of the subject itself; second, the importance of a topic derives from the character of the system that takes up that topic. Again, in both matters I have to show that my generalizations pertain to more than a single case. We turn first to the systemic definition of "Israel": what kind of "Israel" and for what purpose; then we consider the importance, within a system, of an "Israel."

By "Israel" the authorships of the documents of the Essene library of Qumran mean "us" and no one else. We start with that "us" and proceed from there to "Israel." In this way I show that – as with the authorship of the documents of the second phase of the dual Torah – the movement of thought began with the particular and moved outward to the general. The group's principal documents comprised a Community Rule, which "legislates for a kind of monastic society"; the Damascus Rule, "for an ordinary lay existence"; and the War Rule and Messianic Rule, "while associated with the other two, and no doubt reflecting to some extent a contemporary state of affairs, plan for a future age."[33] Among the four,[34] the first two will tell us their authorships' understanding of the relationship between "us" and "Israel," and that is what is critical to the picture of the type of "us" that (as we shall see) is "Israel" at hand.

Stated simply, what our authorships meant by "us" was simply "Israel," or "the true Israel." That is why the group[35] organized itself as a replication of "all Israel," as they read about "Israel" in those passages of Scripture that impressed them. They structured their group, in Vermes's language, "so that it corresponded faithfully to that of Israel itself, dividing it into priests and laity, the priests being described as the 'sons of Zadok' – Zadok was High Priest in David's time – and the laity grouped after the biblical model into twelve tribes."[36] This particular Israel then divided itself into units of thousands, hundreds, fifties, and tens.[37] The Community Rule further knows divisions within the larger group, specifically, "the men of holiness" and "the men of perfect holiness" within a larger "Community." The corporate being of the community came to realization in common meals, prayers, and deliberations. Vermes says, "Perfectly obedient to each and every one of the laws of Moses and to all that was commanded by the prophets, they were to love one another and to share with one another their knowledge, powers, and possessions."[38]

The description of the inner life of the group presents us with a division of a larger society. But one detail among many probative ones tells us that this group implicitly conceived of itself as "Israel" – namely, that the group lived apart from the temple of Jerusalem and had its liturgical life worked out in utter isolation from that central cult. They had their own calendar, which differed from the one people take for granted was observed in general, for their calendar was reckoned not by the moon but by the sun. This yielded different dates for the holy days and effectively marked the group as utterly out of touch with other Jews.[39] The solar calendar followed by the Essene community at Qumran meant that holy days for that group were working days for others and vice versa. The group furthermore had its own designation for various parts of the year. The year was divided into seven fifty-day periods, as Vermes says, each marked by an agricultural festival (e.g., the Feast of New Wine, of Oil).[40] On the Pentecost, treated as the Feast of the Renewal of the Covenant, the group would assemble in hierarchical order: "the priests first, ranked in order of status, after them the Levites, and lastly 'all the people one after another in their Thousands, Hundreds, Fifties, and Tens, that every Israelite may know his place in the community of God according to the everlasting design.'"[41]   There can be no doubt from this passage – and a vast array of counterparts can be assembled – that the documents at hand address "Israel." The priests' blessing of the "Israel" at hand corresponds, therefore, to the priestly blessing of Num. 6:24–6:

> May he bless you with all good and preserve you from all evil.
> May he lighten your heart with life-giving wisdom and grant you
> eternal knowledge. May he raise his merciful face toward you for
> everlasting bliss.[42]

Other rites, involving purification, the common meal (eaten in a state of cultic cleanness), and the like, suggest that we deal with an "Israel" that in its metaphorical thought about itself forms the counterpart to the holy temple in Jerusalem, an "Israel" that, as a social group, constitutes the entirety of the "community of Israel" in the here and now. Vermes makes this matter explicit:

> The Council of the Community was to be the "Most Holy Dwelling of Aaron" where "without the flesh of holocausts and the fat

of sacrifice," a "sweet fragrance" was to be sent up to God, and where prayer was to serve "as an acceptable fragrance of righteousness."[43]

It follows, as Vermes says, that "the Community [we should read: this "Israel"] itself was to be the sacrifice offered to God in atonement for Israel's sins."[44]

To complete the case that the Essenes of Qumran conceived a political "Israel," namely, themselves, it suffices to ask how the word "Israel" is used in their writings. A few examples, chosen at random, tell the entire story:

> *The Community Rule:*
> But the God of Israel and his angel of truth will succor all the sons of light [meaning, the group] . . . [45]

> No man shall walk in the stubbornness of his heart . . . but he shall circumcise in the Community the foreskin of evil inclination and of stiffness of neck, that they may lay a foundation of truth for Israel, for the Community of the everlasting Covenant. They shall atone for all those in Aaron who have freely pledged themselves to holiness, and for those in Israel who have freely pledged themselves to the House of Truth, and for those who join them to live in community and to take part in the trial and judgment and condemnation of all those who transgress the precepts.[46]

> But when a man enters the Covenant to walk according to all these precepts that he may join the holy congregation, they shall examine his spirit in community with respect to his understanding and practice of the Law, under the authority of the sons of Aaron who have freely pledged themselves in the Community to restore His covenant and to heed all the precepts commanded by Him, and of the multitude of Israel who have freely pledged themselves in the Community to return to his covenant. . . .[47]

> When these become members of the Community in Israel according to all these rules, they shall establish the spirit of holiness according to everlasting truth. . . . At that time the men of the Community shall set apart a House of Holiness in order that it may be united to the most holy things, and a House of Community for Israel, for those who walk in perfection.[48]

It seems to me that these references to "Israel" repeatedly take for granted that "Israel" is equivalent to either the caste, "Israel" as against the Levites and priests or, more commonly, the group at hand, that is, "Israel" as "us." It is possible that the writers take account of an "Israel-out-there," but Vermes's translation repeatedly suggests otherwise. For, as he reads the texts, "Israel" is repeatedly modified by "Community," standing in apposition.

References in the other important statement suggest that the group identifies itself in particular with the remnant of Israel, the plant that sprang from Israel, the remnant that was not destroyed after 586 C.E.[49]

> *The Damascus Covenant:*
> None of the men who enter the New Covenant in the land of
> Damascus and who again betray it and depart from the fountain
> of living waters shall be reckoned with the Council of the people
> or inscribed in its Book from the day of the gathering in of the
> Teacher of the Community until the coming of the Messiah out
> of Aaron and Israel.[50]

Essentially, "Israel" encompasses those who are within the Covenant, pure and simple. And that Covenant encompasses all those in the group that stands behind these documents and no one else.

This survey has carried us far from our original question. Let me return to the proposed law – that what an "Israel" is depends on who wants to know. This proposition was spelled out in Chapters 5 and 10. Now we see that Philo has given us a philosophical "Israel." And we now find the same phenomenon once more. The authorships of the documents preserved by the Essenes of Qumran define "Israel" not as a fictive entity possessing spiritual traits alone or mainly, but as a concrete social group, an entity in the here and now, that may be defined by traits of persons subject to the same sanctions and norms, sharing the same values and ideals. Builders of a community or a polis, and hence, politicians, the authorships of the Essenes of Qumran conceived and described in law a political "Israel." Their "Israel" and Philo's bear nothing in common.

The one "Israel" – the Essenes' – constitutes a political entity and society. The "Israel" of the Essenes is the "Israel" of history and eschatology of Scripture, as much as the "Israel" of the authorship of the Yerushalmi, Genesis Rabbah, and Leviticus Rabbah refers back to the "Israel" of Genesis and Leviticus. The other "Israel" – Philo's – comprises people of shared intellectual traits in a larger picture of how God is known, as much as the "Israel" of the authorship of the Mishnah and related writings exhibits taxonomic traits and serves a function of classification. Both sets of politicians present us with political "Israel"s, that is, each with an "Israel" that exhibits the traits of a polis, a community ("people," "nation"). Both sets of philosophers offer a philosophical "Israel," with traits of a taxonomic character – one set for one system, another set for the other – that carry out a larger systemic purpose of explanation and philosophical classification. We have, therefore, not a generalization of a particular case, but a rule that can be tested in three cases.

vi. The Cases of Paul, Philo, the Essenes of Qumran, and the Sages of the Dual Torah

> Proposition 3: *The systemic importance of the category "Israel" depends on the generative problematic – the urgent question – of the system builders, and not on their social circumstance. The place of "Israel" within the self-evidently true response offered by the system will prove congruent to the logic of the system and that alone.*

The proposition is that the systemic question – the precipitating crisis that leads several generations of intellectuals to rethink the grounds of social being and to reconsider all fundamental questions in a new way – determines the importance of any category within the system. The negative version of the same law is obvious. The paramount character of a category in the social facts-out-there, in the streets and households (in the case of the social entity), has slight bearing upon the proportions and order of the system. Stated in the positive, the rule is that the systemic logic-in-here dictates all issues of proportion, balance, and order. We therefore ask ourselves how on objective grounds and by appealing to data, not mere impressions, we may assess the relative importance of a given systemic structural category when we compare one system with another.

Whether "Israel" takes an important place in a system is decided by the system and its logic, not the circumstance of the Jews in the here and now. Systemopoeia is a symbolic transaction worked out in imagination, not a sifting and sorting of facts. But how do we know whether any systemic component plays a more, or a less, important role? A judgment on the importance of a given entity or category in one system by comparison to the importance of that same entity or category in another need not rely upon subjective criteria. A reasonably objective measure of the matter lends hope to test the stated law. That criterion is whether the system remains cogent without consideration of its "Israel." Philo's does, the Mishnah's does, Paul's does not, the Essenes' does not, and the second stage in Judaism's does not.

The criterion of importance therefore does not derive from merely counting up references to "Israel." What we must do is to assess the role and place of the social entity in a system by asking a simple question. Were the entity or trait "Israel" to be removed from a given system, would that system radically change in character or would it merely lose a detail? What is required is a mental experiment, but not a very difficult one. What we do is simply present a reprise of our systemic description. Let me state some bald facts. First, without "Israel," Paul would have had no system. The generative question of his system required him to focus attention on the definition of the social entity "Israel." Paul originated among Jews but addressed both Jews and gentiles, seeking to form the lot into a single social entity "in Christ Jesus." The social dimension of his system formed the generative question with which he proposed to contend. Second, without "Israel," Philo, by contrast, can have done very well indeed. For even our brief and schematic survey of the Philo described by Wolfson and Goodenough has shown us that, whatever mattered, "Israel" did not. It was a detail of a theory of knowledge of God, not the generative problematic even of the treatment of the knowledge of God, let alone of the system as a whole (which we scarcely approached, and had no reason to approach). We may therefore say that "Israel" formed an important category for Paul and not for Philo. Accordingly, the judgment of the matter rests on more than mere word counts, on the one side, or exercises of impression and taste, on the other. It forms part of a larger interpretation of the system as a whole and what constitutes the system's generative problematic.

But this rapid experiment in imagination hardly concludes the assessment or bears the burden of proof that the relative importance of the social component of a system may be gauged in objective terms. Far from it. It is not only the problematic, but the topical program and category structure and organization of a system that will provide probative testimony to issues of importance or peripherality. And these matters constitute statements of an entirely factual order. Specifically, I appeal simply to the "table of contents" that a book stating a system would offer. That is, after all, something that the corpus of writings of a system – its canon – allows us to compose for ourselves. What the cases of Philo and Paul present is a quite simple criterion, which is the shape and proportion of the categorical structure of a system. We therefore can define the categories of a system – whether they concern this or that, whether they focus on one thing or some other – simply by listing the titles of books deemed canonical, the titles of chapters or tractates, and, for the classification of systems, the types of such titles, the character of the encompassing program. We begin by asking whether and how systems may be shown symmetrical to one another, then attend to the assessment of the importance or unimportance of a given systemic component, for example, the social entity.

The categorical imperative of a system is illustrated, first of all, by the Judaism of the dual Torah in its two phases. A literature that is made up of Mishnah tractates and supplements to those tractates and that does not contain a single "tractate" organized around a book of Scripture is different from a literature that encompasses Scripture "tractates." The Judaism of the dual Torah at its first phase is categorically quite symmetrical with the Judaism of the dual Torah at its second. For the former is organized around Mishnah tractates (e.g., Tosefta) and Scripture "tractates" (e.g., Sifra and the two Sifrés), and the latter is organized in the same way, with its Yerushalmi and Bavli to the Mishnah tractates chosen for study and its Genesis Rabbah and Leviticus Rabbah for its Scripture "tractates." These systems then are symmetrical as to their literary categories, even though, as I have suggested, they are asymmetrical in other ways. But, by contrast, how are Philo's and Paul's and the Essenes' systems categorically symmetrical? They are, of course, not at all symmetrical. And were we to ask Philo to list his categories, all he would do is point us to the titles of his tractates, none of which coincides with any title we might (hypothetically) hear from Paul.[51] Now to the point at hand: Would Paul give us a "tractate on Israel"? Indeed, he would. In fact, in Rom. 9–11, he has, and not only there. Would Philo offer us a "tractate on Israel"? His system does not present one, because, within its logic, structure, proportion and order, it does not require one. For Philo "Israel" forms at best a chapter in the tractate on ontology. It follows that "Israel" in fact – not merely in subjective impression – plays a far more critical role within Paul's Judaic system than within Philo's.

With that criterion in hand, we turn to the Essene community at Qumran, this time wanting to know whether the system as a whole, as described by Vermes,[52] treats as systemically critical or as merely tangential the matter of who, and what, is "Israel." When the library of the Essenes of Qumran takes up the issue, it turns to what, to the authorships at hand, is its central question. Indeed, we may say that if the generative problematic of the Mishnah is defined by the exegesis of sanctification in the here and now of "Israel"'s everyday reality, accounting for the excruciating detail to which the Mishnah subjects its audience, the precipitating issue of the Essene system revealed in the library of Qumran is defined by the exegesis in detail of "us" as "Israel." That issue holds together the principal documents and comes to expression even in a variety of fragments.

In wanting to ask about the (relative) importance of "Israel" in the system as a whole, we must realize that when the authorships of the

Essenes wrote about "Israel," they meant "us," that is, themselves, and when – more to the point – they wrote about their community, they thought that they described and legislated for "Israel." It follows that when their topical program treats the community, the issue is "Israel." The reason is that the system, and therefore also the group, begins with the position that the social entity of the system forms "Israel," the saving remnant, all that is left. What is urgent to the group is the explanation of who that group is by comparison with and contrast to others claiming the same status, the status of "Israel." That is what is urgent. The social circumstance of the system builders is not the surface consideration; the logic of the system dictates discourse.

By the stated criterion, then, two of the principal documents, the Community Scroll and the Damascus Covenant, constitute two sustained tractates on "Israel."[53] The one, to generalize somewhat, tells us a great deal about the organization of the social entity, the other, about the qualifications and conduct of membership – the one therefore about "Israel" the entity, the other about an "Israel" within the larger entity and representative of it, "Israel" writ large, "Israel" writ small. For example, the Community Scroll spends much time describing the institutions of the community beginning with the Council of the Community or assembly of the Congregation.[54] Vermes states, "From a passage ordering all the members to sit in their correct places . . . , it would seem to have been a gathering of the whole community, under the priests and men of importance, with the guardian at the head."[55] Various rules governed the social requirements and sanctions of this "Israel" – for example, grounds for expulsion. A central topic, as I have already indicated, was the common meals and how they were conducted. The importance of the meal may be gauged from the fact that a recurrent sanction involved ostracism, meaning exclusion from the pure meal. A further set of elaborate rules governed entry into the community (what I have called a novitiate) for a year, followed by a further year of trial.[56] Ample attention, moreover, is paid to the supreme authority of the "Israel," its administration, power, responsibilities, and the like. The Guardian of the community forms a central topic. A sizable body of rules of public conduct is included; indeed the Damascus Covenant presents a set of small but highly systematic pictures of socially permitted behavior of various sorts.

If, therefore, we ask whether "Israel" is critical to the Essenes of Qumran, a simple fact answers our question. Were we to remove "Israel" in general and in detail from the topical program at hand, we should lose, if not the entirety of the library, then nearly the whole of some documents, and the larger part of many of them. The Essene library of Qumran constitutes a vast collection of writings about "Israel," its definition and conduct, history and destiny. We cannot make an equivalent statement of the entire corpus of Philo's writings, even though Philo obviously concerned himself with the life and welfare of the "Israel" of which, in Alexandria as well as world over, he saw himself a part. The reason for the systemic importance among the Essenes of Qumran of "Israel," furthermore, derives from the meanings imputed to that category. The library stands for a social group that conceives of itself as "Israel" and that wishes, in these documents, to spell out what that "Israel" is and must do. The system as a whole forms an exercise in the definition of "Israel" as against that "non-Israel" composed not of gentiles but of erring (former) Israelites. The saving remnant is all that is left: "Israel."

To revert to the system at hand, "Israel" forms a consequential category in both phases of the Judaism of the dual Torah, but for different reasons and, consequently, in different ways. The former of the two, the Mishnaic phase, presents us with no tractate of "Israel," whereas I read Genesis Rabbah and Leviticus Rabbah as remarkably cogent statements on, and of, an "Israel." True, were we to count the number of references to "Israel," proportionate to a given document, in writings of the one phase as against the other, I do not imagine that the result would produce important variation. But that hardly matters to our inquiry. "Israel" is important in the programs of the Mishnah and the Yerushalmi. In each case, the grounds for Israel's importance is particular to the systemic statement. The logic of the Mishnah tells its authorship that "Israel" is sanctified, and the modes and aspects of sanctification – of "Israel" – then form the imperative that dictates categories for inquiry, classifications for analysis. That same categorical imperative operates, in the nature of things, in the Yerushalmi. But it does not govern. A different generative problematic dominates, and that is what imparts to "Israel" the obviously critical importance it enjoys in the documents of the second phase of the Judaism of the dual Torah. The problematic addresses the issue not of sanctification but of salvation as a consequence of sanctification. Then the tractates remain those of sanctification, but the paramount issue of sanctification finds itself a partner in an equally prominent concern for salvation.[57] While each phase in the Judaism of the dual Torah therefore pursued its own logic, dictated by its own generative problematic, on account of that logic each system would accord to "Israel" a systemically critical role. "Israel" in the one stage requires a literature of one sort, exegetical of sanctification in the natural life, "Israel" in the next stage generates a literature of another sort, requiring the genre of storytelling, for example, to deliver a message of history and salvation. The circumstance of the authorship of the Mishnah was dictated by the experience of defeat, and nothing had changed by the turn of the fifth century. But the interests of the authorships at the end of the fourth century led them to press a different (if related) range of questions. And the rest follows.

Thus, we do have a rule and not the mere generalization of a particular case. Our survey of four Judaisms yields a single rule. If we wish to know whether "Israel" will constitute an important component in a Judaism, we ask about the categorical imperative and describe, as a matter of mere fact, the consequent categorical composition of that system, stated as a corpus of authoritative documents. A system in which "Israel" – the social entity to which the system's builders imagine they address themselves – plays an important role will treat "Israel" as part of its definitive structure. The reason is that the system's categorical imperative will find important consequences in the definition of its "Israel." A system in which the system's builders work entirely on other questions than social ones and explore the logic of issues different from those addressing a social entity, will not yield tractates on "Israel" and will not accord to the topic of "Israel" that categorical and systemic importance that we have identified in some Judaisms. Discourse on "Israel" in general (as in the second phase of the Judaism of the dual Torah) or in acute detail concerning internal structure (as in the Essene writings of Qumran) comes about because of the fundamental question addressed by the system viewed whole.

Let me point to a negative consequence of the present rule. The point of systemic differentiation is not the social character or status of the system builder(s). For an authorship that forms a collectivity need not be expected on that account to appeal to a palpable and social "Israel," and an individual author may not be supposed on account of his individuality to turn to an abstract category. Our cases contradict that false hypothesis. Paul was an individual, and for his system "Israel" constituted a massive presence. Philo also was an individual, and for him, "Israel" constituted a useful detail. The authorship of the Mishnah by definition formed a social group, but their "Israel" supplied a taxonomic category. The authorship of the Yerushalmi, Genesis Rabbah, and Leviticus Rabbah constituted, also by definition, a group, and their document everywhere claims to present the consensus of a group. And that authorship focused upon "Israel" in much the same way and terms as did the author Paul. So the social circumstance of systemic composers is not by itself a considerable variable. It is merely one point of possible correlation. The character of systemic logic, the substance of the generative question, is the independent systemic variable. But, as I shall argue, that too is not the end of matters. For if the author's or authorship's social status presents no independent variable, the generative question presented by the group's social circumstance – I propose – does.

NOTES

1 System builders, as we see, do not find themselves bound to remain with an inherited repertoire, though they may survey the possibilities made available by it.

2 This then forms the converse and conclusion of proposition 1.

3 In the closing part of this chapter I spell out my more general theory of the order and shape of systemic formation.

4 My picture of Paul's thought is meant to give the consensus of learning at this time. I mean to illustrate my theoretical model by reference to that consensus. I owe thanks to my colleague at Brown University, Stanley Stowers, for reading this section of the book. He has a quite different interpretation of Paul on "Israel," which is to be dealt with once it has been published.

5 I had the advantage of the comments on my treatments, in this and the following sections, of the Essenes of Qumran, Paul, and Philo of Professors Bruce Chilton, Bard College; Robert Berchman, Michigan State University; Stanley Stowers, Brown University; and Burton Mack, Claremont Graduate School.

6 Adolf Harnack, *The Mission and Expansion of Christianity in the First Three Centuries,* trans. and ed. James Moffat (London; repr., Gloucester: Pete Smith, 1908), pp. 241, 244.

7 Stowers sees these as coordinate but separate.

8 In "Fences and Neighbors," in *Approaches to Ancient Judaism,* ed. W. S. Green (Missoula, Mont.: Scholars Press for Brown Judaic Studies, 1978) 2:1–25 = Jonathan Z. Smith, *Imagining Religion. From Babylon to Jonestown* (Chicago: University of Chicago Press, 1982), pp. 1–18.

9 Or, as Stowers sees it, what gentiles' being blessed through Abraham means.

10 I owe this formulation to Robert Berchman.

11 Once more I depend upon generous colleagues to save me from needless error based on mere ignorance. I owe special thanks to Robert Berchman.for the reading of this section.

12 That is not to suggest that Philo does not see Jews as a living social entity, a community. The opposite is the case. But when he constructs his philosophical statement, the importance of "Israel" derives from its singular capacity to gain knowledge of God, which other categories of the system cannot have. When writing about the Jews in a political context, Philo does

not appeal to their singular knowledge of God, and when writing about the Jews as "Israel" in the philosophical context, he does not appeal to their forming a this-worldly community.

13 Harry Austryn Wolfson, *Philo: Foundations of Religious Philosophy in Judaism, Christianity, and Islam* (Cambridge: Harvard University Press, 1948), 2:51–2.

14 Ibid., p. 51.

15 Goodenough's critique of Wolfson for his insistence upon finding rabbinic parallels to Philo's ideas seems to me absolutely on target, beginning, middle, and end. That critique is now in print in Ernest S. Frerichs and Jacob Neusner, eds., *Goodenough on History of Religion and on Judaism* (Atlanta, Scholars Press for Brown Judaic Studies, 1986). Wolfson extended to Philo the interpretive system of George Foot Moore's *Judaism: The Age of the Tannaim* (Cambridge: Harvard University Press, 1954), composing of the whole – rabbis, Philo -- a single, unitary, and normative statement, a Judaism.

16 Wolfson, *Philo*, p. 52.

17 Ibid., p. 84.

18 Ibid., pp. 91–2. The issue of whether this is direct knowledge of God's essence or indirect knowledge of God's existence is not important to our inquiry.

19 Ibid., pp. 322–438.

20 Ibid., p. 356.

21 Ibid., p. 357.

22 Ibid., p. 358.

23 Ibid., p. 84.

24 Ibid., p. 397.

25 Ibid., pp. 400–1.

26 Ibid., p. 432.

27 Erwin R. Goodenough, *By Light, Light: The Mystic Gospel of Hellenistic Judaism* (New Haven: Yale University Press, 1935), p. 136.

28 Ibid., p. 136.

29 As to circumcision, Smith, "Fences," p. 14, points out that Philo legitimates circumcision against unnamed critics: "It cannot, if Egyptian, be foolish . . . the removal of the foreskin is symbolic of the excision of pleasure or conceit," that is to say, yet another philosophical reading of a taxon.

30 I take as fact the current consensus identifying the Essenes with the community that valued the books found by the Dead Sea. I have no vested interest in the matter, which has slight bearing upon our inquiry.

31 While the monographic literature on the Essene library and community of Qumran is truly formidable, the systemic description, analysis, and interpretation of that community has yet to begin. I cannot point to a single sustained and encompassing account of not the literature but the religious system, the Judaism, of the Essenes of Qumran, read inductively. Vermes's summary of knowledge, cited below, seems to me definitively to show (to the time of his writing) not only what has been accomplished, but also what awaits attention. I think the reason we do not have a picture of the Judaism of the Essenes of Qumran is that most scholars who have worked on the subject have come from the disciplines of philology, text criticism, history, or theology, not the history of religion, and a great many of them have found the library of Qumran of special interest in the theological study of the earliest Christian writings. That is an important topic, but it is, from the viewpoint of the history of religions, epiphenomenal (that is, rather beside the point).

32 I rely on his *The Dead Sea Scrolls: Qumran in Perspective* (London: Collins, 1977), and, for the texts, his *The Dead Sea Scrolls in English*, 2nd ed. (Harmondsworth: Penguin, 1975).

33 Vermes, *Perspective*, p. 87. The temple scroll, published after Vermes's account, is asymmetrical to our question, and can be set aside for the moment. But further study on our issue will certainly demand a rereading of that document for the purpose of its picture of "Israel." This first statement of the larger theses and hypothesis suffices with the first two items.

34 I do not mean to neglect the numerous other important writings, but the ones at hand suffice for the limited purpose of this exercise.

35 To call them a "sect" is inappropriate, because we do not know what type of group they were, and, from our perspective, the question is irrelevant. A group in its larger context constitutes a sect only if we have decided that that group is not what it conceives itself to be, which is, in this case, not the sect but the entirety of society ("church"). We need not make such an assessment in our context – and in fact, cannot.

36 Vermes, *Perspective*, p. 88.

37 Why using as the base 10 rather than the scriptural and Mesopotamian base 6 I cannot say, but the analogy to the Iranian preference for base 10 (e.g., the *hazarapats*) should not be missed, for whatever it is worth.

38 Vermes, *Perspective*, p. 89.

39 Ibid., p. 176.

40 Ibid., p. 177.

41 Ibid., p. 178.

42 Ibid.

43 Ibid., p. 181.

44 Ibid. See also B. Gärtner, *The Temple and the Community in Qumran and the New Testament* (Cambridge: Cambridge University Press, 1965).

45 Vermes, *Scrolls in English*, p. 76.

46 Ibid., pp. 78–9.

47 Ibid., p. 80.

48 Ibid., p. 87.

49 Cf. Vermes, *Scrolls in English*, p. 97 for an explicit statement here paraphrased.

50 Ibid., p. 106.

---

51 This is pure surmise on my part and should be received as such.

52 Vermes, *Scrolls in English,* p. 97.

53 That is not to suggest there are no others. I point to these merely as examples.

54 Vermes, *Perspective,* p. 91.

55 Ibid.

56 Neusner, "The Havurah in the Second Jewish Commonwealth," *Harvard Theological Review* 30(1960): 194–216. See also Vermes, *Scrolls in English,* pp. 95–7, who seems to have missed this item. But his bibliography throughout is the starting point for all research.

57 I do not see that the difference in the choice of Mishnah tractates important in the Yerushalmi , those of Agriculture, and neglected in the Yerushalmi, the ones of Holy Things, is to be explained in this way. The Bavli, for its part, treats the tractates of Holy Things, the everyday cult and support of the temple, and neglects Agriculture. Both Agriculture and Holy Things constitute sustained exegeses of sanctification in particular dimensions of the common life, and from the present perspective I see no difference between them. People generally suppose that the Bavli neglects Agriculture because the rules of Agriculture apply only in the Holy Land of Israel. But why should the authorship of the Yerushalmi – by the same criterion of explanation – have ignored Holy Things, because, after all, the temple was to be rebuilt in Jerusalem? So the whole matter does not find illumination within the distinctions I offer here.

CHAPTER 12

Society and System

i. How History Matters in Systemic Analysis: The Case of an "Israel"

In stressing the importance of the systemic logic, which tells the framers of a system what they wish to know and how they are to find it out, we must wonder how history – that is to say, chance and circumstance, events of inescapable effect, the encompassing society beyond – shapes the formation of a system. On the one side, different groups of people, represented by diverse writings, responded to the same historical events by composing quite different systems. On the other, people living in the same age and in the aftermath of the same events took quite distinct and contradictory views of the weight and meaning of events. To the authorships of the Gospels, for example, the destruction of the temple carried considerably less weight than that event bore for Josephus and the writers of 4 Ezra and 2 Baruch. Among the Jews of the Land of Israel in the fourth century, sages clearly represented one powerful response to Constantine. But another response, produced by considerable numbers, was to accept what might be called the logic of history – and to convert to Christianity, apparently proven by events to have been, and now to be, God's truth. Accordingly, we cannot claim that circumstances impose their logic upon all system builders. But we also cannot allege that circumstances make no difference at all in the framing of systems. In dealing with this final concern, the relationship between society (including history) and system, I offer a simple hypothesis. It is that the system builders' social (including political) circumstance defines for them the generative problematic that imparts self-evidence to the systemically definitive logic, encompassing its social component. But the same social (including political) circumstance hardly defines for others, in the same time and place, what they identify as the generative problematic requiring urgent consideration, and the self-evidence of the solution to that inescapable crisis worked out by one group will strike another as not particularly compelling or even interesting.

Logic, self-evidence, the givenness of data, the importance self-evidently inhering in one set of facts and lacking in another – these form the systemic process and define its propositions. But they constitute the means by which the urgent question receives its ineluctable answer. They do not define the question. Context and circumstance do. But that is all they do – set the question some may identify as compelling. That simple statement in my judgment forms the self-evident result of this study. The circumstance of the destruction of the Jerusalem temple in 70 C.E. and the calamity that followed the war led by Bar Kokhba "three generations" later in 132–5 C.E. rendered acute the chronic issue of sanctification.[1] And the rest followed. The context of the political revolution in the standing and status of Christianity defined for Jews the central concerns of the fourth and fifth centuries. The question they could not avoid and had to work out derived from that context. I hardly need belabor the point. Rather, let me test the three propositions laid out in Chapter 1 by appeal to other cases than the one that has held our attention and, at the end, spell out the problem and problematic of the consequent hypothesis. For at stake, in the end, is a theory of self-evidence: What makes the truth self-evidently true?

ii. The Cases of Paul, the Essenes of Qumran, and the Sages of the Dual Torah

> Hypothesis: *The system builders' social (including political) circumstance defines the generative problematic that imparts self-evidence to the systemically definitive logic, encompassing its social component.*

The systemically generative circumstance finds its definition in the out-there of the world in which the system builders, and their imagined audience, flourish. Extraordinary political crises, ongoing tensions of society, a religious crisis that challenges theological truth – these in time impose their definition upon thought, seizing the attention and focusing the concentration of the systemopoieic thinkers who propose to explain matters. Systems propose an orderly response to a disorderly situation, and that is their utility. Systems then come into existence at a point, and in a context, in which thoughtful people identify questions that cannot be avoided and must be solved. Such a circumstance, for the case at hand, emerges in the polis, that is, in the realm of politics and the context of persons in community, in the corporate society of shared discourse. The acute, systemopoieic question then derives from out there; the system begins somewhere beyond the mind of the thoughtful intellects who build systems. Having ruled out the systemopoieic power of authors' or authorships' circumstance, therefore, I now invoke the systemopoieic power of the political setting of the social group of which the system builders form a part (in their own minds, the exemplification and realization).

Let me explain the hypothesis with which this comparative study concludes. Systemic logic enjoys self-evidence. But it is circumstance that dictates that absolute given, that sense of fittingness and irrefutable logic, that people find self-evident. By circumstance I do not mean the particular setting within which an authorship finds itself, for, as I just said, a collective authorship or an individual writer may produce an abstract or a concrete "Israel." How then does circumstance shape matters? System building forms a symbolic transaction and, by definition, represents symbol change for the builders and their building. On the one hand, it is a social question that sets the terms and also the limits of the symbolic transaction, so symbol change responds to social change (at least for some). On the other hand, symbol change so endures as to impose a new shape upon a social world, as we can show was the case at Qumran for the Essenes and in the aftermath of Constantine for the Jews who then constituted "Israel." It follows that social change comes about through symbol change. How shall we account for the origin of a system? We can show correlation between a system and its circumstance and, it must follow, between the internal logic of a system and the social givens in which the system flourishes. But, as I shall argue presently, correlation is not explanation. And the sources of explanation lie beyond the limits of cases, however many. The question facing system builders carries with it one set of givens, not some other, one urgent and ineluctable question, which, by definition, excludes others. The context of the system builders having framed the question before them, one set of issues and not some other, issues of one type rather than some other, predominates. Now to the cases at hand.

Matters in regard to Paul's and the Essenes' systems hardly require detailed specification. Paul's context told him that "Israel" constituted a categorical imperative, and it also told him what about "Israel" he had to discover in his thought on the encounter with Christ. The Essenes of Qumran by choice isolated themselves and in that context determined upon the generative issue of describing an "Israel" that, all by itself in the wilderness, would survive and form the saving remnant.

Paul, all scholarship concurs, faced a social entity ("church" or "Christian community") made up of Jews but also gentiles, and (some) Jews expected people to obey the law (e.g., to circumcise their sons). Given the natural course of lives, that was not a question to be long postponed, which imparts to it the acute, not merely chronic, character that it clearly displayed even in the earliest decade beyond Paul's vision.[2] And that fact in my judgment explains why, for Paul, circumcision formed a critical taxic indicator in a way in which, for Philo, for the Mishnah, and other Judaic systems, it did not.

The circumstance of the Essenes of Qumran is far better documented, because that community through its rereading of Scripture tells us that it originated in a break between its founder(s) and other officials. Consequently, my characterizing the Essenes of Qumran hardly moves beyond the evidence in hand. They responded to their own social circumstance, isolated and alone as it was, and formed a community unto itself – hence seeing their "Israel," the social entity of their system, as what there was left of Scripture's "Israel," that is, the remnant of Israel.[3]

The sages of the dual Torah made their documentary statements in reply to two critical questions, the one concerning sanctification, presented by the final failure of efforts to regain Jerusalem and restore the temple cult, the other concerning salvation, precipitated by the now-unavoidable fact of Christianity's political triumph.[4]

Once each of the three Judaisms for which a precipitating (in my jargon, systemopoieic) crisis can be identified passes before us, we readily see how the consequent program flowed from the particular politically generative crisis.[5] The case of the sages in both phases in the unfolding of the dual Torah is the obvious example of the interplay of context and contents. There we see with great clarity both the precipitating event and the logic of self-evidence out of which a system spun its categorical program. That program, correlated with the systemopoieic event, would then define all else. If sanctification is the issue imposed by events, then the Mishnah will ask a range of questions of detail, at each point providing an exegesis of the everyday in terms of the hermeneutics of the sacred: Israel as different and holy within the terms specified by Scripture. If salvation proves the paramount claim of a now-successful rival within "Israel," then the authorship of Genesis Rabbah will ask the matriarchs and patriarchs to spell out the rules of salvation, so far as they provide not merely precedents but paradigms of salvation. The authorship of Leviticus

Rabbah will seek in the picture of sanctification supplied by the book of Leviticus the rules and laws that govern the salvation of "Israel." The history of an "Israel" that is a political entity – family, sui generis, either, both, it hardly matters – will dictate for the authorship for which the Yerushalmi speaks a paramount category.

Yet an element of a priori choice proves blatant in the three systems upon which we have come to focus. And that matter of selectivity points toward symbol change as the prior fact, social change as the consequent fact. That is to say, social change forms a necessary but not sufficient explanation. There is a simple fact that seems to me to validate that judgment. It is that many Jews confronted the social change to which the system builders responded in the way they did. But, by definition, only the system builders[6] reached the conclusions that they reached and composed the system that they created. There were other Jews who reached other conclusions (or none at all). Hence social crisis tells us the problem that engaged the system builders, but the character and structure of the crisis, viewed by itself, could not tell us the system that they would build.

Sages formed a group of Jews who identified the critical issue as that of sanctification, involving proper classification and ordering of all of the elements and components of Israel's reality. Not all Jews interpreted events within that framework, however, and, it follows, circumstances by themselves did not govern. The symbol change worked for those for whom it worked, which, ultimately, changed the face of the Jews' society. But in the second and fourth centuries there were Jews who found persuasive a different interpretation of events – whether the defeat of Bar Kokhba or the conversion of Constantine – and became Christian.[7]

Nor did all Christians concur with Paul that Jews and gentiles now formed a new social entity, another "Israel" than the familiar one; the same social circumstance that required Paul to design his system around "Israel" persuaded a later set of authorships to tell the story of Jesus' life and teachings, a story in which (as in the Mishnah's system) "Israel" formed a datum, a backdrop, but hardly the main focus of discourse or the precipitating consideration. It took a century for Paul's reading of matters to gain entry into the canon, and before Luther, Paul's system was absorbed and hardly paramount.

So too with the Essenes. Diverse groups in the age in which the Essenes of Qumran took shape and produced their library, hence the system expressed in their books, formed within the larger society of the Jews in the Land of Israel. And not all such smaller groups seized upon the option of regarding themselves as the whole of (surviving) "Israel." Many did not. One such group, the Pharisees, presents an important structural parallel, in its distinctive calculation of the holy calendar, in its provision of stages for entry into the group, in its interest in the rules of purity governing meals that realized in a concrete communion the social existence of the group, and in diverse other ways.[8] The Pharisees did not regard themselves as co-existent with "all Israel," even while they remained part of the everyday corporate community. They proposed to exemplify their rules in the streets and marketplaces and to attain influence in the people at large. So merely forming what we now call a sect did not require a group to identify itself as "all Israel," as did the Essenes of Qumran.[9]

When we point to the correlation between problem and program, context and contents, we do not explain matters. We only beg the question. True, the system builders' social (including political) circumstance defines the generative problematic that imparts self-evidence to the systemically definitive logic, encompassing its social component. But that important point of correspondence cannot by itself account in the end for the particular foci and the generative problematic of a system. I claim that a single political problem, a crisis that we can identify and describe, persuaded one group of the self-evidence of a given set of cogent truths, which yielded, for an author or authorship, the materials of a systematic rereading of all things in light of some one thing – thus, the documents that form the canon of that system.[10] But that same circumstance did not impose upon another group in the same time, place, and situation the same sense of the self-evidence of that system's matters identified as important and read in one way and not in some other. Paul had opposition within precisely the sort of groups that he identified as the center of interest – mixed groups of Jews and gentiles. Different groups responded in diverse ways to the same crisis, which is proved by the fact that diverse systems, reaching documentary expression in canons of varying contents, did emerge from the same circumstances and did appeal to precisely the same foundation document, the Hebrew Scriptures. Issues of the first century and the destruction of the temple, issues of the fourth century and the conversion of the government of Rome to Christianity – these generated more than a single canon, as the history of the West testifies.

Because I have focused upon the Judaism of the dual Torah, let me spell out the insufficiency of appeal to the precipitating circumstance in explaining the character of that system. The sages' Mishnah and Yerushalmi and related writings, at both of the two phases in their unfolding, solved the problem on which they focused for sages. But others did not necessarily concur on either the urgent question or the self-evident answer. To take one example, some Jews in the second century did conclude that "Judaism" was over. Justin's Trypho may typify these Jews, and it may well be that among those who adopted the Gnostic way of seeing things and rejected both the Creator-God and the Torah were Jews disgusted by the perfidy of destruction and disappointment.[11] To take another example, Avi-Yonah plausibly maintains that in the fourth and fifth centuries, Christians became the absolute majority of the population of the Land of Israel, and Jews formed a minority.[12] The political triumph of Christianity may have persuaded numbers of Jews that their ancestors had erred in rejecting Jesus as Christ the King of the world, as he now appeared to be. That that issue proved paramount I believe is a fact, and that in consequence Jews did adopt Christianity and therefore rejected the sages' explanation of matters seems to me a reasonable view of matters.[13]

To conclude: When we appeal to the shared experience, hence social circumstance, to account for the power of self-evidence that lends strength to a system, holding together the system's identification of the urgent question with the obvious truth of the self-evident answer to that question, we prove our hypothesis by repeating it. That tells us that we have come to the end of our inquiry. For the concluding hypothesis may be illustrated but not proved. The reason is that the hypothesis with which we conclude derives from our interpretation, specifically, of the correlation we observe between circumstance and system. But that correlation does not encompass all of the systems that, in the same circumstance, we can imagine were taking shape. More to the point, it certainly does not accord with all of the facts we do have concerning Jews' reading of the circumstances in which, for some, a given system did prove ineluctable. That is why, beyond the stated hypothesis, we cannot move along the lines of analysis undertaken here. "Israel" and how the social entity of a given system is imagined and transformed into metaphor – these matters form components of systems. They show us one important way in which a system is bonded and made coherent. When we wish to describe the larger points of harmony and coherence within a given system, we do well to investigate the social metaphors that come to concrete expression in diverse documents and statements of that system. When we wish to analyze the connections among the documents that make up the designated canon of a system, the work of comparison and contrast of views of "Israel" provides ample results of interest. That analytical inquiry yields perspective upon what we have described. Finally, when we propose to interpret diverse Judaisms and so show what makes one Judaism cohere and form a continuity, on the one side, but differ from some other Judaism, on the other side, the comparison of "Israel"s forms a considerable source of interpretative possibilities, as we have seen in the present chapter. These things we can do.

The upshot is simple, if not very satisfying. What we cannot do in this context is explain. That is, to account for the relationship between systemically definitive logic, which enjoys the standing of self-evident truth, and the context and circumstance in which a system originates and to which (I would regard as obvious) a system may be shown to respond, we must move beyond all our cases, altogether. So when we move from description, analysis, and interpretation to the larger matter of explanation, we complete the work that we can do, and that I set out to do. We come, however, not to an impasse but to a proper conclusion of a work correctly limited and appropriately defined. For the explanation of the whys and, especially, the wherefores of Judaic systems must derive from sources of theoretical thought other than the ones of (mere) description, analysis, and interpretation of Judaic texts in particular or even of the facts of religion in general.

There are two sources of explanation, each valid in its realm. Why a given system takes the shape that it does and not some other is a question answered, within the system of the dual Torah, by appeal to theology and, beyond the system of the dual Torah, by appeal to sociology, anthropology, the historical and political sciences, psychology, economics – to any and all of the sciences of social explanation of action and of intellect that propose to make sense in general of the particularities of human expression in society. To these sciences Judaism makes a rich contribution of suggestive cases and interesting examples, occasions for the testing, in a particular case, of a hypothesis of general intelligibility.

But theology of Judaism also proposes to explain things and does explain things. The sages of the Judaism of the dual Torah, working out through metaphors a theory of what and who they and their social world were, proposed for their part to answer that very question, namely, to account through general laws, everywhere applicable, for what and who they were as a social entity. They were "Israel" individually and collectively, responding to the Torah that was Heaven's projection onto earth, the account of what it meant to be humanity "in our image, after our likeness." I cannot imagine, within the science of social explanation of action and of intellect, a more encompassing statement.[14]

iii. Society and System

We cannot, in the end, explain the origin of Judaic systems. Stated in
general terms, the issue is whether symbol change generates (for
some) social change, or social change precipitates symbol change. In
the setting of this argument, it is whether society sets the issue, which
the system then works out, or whether the inner logic of the system
dictates the proportions and order and logic, which, as a matter of
fact, serves very well where and when it serves. But that impasse in
finding the reason why need not impede our reaching one solid
conclusion concerning systems and the symbolic transactions realized in them. At the end I can offer only my own judgment of
matters. It is that, in systemic formation, the social entity takes
priority. History then makes its contribution to the facts that the
social entity confronts, and that is all that history contributes.

Systems begin in the social entity, whether of two persons or two
hundred or ten thousand – there, and not in their canonical writings,
which come only afterward, or even in their politics. The social
group, however formed, frames the system, the system then defines
its canon within, and addresses the larger setting, the polis without.
For our part, to be sure, we describe systems from their end products, the writings that are our sole entry. But we have then to work
our way back from canon to system. We cannot be so deceived as to
imagine either that the canon is the system, or that the canon creates
the system. The canonical writings speak in particular to those who
can hear, that is, to the members of the community who, on account
of that perspicacity of hearing, constitute the social entity or systemic
community. The community then comprises that social group the
system of which is recapitulated by the selected canon. The group's
exegesis of the canon in terms of the everyday imparts to the system the power to sustain the community in a reciprocal and self-
nourishing process. The community through its exegesis then
imposes continuity and unity on whatever is in its canon.

Although we cannot account for the origin of a system, we can explain its power to persist. This power derives from interchange and
movement, like electricity from magnetism via a dynamo, specifically
as a symbolic transaction. It is one in which social change comes to
expression in symbol change. That symbolic transaction specifically
takes place in its exegesis of the systemic canon, which, in literary
terms, constitutes the social entity's statement of itself.[15] So, once
more, the texts recapitulate the system. The system does not recapitulate the texts. The system comes before the texts and defines
the canon. The exegesis of the canon then forms that ongoing social

action that sustains the whole. A system then selects and orders its texts, imputes to them as a whole cogency, one to the next, that their original authorships have not expressed in and through the parts. A system expresses through the composition formed of the documents its deepest logic, and it also frames that just fit that, we have observed, joins system to circumstance. The whole works its way out through exegesis, and the history of any religious system – that is to say, the history of religion writ small – is the exegesis of its exegesis. And the first rule of the exegesis of systems is the simplest, and the one with which I conclude: The system does not recapitulate the canon. The canon recapitulates the system.

The system forms a statement of a social entity, specifying its worldview and way of life in such a way that, to the participants in the system, the whole makes sound sense, beyond argument. So in the beginning are not words of inner and intrinsic affinity but (as Philo would want us to say) the Word: the transitive logic, the system, all together, all at once, complete, whole, finished. Then the world awaits only that labor of exposition and articulation that the faithful, for centuries to come, will lavish at the altar of the faith. That is why, as Jonathan Z. Smith has said, the history of religion is the exegesis of exegesis.

A religious system therefore presents a fact not of history but of immediacy, of the eternal, social present. The issue of why a system originates and survives, if it does, or fails, if it does, by itself proves impertinent to the analysis of a system. A system is like a language. A language forms an example of language if it produces communication through rules of syntax and verbal arrangement. That paradigm serves full well however many people speak the language, or however long the language serves. Two people (two hundred, ten thousand) who understand each other form a language community, even – or especially – if no one understands them. So too by definition religions address the living, constitute societies, frame and compose cultures. For however long, at whatever moment in historic time, a religious system always grows up in the perpetual present, an artifact of its day, whether today or a long-ago time. The only appropriate tense for a religious system is the present. A religious system always *is,* whatever it was, whatever it will be. Why so? Because its traits address a condition of humanity in society, a circumstance of an hour – however brief or protracted the hour and the circumstance.

When we ask that a religious composition speak to a society with a message of the *is* and the *ought* and with a meaning for the everyday, we focus on the power of that system to hold the whole together: the society the system addresses, the individuals who compose the society, the ordinary lives they lead, in ascending order of consequence. That system then forms a whole and well-composed structure. Yes, the structure stands somewhere, and, indeed, the place where it stands will secure for the system either an extended or an ephemeral span of life. But the system, for however long it lasts, serves. And that focus on the eternal present justifies my interest in analyzing why a system works (the urgent agenda of issues it successfully solves for those for whom it solves those problems) when it does, and why it ceases to work (loses self-evidence, is bereft of its Israel, for example) when it no longer works.[16] The phrase, the *history* of a *system*, presents us with an oxymoron. Systems endure in that eternal present that they create. They evoke precedent, they do not have a history. A system relates to context but, as I have stressed, exists in an enduring moment (which, to be sure, changes all the time). We capture the system in a moment, the worm consumes it an hour later. That is the way of mortality, whether for us one by one, in all mortality, or for the works of humanity in society.

As to the Judaism of the dual Torah, change did not destroy, time did not attenuate, so long as the fundamental issues persisted. The issues of its "Israel," therefore the metaphors that realized that "Israel," moreover, possessed an enduring self-evident aptness, indeed an urgency. For pretty much everyone in the world Jews knew asked the same questions and answered them by appeal to the same set of facts, diversely construed to be sure. The Israel of the Judaism of the dual Torah lived in a timeless world of the everyday, for the *now* of sanctification, and of the future redemption, for the *then* of salvation. And the larger circumstance of that system spoke of God's will for Israel in the now and plan for Israel in the then. So long as the system corresponded to the circumstance, its metaphors for "Israel" proved evocative, and the system survived. But where it came from, why it proved so timely and so enduring for so long as it did, where and when it did – these are things that God knows, and about them we may only speculate.

NOTES

1 I maintain that the reason the issue persists derives from the porous frontiers between "Israel" and other groups. That is the argument of my *Judaism: The Evidence of the Mishnah* (Chicago: University of Chicago Press, 1981) on the persistence, within the Mishnaic system, of the ontology of the Priestly Code. An ongoing social datum, e.g., close identification with

neighboring groups of a group that perceives itself as fundamentally different, or political reality, such as defeat and ongoing subordination, will generate, in the idiom of diverse times and places to be sure, a structurally cogent system, persisting through. That is the reason, I should imagine, for an unchanging ontological system and structure within time and change. I employ that theory in my *Judaism in the Matrix of Christianity* (Philadelphia: Fortress Press, 1986) to account for what changed, and what remained the same, in the unfolding of the Judaism of the dual Torah.

2 I am not equivalently clear on the crisis that provoked and defined Philo's program of stating in philosophical terms the Judaism he proposed to expound and defend. Scholarship generally concurs that he took as his task the labor of mediation, but whether we can characterize that program as a response to an urgent crisis I cannot say.

3 That fact contrasts with the clear premise of the Mishnah's authorship that "Israel" meant "all the Jews," except, of course, for the exceptions. But in no detail do I find in any rabbinic document of late antiquity the conception that the "Israel" of whom the document speaks is the saving remnant, leaving out all nonbelieving or nonconforming Jews. Sages saw themselves as special within the context of a general society to be transformed in the image and after the likeness of sages. That is a totally opposite conception from the one that reads "us" as "all Israel," "all Israel" as "us," and omits everyone else. Paul's system, we note, entertained no such possibility, which was irrelevant to Philo's too. Clearly, one taxic classifier among Judaisms will be the character of the social entity of the system: inclusive or exclusive, in a variety of senses of those words.

4 That is the argument of my *Judaism and Christianity in the Age of Constantine* (Chicago: University of Chicago Press, 1987).

5 Once more, "political" stands for "pertaining to the polis, the corporate community."

6 That is not to neglect those who responded to their judgment of the self-evident and the logical.

7 We return to this matter presently.

8 Indeed, the earliest debates on the identification of the sponsorship of the ancient library dug up at Qumran encompassed the position that the authors were Pharisees in particular. For an encompassing account of the matter, see G. Vermes, *The Dead Sea Scrolls: Qumran in Perspective* (London: Collins, 1977), pp. 116–36.

9 The utility of my proposed taxic indicator for systemic comparison is here illustrated.

10 I underline the matter of canon because of what follows in the concluding section.

11 In my *Judaism: The Evidence of the Mishnah*, pp. 37–43, I go over this matter. I know of no concrete evidence that Jews formed an important part in the Gnostic groups.

12 See M. Avi Yohnah, *The Jews of Palestine: A Political History from the Bar Kokhba War to the Arab Conquest* (New York: Oxford University Press, 1976), pp. 220ff., and my *Judaism in Society: The Evidence of the Yerushalmi. Toward the Natural History of a Religion* (Chicago: The University of Chicago Press, 1983), pp. 9–23.

13 But an account of the sages' opposition as reflected in the polemics mounted by them must encompass, also, the Gnostic position that is the opposite of the recurrent points of emphasis of Genesis Rabbah's authorship's reading of creation.

14 When sages spoke of "image" and "likeness" in comparing humanity to divinity, they meant the personality of God in heaven, the theological anthropology of humanity on earth. These two further studies will go forward.

15 And that is why, of course, we have focused analysis upon the canonical evidences of the Judaism of the dual Torah. The social facts outside, uncovered by archaeology, for one example, are systemically inert and uninteresting.

16 I have performed this analysis in my *Death and Birth of Judaism: The Impact of Christianity, Secularism, and the Holocaust on Jewish Faith* (New York: Basic Books, 1987). These remarks paraphrase the meditation on systemic analysis that forms the appendix of that book.

General Index

Abba bar Kahana, "Israel" as family,
    141
Abbahu, "Israel" as family, 136
Abba Saul, world to come, 73
Abin, "Israel" as way of life, 151
Aha
    fasting for rain, 200
    "Israel" as family, 130
    uniqueness of "Israel," 179
Aibu, birthright of "Israel," 162
Alexander, 100
Aphrahat, claim of Christian inheritance of
    "Israel," 146–50, 153
apostasy and world to come, 75–7
Aqiba, world to come, 73, 75
Aristotle, 100
    Politics, 107
Avi-Yonah, A. M., 245
Azariah, birthright of "Israel," 157

Berekhiah
    birthright of "Israel," 158–9
    "Israel" as family, 130
Birai, "Israel" as family, 141
birthright of "Israel," 157–63

Christianity
    challenge to "Israel," 96–106
    claim to inheritance of "Israel," 145–63,
        214
    diverse writings on claim of "Israel,"
        239–49
    impact of Gospels on Judaism of "Israel,"
        101–2
    "Israel" after the spirit, claim of, 88–9,
        112–43, 186–92, 215–20
    messianism and salvation, 5
    Paul's view of "Israel," 33–4
    political dominance and identification of
        "Israel," 87–91

Church and state, Christianity's challenge to
    "Israel," 96–106
Constantine
    Christianization and claim to be "Israel,"
        186, 189–90
    legalization of Christianity as state
        religion, 98–9, 101, 106
    response of history, 239, 241, 243
culture, sanctification, its doctrine as
    structure of order, 21–8

destiny, dual Torah and Mishnaic system of
    sanctification, 32–5
Diocletian, 98
dual Torah
    doctrine of merit, 47–50, 131–9
    foundation of Judaic system, 3–4
    gentiles and "Israel," 38–58
    interpreting Judaism of sanctification, 21–
        8
    Judaism of, 184–203
    Judaism and Mishnaic discourse on
        "Israel," 38–58
    Mishnaic system for sanctification of
        "Israel," 28–35
    sanctification of Judaism, 21–8
    society and systems, 240–6

Eleazar
    "Israel" as family, 136, 140
    Judaism of dual Torah, 193
Eleazar b. R. Menahem, uniqueness of
    "Israel," 182
Eliezer, world to come, 75
Essene community at Qumran
    Christianity and "Israel" after the spirit,
        219
    Community Rule, 225–8, 232
    Damascus Rule, 225, 228, 232
    defining "Israel," 220, 224–34

252

Index to Biblical and Talmudic References